# Nisei Voices

Norio Yasaki (standing) in a 1929 photograph with his siblings (from left to right) Misako, Joe and Yuriko in Los Angeles. *Courtesy of Federick S. Yasaki.*

# Nisei Voices

## Japanese American Students of the 1930s—Then & Now

**Joyce Hirohata & Paul T. Hirohata, ed.**

*Third Edition*

Hirohata Design — Oakland, California

Hirohata Design would like to acknowledge the help of the California Civil Liberties Public Education Program in the publication of this book. A complete list of financial contributors may be found in the acknowledgments.

Hirohata Design
P.O. Box 720243, San Jose, California 95112-3679 U.S.A
www.niseivoices.com

First edition published 1932. Second edition 1935. Third edition 2004.
(First and Second editions originally published as *Orations and Essays by the Japanese Second Generation of America*, Edited by Paul T. Hirohata)

First impression 2004

ISBN 0-9728149-0-6

Library of Congress Control Number 2003101034

This book is printed on acid free paper.
Printed in the United States of America by Worzalla.
Cover design by Mik Gaspay. Interior composed by Victoria May in Bembo.
All maps created by Ben Pease.

Front cover photographs
Top: Yoshiko Higuchi (bottom row, third from left) in the Monterey Buddhist Women's Organization in 1934. *Courtesy of Tazu Kanda.*
Bottom: George Inagaki, (top row, far left) in the Sacramento Junior Colllege Men's Club in 1932. *Courtesy of Chris Inagaki.*

Spine photographs
From left to right: Toshio Yamagata, Michiko Naito, Kazuya Sanada, Helen Kuwada, Joe M. Nakanishi and Shizu Komae. *Photographs courtesy of individuals pictured, except Yamagata's photo courtesy of Jeannette Sanderson and Kuwada's photo courtesy of Agnes Sasaki.*

Back cover photographs
From left to right: Haruko Fujita, George Nishida, Yukiko Sanwo, Norio Yasaki and Yoshiko Higuchi. *Photographs courtesy of individuals pictured, except Nishida's photo courtesy of Agnes Nakamura, Yasaki's photo courtesy of Frederick Yasaki and Higuchi's photo courtesy of Tazu Kanda.*

Back flap photographs
Top: Joyce Hirohata. © *John Story/San Francisco Chronicle 2001.*
Bottom: Paul Tsunegoro Hirohata. *Courtesy of John K. Hirohata.*

*For my Mother and Father*

Yoshiko Higuchi (fourth from right) helped the Monterey Buddhist Women's Organization basketball team become Coast District Champs in 1931. *Courtesy of Tazu Kanda.*

# Contents

## EDUCATION

## GRADUATION

## INTERNATIONAL RELATIONS

# First Foreword

By any standard, the Japanese Americans (Nisei) were a remarkable people. They grew up in the thirties in near-poverty on marginal California farms and in city slums as members of families where English was rarely spoken. Economic opportunity seldom extended beyond the farm or jobs in a fruit stand. In some areas, when a high school class went on an outing to a public pool, the Nisei were left behind.

Yet, they excelled in their studies and an astonishing number graduated at the head of their high school classes. In 1932 an enterprising Japanese immigrant named Paul Tsunegoro Hirohata, amazed and proud of the scholarship of the Nisei, collected the valedictory speeches of twenty-seven of them, publishing them in *Orations and Essays by the Japanese Second Generation of America*. Three years later he published a second edition containing an additional twenty-two speeches.

In 1999, his granddaughter, Joyce Hirohata of Oakland, California, came across a copy of the book and was impressed enough to wonder what had happened to the forty-nine scholars. Thus began her determined search that led ultimately to *Nisei Voices* which includes a brief report on the lives of each of the forty-nine as well as the text of their speeches.

The common theme that runs through the teenagers' orations are hopes and high emotions extolling the future of the world and

America—an almost incomprehensible attitude in view of the racial prejudices and economic problems they faced. The titles of their speeches range from "George Washington and the Constitution" to "Women and World Peace," "The Influence of the Olympic Games on Greek Art" to "An Appeal for World Friendship."

Unknown to the scholars, in a few years they (and other Japanese Americans) would be betrayed by the America they extolled, rounded up like enemy aliens and imprisoned—guarded by troops who wore the same uniform as many of the Japanese Americans' brothers—without being charged with anything but being ethnic Japanese.

Joyce Hirohata discovered that most of the scholars came through this experience largely unscarred, and although she does not say so, this phenomenon might well be traced to the faith and idealism they had expressed in their valedictory addresses.

Joyce Hirohata, with assistance from her Grandfather, Paul, has served history well by providing us with penetrating insights into the lives, times, youthful hopes and thoughts of a Japanese American generation that is all but gone.

Bill Hosokawa

*A Seattle-born newspaperman since 1937, Bill Hosokawa is the author of twelve books including* Nisei: The Quiet Americans. *His most recent work is* Old Man Thunder, Father of the Bullet Train.

# Second Foreword

ONE OF THE JOYS of historical research is discovering materials that have likely sat undisturbed for many decades, and such seemed to be the case when I stumbled across *Orations and Essays by the Japanese Second Generation of America,* edited by Paul T. Hirohata. As far as I could gather, authors who had written about Japanese Americans had not referenced the work nor had leading scholars heard of the collection or the editor. In reading the book, I quickly realized its value—a relatively rare entry point into the words and thoughts of Japanese American students during the period between World Wars. Up to this point, I had not found much that enabled me to access the mindset of the second generation (Nisei) since many of them were so young at the time. Although orations and essays carry their own limitations as primary sources, the material gathered by Paul Hirohata provided some genuine glimpses into how Japanese Americans of the 1920s and 1930s were trying to make sense of the times and their place in it. I felt fortunate to include some portions of the collection in my book, *Growing Up Nisei.*

Despite its value, the collection as well as its editor raised a number of questions that I could only partially answer. While Paul Hirohata was identified as a representative of the *Japan Times*, I did not have much luck finding out more about who he was or his connection to the material. While I was able to find bits and pieces of information about some of the contributors, many of them remained obscure, hidden as it were by time and by the fact that their stories were part of a buried past. Hence, when I received word from Joyce Hirohata that she was publishing an expanded third edition of *Orations and Essays* renamed *Nisei Voices*, I was glad that she was attempting to fill in many of the blanks that existed. She should be commended for carrying on the legacy of her grand-father, and for making these stories and individuals come to life, even as the era of the Nisei passes.

At first glance, it would seem that these people and events that took place some seventy to eighty years ago have little bearing upon our lives today. Indeed, much has happened in the intervening years, including tremendous change in areas such as technology and media. And yet, the past is linked to the present, and history teaches us that those ties and connections provide important insights to who we are as individuals, communities and societies. The Nisei in the 1920s and 1930s faced real hardships steeped in racial prejudice. For those on the West Coast that racial prejudice would culminate in their incarceration by their own government. Few of the orators and essay writers could have predicted such a fate, but many of them did know through their personal and shared experiences that Japanese Americans were a people set apart—by law, by custom and by being branded as "different." The process of becoming American is as perennial a process as it is complex and contingent. This peek into how select Nisei navigated their era is as relevant today as it always has been.

David K. Yoo

*David K. Yoo is Associate Professor and Chair, Department of History, Claremont McKenna College, and Chair, Intercollegiate Department of Asian American Studies at the Claremont Colleges, Claremont, California.*

# Preface

THIS BOOK was first published in a much more modest form in 1932 by my grandfather, Tsunegoro Hirohata, whom I never knew. He was born on March 19, 1898 in the Fukuoka prefecture on the southern island of Japan. When he was twenty-one years old, he ventured to California to join his father, Kichijiro Hirohata, who was already in the United States.

Grandfather adopted the name "Paul" and supported himself through odd jobs and working as an occasional farmhand. In 1927 he graduated from Whittier College with a sociology degree and became the U.S. correspondent for the *Japan Times*, the oldest English language newspaper in Japan. He also wrote articles for a Japanese American newspaper called the *Los Angeles Daily News*, known today as the *Rafu Shimpo*. Making his base in Little Tokyo in Los Angeles, he became a fixture in the community. Togo Tanaka, one of the first editors of the English section at the *Rafu Shimpo* called Grandfather a "guardian angel of underpaid newspapermen."

Keenly interested in preserving the history of Japanese immigrants in the United States, Grandfather self-published a book about it in the 1930s. Written in Japanese, *Zaibei Fukuoka Kenjinshi* documents the Japanese from the Fukuoka prefecture who came to America. He also wrote another book that is lost to us, *Charles Lindbergh, the King of the Sky*. In between his work as a journalist and author, Grandfather collected speeches from the first Japanese

American students chosen to give commencement addresses in California public schools. He was very proud of these valedictorians and salutatorians and knew he was seeing history being made by the Nisei, second generation Japanese born in the United States. To memorialize their thoughts and ideas, he published their graduation speeches during the Great Depression. He thought the orations were "valuable," revealing the "idealism and emotion" of the second generation. He also wanted the speeches to serve as "reference material" and "stimulate" the ambitions of the younger Nisei.[1]

In 1932 with the help of the *Rafu Shimpo's* newspaper presses, he printed the first edition of *Orations and Essays by the Japanese Second Generation of America* that featured twenty-seven students' speeches. We do not know how Grandfather gathered the writings or how many copies he published, but we do know he sold the book from his home. The first printing was well received and there was a second edition published three years later. Japanese American students in California had continued to excel and twenty-two more speeches were added. Six years after printing the second edition, World War II started and the United States government stripped 120,000 people of Japanese heritage—including the Japanese Americans who were citizens by birth—of their rights, expelling them from their homes along the West Coast, and incarcerating them in concentration camps. By then, Grandfather was no longer in America to witness these events. In 1939 the rumblings of war between Japan and the United States were escalating. After twenty years in this country he returned to Japan, taking his wife and two young American-born children with him. He never returned to the United States and he died in Tokyo in 1965.

In 1954, his son, John Koki Hirohata—my father—emigrated back to America. He eventually married and settled in San Francisco where I was born and raised. One day in 1999 he said to me, "Your grandpa's book is falling apart. I'm going to ask the church secretary to retype it."

"Let me look at it. Maybe I can help you," I replied. Little did I know the offer to help preserve Grandfather's work would take me on such a journey. When I was young, I had studied the small red volume in eighth grade to get ideas for my junior high valedictorian speech, but I never understood its historical significance and forgot all about the book.

Toward the end of 1999, Dad sent me a crumbling family copy of *Orations and Essays*. I looked at it as an adult for the first time.

Paul Tsunegoro Hirohata (standing) with his father, Kichijiro Hirohata, in a portrait taken in the U.S. in the early 1920s. *Courtesy of John K. Hirohata.*

The publication was typeset with care, but I found it uninteresting—just a collection of speeches written in old-fashioned, idealistic language from another era. Not a single photograph or illustration was included to pique my interest. I tried reading the book three times, but kept falling asleep. Finally, on the fourth try, I realized something: in spite of their declarations of love and loyalty to their country, the youths in the volume had been incarcerated as adults during World War II. This realization suddenly changed my view of the speeches. I finally understood how historically important the orations were. Given what happened to the students later in adulthood, I now felt their writings were ironic, sad and poignant.

The internment of the people of Japanese heritage by the United States government was never part of my family history. My grandfather had gone back to Japan before World War II started, and my father returned to the United States well after it had ended. Growing up, I felt completely removed from the incarceration experience and out of utter ignorance would often think, "Why do those people always keep talking about it?" When I realized the valedictorians in *Orations and Essays* probably suffered the same fate as other Japanese Americans living on the West Coast, their incarceration based on ethnicity suddenly became personal. In a strange way, the forty-nine students in the book became like distant relatives to seek out. I wanted to know what had become of them. From the dates of their speeches, I calculated they would be in their eighties and a few might still be alive. My mission became to find them or their surviving family members. I especially wanted to find out if they had been interned and wanted to collect their biographies and photographs to create an expanded, new edition of *Orations and Essays.*

The only information I had to locate the students were their names, schools, school locations and dates the speeches were given. In December 1999 I began my search. I created a flyer that listed the valedictorians' names and enthusiastically distributed copies to every person I knew affiliated with the Japanese American community. During a trip to Southern California in January 2000, I left a bunch of flyers at the Japanese American National Museum in Los Angeles. One of the volunteer docents, Shizu Komae Matsumura, saw her name on it and called me. I had located my first *Orations and Essays* student.

Over the next two years I placed articles in every Japanese American newspaper and mailed over a thousand flyers to Japanese American churches and temples in California. I searched obituaries

Joyce Hirohata with a copy of the 1935 edition of *Orations and Essays. Courtesy of the San Francisco Chronicle (John Story).*

and government records on the Internet, posted my project on Japanese American listservs and created a Web site. These efforts and strong word of mouth produced a steady trickle of phone calls and letters with leads that helped me find the valedictorians. E-mail enabled me to communicate efficiently with those who sent information and also allowed me to work with friends in Japan. In the summer of 2000, when I took a trip to Tokyo, the *Japan Times* newspaper graciously ran an article that helped me find one Nisei student who was living there.

During my research there were many times when few calls came and leads did not pan out, but never did I dream that I would be able to find information on every student. By December 2001 my list was reduced to the last ten people and I received the perfect Christmas present from the *San Francisco Chronicle*. The newspaper ran a prominent story about my research that eventually allowed me to find the remaining Nisei students. It was pure irony—a publication that had once been a leader in producing sensational anti-Japanese headlines turned out to be one of the greatest helps to my project.

Because the Japanese American community was so close before World War II, many students I found knew other people in my search who were from the same area. I was surprised to discover twenty-two of the forty-nine Nisei valedictorians are still alive and they turn between eighty-three and ninety years of age this year. Most of them are healthy, remarkably active and mentally sharp. Only a couple of them were aware that their speeches were once published in a book.

Their reactions to my contacting them were generally positive. As expected, they had different degrees of willingness to talk about themselves and the past. Some, out of modesty, privacy or personality shared few details while others expressed their thoughts, opinions and experiences candidly. Several who were reticent and perhaps naturally a bit suspicious of me at first, became more open as I repeatedly contacted them over the years. But not everyone was happy to be found. Several had their reasons, not expressed to me, for not wanting to participate in the project. Perhaps the old days brought back too many painful memories or maybe they just did not want to be bothered.

For the students who had passed on, I was able to track down their husbands, wives, children, siblings, friends or classmates. Many of these contacts were very supportive, providing as much information as they could, while others knew only the barest of details about the students. One of the most rewarding aspects of this project was sending the valedictorian's children their parents' speeches and hearing the children's reactions and memories of their mothers and fathers.

Many photographs of the students that were taken before World War II were lost or destroyed during their internment and subsequent moves they made throughout their lives. Fortunately, some pictures survived. The individuals themselves, their family members or friends provided almost all of the photographs of the students. I gathered several others from newspapers and yearbooks from California public libraries and schools. Most of the photographs of the World War II detention camps came from the National Archives and Records Administration in Washington D.C.

Today, only a few fragile, decaying copies of *Orations and Essays* remain at the University of California at Los Angeles and Berkeley, and in private collections. In publishing this third edition, my goal is to preserve the speeches given by the first Japanese American valedictorians and make them widely accessible. I also want to document and celebrate the lives of these outstanding people.

This new edition is divided into two parts. Part 1 tells the story of the students' lives as a group, especially putting them in the context of American society and the Japanese American community before and during World War II. The information for part 1 was gathered through in-person, written or telephone interviews. Newspaper articles, books, public records and yearbooks provided additional resources. Part 2 contains the text of the graduation speeches that the Nisei valedictorians gave in the 1920s and 1930s.

Adjacent to the orations, I have included photos and a short biography of each student.

When I first started this project, I was hoping to collect in-depth life stories and juxtapose them next to each person's speech. As I began to gather the data, however, it soon became apparent that I could find volumes of information about some students but only a few facts about others. In addition, most people were not comfortable with me delving deeply into their personal lives. One valedictorian expressly said, "Don't single me out."

While the students' life experiences were varied and unique, they very much paralleled and affirmed the experience of Japanese Americans as a whole before and during World War II. Because of these factors, it made sense to treat the valedictorians as a group. For part 1, I wrote what I call a "collective narrative." Instead of focusing on individuals, I tried to create a "collage" or "mosaic" of the cohort. Although much has already been written about Japanese Americans and their incarceration during World War II, I still wanted to tell the story of these specific students within the context of those times. Readers who are already familiar with Japanese American history may wish to jump directly to the epilogue that follows the valedictorians after the war, at the end of part 1.

My research validated that much of the students' upbringing and life experiences mirrored what their generation faced. As a result, I attempted to make it clear when I was referring to the valedictorians as opposed to Nisei in general. When I use the term "Nisei" or "Japanese Americans," I am referring to not just the students, but to all those of their generation. When I write specifically about the people of *Orations and Essays*, I call them "valedictorians" or "students."

Part 2 of this book contains the forty-nine commencement speeches given in California by the students between 1923 and 1935. In this edition, I am pleased to add a fiftieth speech by Joe Masao Nakanishi, the 1939 valedictorian of Alhambra Union High School in Martinez, who turns eighty-four this year.

In the earlier editions of *Orations and Essays*, the speeches were presented in no discernable order. Here, I have organized them by topic. The topics are alphabetically listed in the contents and within each topic category the orations are listed alphabetically by the valedictorians' last names. To help readers find specific students easily, the appendix A contains lists of the valedictorians sorted alphabetically by last name, by school, by city and by year.

For this edition, the text of the orations was not edited except to correct misspellings and obvious errors of punctuation. Sentence structure was altered only when necessary for comprehension. The 1932 edition contained twenty-seven speeches and twenty-two more were added in 1935. Part 2 of this book is comprised of all the speeches from the 1935 edition. My additions to the original material are: the introduction to part 2; Joe M. Nakanishi's speech; all photographs; and the brief biographies provided in the sidebars. Any material from the 1932 and 1935 editions not included in part 2 can be found in appendix B.

One of the major problems all Japanese Americans faced in the first half of the twentieth century was their fight to be seen as Americans, not foreigners. As we begin the twenty-first century, many people still continue this struggle. I hope this book will inspire us to overcome our obstacles and challenges, whatever they may be, and help us appreciate former generations who made the United States of America the great country that it is.

*Two pages of the table of contents from the 1935 edition of* Orations and Essays by the Japanese Second Generation of America.

I would also like this book to serve as a reminder to never repeat the racist times and hysteria that led to the expulsion and incarceration of people of Japanese heritage during World War II. Since the September 11th tragedy and war against Iraq, Arab and Muslim Americans have been attacked and their civil liberties violated, echoing what happened more than sixty years ago to the people of Japanese ancestry in the U.S. We must learn from our history so that our country can avoid making the same mistakes again.

Even though I never knew my grandfather, preserving and adding to his work makes me feel closer to him. I hope he would be very happy and pleased with this new edition if he were alive.

Joyce Hirohata
June 2003
Oakland, California

## Notes

1   See appendix B for the English translations of the preface to the first and second editions of *Orations and Essays* written in Japanese by Paul Tsunegoro Hirohata.

# Acknowledgments

THIS PROJECT was truly a team endeavor. Without the help of many individuals and groups, this book would not have been published. I would first like to sincerely thank the following people and organizations that promoted this project, playing an invaluable role in helping me find the Nisei students of *Orations and Essays*: Hiro Takenaga, *Asahi Japan*; Yoshiko Urayama, *Chicago Shimpo*; Warren Iwasa, *Hawaii Herald*; J.K. Yamamoto, *Hokubei Mainichi*; Toshiaki Ogasawara and Yoshikazu Ishizuka, *Japan Times*; Bill Schechner, *KPIX Channel 5 News*; Kenji Taguma, *Nichi Bei Times*; Jeffery Kimoto, *Nikkei West*; George Kihara, *Nisei Post 8985 VFW*; Mick Matsuzawa, *North American Post*; Paul Nagano, *NCJCCF Domei Newsletter*; Caroline Aoyagi and Martha Nakagawa, *Pacific Citizen*; Nina Thorsen and Nguyen Qui Duc, *Pacific Time from KQED Radio*; Michael Komai and John Saito, *Rafu Shimpo*; Alissa Hiraga, *Rafu Shimpo Magazine*; Yoriko Imada, *Rocky Mountain Jiho*; and Charles Burress, *San Francisco Chronicle*.

I extend my heartfelt appreciation to all the individuals who gave me information and leads in my search for the valedictorians. I would especially like to acknowledge Harry Honda, Dr. Andrew Kim and Nancy Matsuda for their help.

My thanks also to the Japanese American National Museum in Los Angeles and National Japanese American Historical Society in San Francisco for their resources. I would also like to extend my gratitude to Diane Matsuda and Dr. Kevin Starr of the California Civil Liberties Public Education Program for supporting this project.

I extend sincerest thanks to the valedictorians themselves for sharing their lives and pictures for this book. For additional information and photographs of the students I am indebted to the family members and friends of the Nisei students.

To the financial contributors to this project, I extend my utmost gratitude: the California Civil Liberties Public Education Program, Jocelyn and Gary Chu, Kiku Tanaka, John and Harumi Hirohata, Yoko and David Hayashi, Chiaki and Sumiko Tanaka, Seigo and Tamiko Hirohata, the Don and May Iwahashi Scholarship, the Rod Ishii Scholarship, the daughters of valedictorians Frank Yamakoshi and Helen Kuwada, (Agnes Sasaki, Esther Ura, Shirley Baskin, Lois and Carole Yamakoshi).

For their suggestions to improve the manuscript, I am grateful to Jere Takahashi, Jocelyn Chu, Yo Hironaka and Gail Tanaka, board member of the San Francisco chapter of the Japanese American Citizens League and granddaughter of valedictorian Haruko Fujita. Many thanks go to Dean Yabuki for his excellent advice and for helping me obtain photographs from the National Archives and Records Administration.

I cannot express enough appreciation to my team who helped me create this book and made it such an enjoyable process. For championing the project in its early stages with unwavering commitment, I am indebted to Gail Tanaka. Many thanks go to my editor, Gil Asakawa, for his expertise, unending encouragement and going above and beyond his role. I am extremely grateful to Shelly Keller who copy edited the manuscript and assisted in so many other ways. For their important contributions I would like to acknowledge Mik Gaspay who produced the cover and Victoria May who created the layouts of the interior pages of this book. Many thanks go to Toshi Uesato for the English translations of the Japanese text, Ben Pease for making the maps, and Bill Hosokawa and David Yoo for writing the forewords.

I would like to express my deepest gratitude to my family, in particular my parents and J.S.H., and in-laws, Carmen and Sam, for their care and encouragement. A very special "thank you" goes to my husband, Mark, for his love and support. Lastly, I would like to thank Jesus Christ for putting me on the earth to do this project and for giving me the courage and strength to complete it.

# PART ONE

# Living in Two Worlds

Kozue Fujikawa (foreground kneeling, second from left) photographed here before a 1933 performance of Puccini's Madam Butterfly at the Hollywood Bowl near Los Angeles. The small child (right) is her younger sister, Chizuko, who was also in the opera. *Courtesy of Chizuko Sanford*.

# Introduction to Part 1

PART 1 of this book documents the lives of fifty academically gifted second generation Japanese, or Nisei, from childhood in the 1930s until the end of World War II. What was it like for them to grow up in California and attend public schools? Chapter 1 tries to capture that period of their lives. In chapter 2 the valedictorians enter young adulthood. Some went to college in the U.S. and others went to Japan. Several did not go on to higher education and married and started families. The chapter ends with the attack on Pearl Harbor and records the students' feelings and reactions to the start of the war between the country of their birthright and the country of their heritage.

Chapter 3 describes the incarceration of people of Japanese ancestry in the spring of 1942. Many of the students were held in temporary camps all over California. Those valedictorians who left California before internment began, relocated to states away from the West Coast. Chapter 4 describes their experiences as well as those of students who were in Asia or serving in the U.S. Military.

After several months in temporary camps, people of Japanese heritage were moved to ten permanent concentration camps in the interior of the United States. Chapter 5 describes how the valedictorians coped, providing an account of the turmoil they experienced when filling out a government "loyalty questionnaire" in 1943.

Chapter 6 discusses how students gained permission to leave the internment camps to continue their education or volunteer for the U.S. military. Other valedictorians left the centers well before the war was over, relocating to the Midwest.

In 1944 people of Japanese ancestry were allowed to return to the West Coast, but many students remained in the camps until they were closed after the war. Chapter 7 follows the valedictorians' return to California. With determination they slowly rebuilt their lives and raised their children. This chapter also provides an account of a few students who were still in Japan and Manchuria when the war ended.

When World War II was over, the valedictorians in this volume were between twenty-five and thirty-eight years old. They were still young enough to rebuild their lives, but many of their parents' generation were broken by the trauma of the incarceration. The after-affects of the incarceration reverberated for generations, still touching families to this day. Just when the internment camps seem like a relic of the past, the September 11th attacks of 2001 sparked fear and hatred, but this time toward another ethnic group. Once again, American civil liberties and freedoms are being threatened.


## GLOSSARY

**Issei** *(pronounced "ee-say")*
First generation Japanese immigrants from Japan

**Nisei** *(pronounced "nee-say")*
Second generation, U.S.-born, American citizen children of the Issei

**Kibei** *(pronounced "kee-bay")*
A Nisei who was primarily educated in Japan

# 1. Growing up in Two Worlds

*There is another group of people whom we must thank and love most dearly. They are those who were a haven in every storm, those who toiled unceasingly so that we might have the best. How often we realize that our education has meant many sacrifices to them. . . . To you, dear fathers and mothers, we extend our most heartfelt thanks.*

Ayame Ichiyasu
San Francisco High School of Commerce, 1933

JOHN AISO, one of the older valedictorians in this volume, was born in 1909 in Burbank, California. His father came to the United States from the Shizuoka prefecture in 1898 and provided for six children by working as a gardener from 4:00 in the morning until 8:00 at night. There were no pickup trucks or electric lawn mowers at that time. His father rode a bicycle to work, carrying a lawn mower on his left shoulder and hanging a fifty-foot garden hose on his handle bars.[1]

Aiso's mother came to California during the Russo-Japanese War (1904–1905). Out of her meager earnings as a laundrywoman, she purchased pictures of George Washington, Abraham Lincoln and Jesus Christ. She hung them in the family's parlor and instructed Aiso to emulate the admirable qualities of these historical characters.[2] But no matter how much Aiso's mother believed in American ideals or how hard his father worked, they could never become American citizens. In 1790 the United States Congress decreed that only "free white persons" and "persons of African descent" could become naturalized.[3]

Although the Issei, first generation Japanese immigrants, were barred from citizenship, it was the birthright of their daughters and sons, the Nisei, which means second generation. As the Nisei grew up, they were encouraged to be loyal citizens *and* be proud of their Japanese heritage.[4] Aiso said his parents constantly reminded him

The Nisei went to public schools with students of all ethnicities. Kameko Yoshioka (third row from top, center) attended Edison Technical High School in Fresno, California in 1932. *Courtesy of Lisa Sato.*

that his conduct would "mold the image in which all Japanese persons would be held."[5] For children growing up in a society that was not ready to accept them, becoming a "bridge" between American and Japanese culture was a difficult task.

Like their parents, the students in this book were pioneers. They excelled academically—some despite the handicap of prejudice. The fifty students featured in this book were the first Japanese American valedictorians and salutatorians in California public schools in the 1920s and 1930s. Molded by the American educational system, they were patriotic youths who also reflected the aspirations and hopes of their parents.

Being top in their class was a testimony to the valedictorians' hard work. This is especially true, considering that for almost all of them, Japanese was their first language and public school was their first real introduction to American culture. Their parents did not

Many Nisei grew up in rural farming areas. George Inagaki (third row from top, far left) attended the El Dorado School in Florin, California in 1921. *Courtesy of Chris Inagaki.*

speak English well and some of the students were isolated because their families lived on farms and in rural areas. If there were no English-speaking children nearby, some Nisei were not exposed to English until kindergarten and, as a result, were held back one school year.

Charles Inouye, a 1932 graduate of Sequoia High School in Redwood City, California, said in his graduation speech, "When I came to Sequoia, being ignorant of many of the American customs and not being able to speak as fluently as others, I felt somewhat out of place." Florence Akiyama, born in Fresno, California in 1914, had a similar experience. In her 1932 Sanger High School Valedictory address, "What High School Means to a Japanese Girl," she said, "High school education means the absorption of the American spirit, I mean not only the attitude toward America but also the customs and the innate ability to speak and think in the English language. . . . In short, I have had to learn two languages and two customs."

At school the students learned American values and spoke English. They lived in an almost exclusively Japanese environment at home, although most admitted they spoke English with siblings. After regular school or on Saturdays, many Nisei also attended special Japanese schools to improve their Japanese language skills.

Not only was citizenship unavailable to their parents, laws such as the Alien Land Law were passed to bar the Issei from landownership, a direct attempt to cut off their farming livelihood. They also suffered from threats and violence by racist mobs. Newspapers such as the *Chronicle* in San Francisco ran sensational anti-Japanese articles under headlines such as: JAPANESE A MENACE TO AMERICAN WOMEN; BROWN MEN ARTISANS STEAL BRAINS OF WHITES; and BROWN MEN AN EVIL IN THE PUBLIC SCHOOLS.[6] With all the prejudice Japanese Americans faced elsewhere, educational institutions should have been a safe haven and learning environment. But that was not always the case. In 1906 the San Francisco Board of Education tried unsuccessfully to force the Nisei into segregated Oriental Schools created for Chinese American children.[7]

Given the racial climate in California in the early 1900s, some students in this book aroused extreme controversy just for being Japanese American. Aiso became the valedictorian of Hollywood High School and Brown University, and later graduated from Harvard Law School. Before achieving those honors, in 1923 he made front-page news in the Los Angeles press at the age of twelve while attending Le Conte Junior High School in Hollywood. His

Florence Akiyama (bottom row, right) in the 1932 Sanger High School yearbook, the *Echo. Courtesy of the Sanger Depot Museum in Sanger, California.*

John Aiso (left) accompanied classmate Herbert Wenig to Washington D.C. in 1926 as Wenig's coach and traveling companion. *Courtesy of Emi Gauville.*

classmates elected him student body president, but their angry parents protested, saying, "No child of mine is going to be under a Jap." Aiso was not allowed to take office and student government was suspended until he graduated. A number of teachers sympathized with him and encouraged him saying, "John, don't give up. No one can stop a good man."[8]

At Hollywood High School, Aiso again faced rejection because of his heritage. He tried to enroll in a Junior Reserve Officer's Training Corps (ROTC) program but the Army instructor refused his application saying, "The American Army doesn't need any Japs." So Aiso joined the debate team instead. In no time he became the captain but racism would continue to stifle his success.

In 1926, Hollywood High School held a speech contest. The winner would travel to Washington D.C. to compete in a national competition, sponsored by several major newspapers. Aiso won first place and in June, the faculty selected him to be the graduating class valedictorian. Afraid that parents and students would protest a Japanese American student dominating two high honors, the principal of Hollywood High School forced Aiso to choose between the contest and the valedictory address. Amidst the controversy and flurry of newspaper articles in the *Los Angeles Times, The Washington Post* and *The Washington Star*, as well as the Japanese American press, Aiso reluctantly forfeited competing in the national contest.[9]

Not all students faced such public scandals, but some still encountered prejudice. Kiyoshi Ichiyasu remembers how his older sister, Ayame, almost lost her rightful honor at the San Francisco High School of Commerce. "During the faculty's valedictorian selection meeting, objection to Ayame was, 'Her voice wouldn't carry,'" he said. "The main reason was the fact that the atmosphere was anti-Japanese. It did not matter she was American and she excelled at school." Non-prejudiced faculty prevailed and in 1933 Ayame Ichiyasu became the first Japanese American valedictorian at that school.

Pearl Kurokawa faced a similar situation when she was about to graduate from Arroyo Grande Union High School in 1932. Her father came home and told her he had overheard a group of school trustees talking in the café where he always had coffee. Because Kurokawa was Japanese, the board members were planning to give the valedictory speech to the Caucasian student whose grades were second highest. Kurokawa told her father, "You know, they can't do that." She did volunteer work in the principal's office, and knew all the students' grades and told her father, "I know my grade is top." After hearing this, her father boldly went back to the café and confronted the trustees with this information. "And when they heard that, they couldn't very well not ask me. So I was asked," she said.

The experience surprised her. She was unaware of the school administration's feelings and it was the first time she experienced anti-Japanese racism. Until then, hers had been a very positive school experience.

Most of the students reported they were not treated differently because of their ethnicity and their classmates were friendly. "At Brawley Union High School, the Nisei at that time were active in varsity sports, football especially," valedictorian Matilde Honda recalled. "Our Caucasian friends were appreciative of our accomplishments, but did not invite us to their homes or social functions."

Beyond the school walls, Nisei rarely socialized with non-Japanese classmates. Frank Chuman was an exception. His experience at Los Angeles High School was very different from the other valedictorians featured in this book and not the norm for Japanese

## Hanford Honors Students To Be Closing Orators

HANFORD (Kings Co.), April 23.—Miss Martha Ann Buckner of Hanford and Kiyoshi Nobusada of Armona, the students with the highest scholastic standings, have been selected as salutatorian and valedictorian, respectively, of the Hanford High

**Martha Buckner**

School graduating class.

Nobusada, a son of Mr. and Mrs. T. Nobusada, Armona merchants, had an exceptionally high standing. Graduating from grammar school at Armona with highest honors, he finished high school

**Kiyoshi Nobusada**

with the same record. He is a member of the Alpha Omega Omicron national honor society and a charter member of the Quill and Scroll journalistic honor society here. He is business manager of The Janus, high school yearbook, and last year held the same position for The Meteor, the school newspaper. In athletics he was on the basketball squad during his sophomore and junior years, and this year and last played on the varsity baseball team. He was president of the class as a sophomore.

Valedictorians were featured in the local press as well as in Japanese American newspapers. Clipping of Kiyoshi Nobusada in 1934. *Courtesy of Yemi Nobusada.*

Americans at that time. Unaware of his unpopular Japanese heritage, Chuman led a full social life including occasional dates with non-Japanese girls. Breaking the stereotype of the studious Asian nerd, he learned to play poker and smoke cigarettes from classmates who invited him to their homes.

The majority of teachers and school administrators the Nisei students encountered were not prejudiced but were supportive and encouraging. Some educators went out of their way to be especially kind. Even though Michiko Naito only attended Lovell Grammar School in Orosi, California for her graduation year in 1934, her teacher checked Naito's grades from her previous school and gave her the valedictory honor. Naito said she felt bad for the boy who was originally scheduled for the farewell address. The same teacher attended Naito's high school graduation and encouraged her to continue her education. When Naito was later incarcerated in the detention camps, the teacher wrote to her and shipped packages of pecan nuts and persimmons.

Some students were too busy working on the family farm or attending Japanese school to pursue many extracurricular activities, but those who did participate engaged in sports, student govern-

Above: Michiko Naito with her parents in 1920. *Courtesy of Michiko Naito.*

Below: Yoshiko Higuchi (first row, fourth from left), president of the Monterey Buddhist Women's Organization in 1934. *Courtesy of Tazu Kanda.*

ment and honor societies. Going to the local dance hall or attending Sunday service at a non-Japanese church was another matter
entirely. Racial barriers blocked the students from participating in
mainstream society. So the Japanese American community created
its own rich subculture of churches, temples and social clubs that
held picnics, festivals, dances and special events. Groups such as the
Young Women's Buddhist Association and its male counterpart
enabled the Nisei to have fun and experience leadership roles for
the first time while creating a small tightly-knit world.[10]

When the students ventured out of the Japanese American
community, they were often met with humiliation and disappointment. Shizue Ohashi, the Canoga Park High School valedictorian in
1932, was a tomboy in a family of five girls. She recalled being
invited to a Caucasian friend's swimming party but was not allowed
to enter the Pasadena public pool. " I couldn't understand why, but
my older sister did. She just said, 'Keep quiet.' " The two sisters waited outside the fence as their friends went swimming without them.
The rejection was confusing and frustrating because near her home,
Ohashi swam at the public city pools called "plunges" without
interference. But in Pasadena, the pools were privately run and did

George Inagaki (top row, third from left)
with the Sacramento Junior College Men's
Club in 1932. *Courtesy of Chris Inagaki.*

not admit Asians. "That was my first feeling of discrimination . . . from a big social aspect," Ohashi said.

Kazuya Sanada, born in San Francisco in 1916, recalls a similar incident in the city with his Boy Scout troop at the Sutro Bath pools at the Cliff House. He said, "I went there in my scout uniform and all were allowed in except me. They asked me if I had a 'health certificate.' They wouldn't let me in." Outraged, the scoutmaster called the group back and they left. Not only were Japanese Americans excluded from swimming pools, they were barred from restaurants, dance halls, hotels and barbershops. Real estate agents would not rent apartments or homes to them. Although not as severe as the African-Americans' experience in the South, segregation was a way of life for Asians in California. Outside of the Southern states, California passed more "Jim Crow" laws imposing racial segregation than any other state in the U.S.[11]

Navigating through adolescence was hard enough, but Japanese Americans experienced the added burden of trying to feel proud of their heritage in a world that despised it. Nisei author Yoshiko Uchida who grew up in Berkeley, California poignantly described the inner conflict in her book, *Desert Exile*:

Kiyoshi Nobusada (second row from bottom, far right) with the Armona Grammar School in Kings county, California circa 1930. *Courtesy of Yemi Nobusada.*

Society caused us to feel ashamed of something that should have made us feel proud. Instead of directing anger at the society that excluded and diminished us, such was the climate of the times and so low our self-esteem that many of us Nisei tried to reject our own Japaneseness and the Japanese way of our parents.[12]

Shizu Komae, who was born and raised in Los Angeles, said she sometimes asked herself, "What am I? Am I Japanese or am I American?" The way society treated her made her wonder. "Because no matter how American you are inside, people don't know. They just take one look at you and say '&^%$ Jap!' or something like that."

## NOTES

1  John Aiso, "Remarks by Justice Aiso at the "Jokun" Recognition Banquet, 1985," in Tad Ichinokuchi, *John Aiso and the MIS* (Los Angeles, CA: MIS Club of Southern CA, 1988), 28.

2  Ibid.

3  Frank F. Chuman, *The Bamboo People: The Law and Japanese-Americans* (Chicago, IL: Japanese American Research Project, Japanese American Citizens League, 1981), 66.

4  Paul T. Hirohata, ed., translation of preface to *Orations and Essays by the Japanese Second Generation of America* (Los Angeles: Los Angeles Daily News, 1935), vi.

5  Ichinokuchi, *John Aiso and the MIS*, 29.

6  Bill Hosokawa, *Nisei: The Quiet Americans* (New York, NY: William Morrow, 1969), 82.

7  Chuman, *The Bamboo People*, 24.

8  Ichinokuchi, *John Aiso and the MIS*, 5.

9  Ibid., 6-7.

10  David Yoo, *Growing Up Nisei: Race, Generation, and Culture among Japanese Americans of California, 1924-49* (Urbana, IL: University of Illinois Press, 2000), 46-48.

11  Jim Crow Legislation Overview, By Susan Falck, M.A., Research Associate, California State University-Northridge, California, available at <www.jimcrowhistory.org/resources/lessonplans/hs_es_jim_crow_laws.htm>.

12  Yoshiko Uchida, *Desert Exile: The Uprooting of a Japanese-American Family* (Seattle, WA: University of Washington Press, 1982), 42.

After high school graduation, the valedic-torians looked toward the future with high hopes. Haruko Fujita in a portrait taken in Los Angeles to celebrate her wedding engagement in 1939. *Courtesy of Haruko Fujita. Photographer, Toyo Miyatake.*

# 2. Beginning of the Test

*Moreover, at present the colleges are overcrowded, and there is no place for the loafer there. The incapable, ill-prepared student would only be wasting his time, energy, and money by entering college.*

Matilde Honda
Brawley Union High School, 1933

VALEDICTORIAN Shizue Ohashi remembered a scenario that was typical in her day: a Nisei friend had graduated from the California Institute of Technology but could only get a job at a fruit stand. Japanese Americans were eager to attend universities after high school, but investing in degrees didn't lead to the American Dream. Racial prejudice blocked them from working in their desired careers and college graduates often found themselves stuck doing menial jobs such as gardening or working in the produce business.

In spite of the obstacles and uncertainties of life after college graduation, many valedictorians in this book hoped for the best, going on to higher learning after high school. Twenty-eight students out of fifty (56%) graduated from four-year universities.[1] Eleven of these graduates (39%) were female. With modest family incomes and the hard times of the Depression, higher education was both a luxury and a sacrifice. The University of California at Los Angeles and Berkeley were the most popular choices, where tuition in the 1930s was about $29 per semester.

Six women and six men (43%) of the twenty-eight students who finished four years of college went on to earn post-graduate degrees. Knowing the difficulty the Nisei would face in the professional job market, some Issei thought the second generation should get as much education as possible and specialize in a line of work.[2] Most Issei toiled as farmers, gardeners and small business owners.

They hoped that if their children became experts in a particular field, this would make the Nisei more employable and increase their chances for white-collar employment in mainstream society.

Most valedictorians reported positive experiences in college but some still dealt with anti-Japanese prejudice, especially when it came to housing. Pearl Kurokawa was taking her last year of public health nursing at the University of California, San Francisco, renting an apartment from a landlord who didn't want Kurokawa's ethnicity identified. To hide the fact that a Japanese tenant was living in the building, the landlord changed the spelling of Kurokawa's name on the mailbox. "Kurokowski would have made me Russian or something, I guess," Kurokawa said.

Frank Chuman, who played poker in high school, continued to have a full, active social life at University of California, Los Angeles. He felt he could do anything and was still "naïve," as he described himself. His dream, unknown to his father, was to become a United States Foreign Service officer. Chuman's father had almost entered the Japan Foreign Service but had abandoned that ambition after immigrating to America. At the University of California, Los Angeles, Chuman prepared himself for his future career. He majored in political science and studied French, the international language at that time. When he was about to graduate in 1938, the dean of the political science department, who was a retired foreign service officer, heard of Chuman's desire to go to Georgetown University's School of Foreign Service. He called Chuman into his office and told him not to bother because even if he passed the rigorous entrance exam, he would never be appointed because of his race. Chuman said, "When I heard that, I was, frankly, devastated. Really crushed. What can I do? . . . I'm here. I want to go there. I'm brimming with ambition to try to please my father."

As painful as the rejection was, it became an opportunity for a different path. After graduation, while working as a messenger for the Los Angeles County Probation Department, Chuman became interested in law. In 1940 he entered the University of Southern California Law School. He was the only Japanese American student; the last one before him had graduated eight years prior. Chuman continued to work for the Probation Department and was promoted, to clerk. Even while holding a full-time job and doing demanding academic work, Chuman made time for fun. He frequently played poker and golf and went to dances with his classmates. "I'm not a scholar," he said.

Top: Jimmie Hamasaki in his graduation photo from Meiji University in Japan in 1941. *Courtesy of Clara Hamasaki.*

Bottom: Kiyoshi Murakami in ROTC uniform at UCLA circa 1935. *Courtesy of Irene Yamaguchi.*

In the 1930s several thousand Nisei went to Japan, mostly to study the Japanese language and look for better employment opportunities. Unfortunately, they were treated as foreigners and as children of low-class peasant immigrants.[3] Still, four male valedictorians—Jimmie Hamasaki, Kiyoshi Murakami, Goro Murata and Toshio Yamagata— took the risk and went to Japan for education and better jobs.

Born in Guadalupe, California in 1916, Jimmie Hamasaki graduated from nearby Santa Maria Union High School in 1934. After working a year for expenses, he went to Japan and was admitted to Meiji University in Tokyo. In early 1941 he graduated with a law degree.

Kiyoshi Murakami had difficulty getting into Japanese law school because he had completed college in the U.S. After graduating from the University of California, Los Angeles as a political science major, he went to Tokyo and passed the entrance exam for Chuo University Law School. However, the university refused to admit him because he had not been educated in Japan. Murakami's Buddhist priest thought this was very unjust and approached the Ministry of Education about the ruling and won the case. The decision was reversed and Murakami made history as the first Nisei accepted into Chuo University without being educated in Japanese schools.

The eldest valedictorian in this book, Goro Murata was born in Montebello, California in 1907. In 1926 he graduated from Montebello High School and four years later earned his bachelor's degree at nearby Whittier College. He became interested in Japan after the Olympics were held in Los Angeles in 1932 and two years later traveled to Tokyo. The oldest English language newspaper in the country, the *Japan Times & Mail*, today called the *Japan Times*, gave him a job and he became a newspaperman.

Orphaned at the age of six, Toshio Yamagata was taken from Fowler, California to Japan by relatives. He lived there for nine years, returning to California in 1927. This made him a Kibei, a Nisei who was educated in Japan and returned to America. According to his daughter, Jeannette, Yamagata had to relearn English when he came back to the United States. He became a commencement speaker for the 1933 Fowler High School senior class and in 1939 earned a B.S. in Commerce from the University of California, Berkeley. After graduation he found his diploma was worthless. His daughter wrote, "My father did say that due to discrimination, he could find no work in his field in the U.S. He

Toshio Yamagata (left) and brother, Goro, in 1928. *Courtesy of Jeannette Sanderson.*

Left: Helen Kuwada married Frank Yamakoshi in 1937 at the San Jose Buddhist Church in Northern California. *Courtesy of Agnes Sasaki.*

Above: Helen Kuwada with the family car at a Young Women's Buddhist Association function in Gilroy, California in 1935. *Courtesy of Agnes Sasaki.*

decided to go to Japan where he knew that bilingual workers would be needed for office work."

After working on a fruit farm and earning money as a Japanese language teacher and Buddhist Sunday school teacher, by 1940 Yamagata had saved enough money for ship fare. When he arrived back in Japan, the first job he acquired was as an office clerk in the city of Nagoya. "When a better offer came up to work in Harbin, Manchuria, he took it," his daughter said. "He became a civilian employee of the [Japanese] army. His job was to translate books and other printed matter for the Japanese occupation forces."

Since most of the valedictorians in this book went to college, they didn't marry until later in life. But for those with limited finances and the need to help their families at home and on the farm, higher education was just not possible. Of the seven female commencement speakers who did not attend college, six married soon after high school. Helen Kuwada of Gilroy, California married a fellow Nisei from this volume, Frank Yamakoshi who was from the same town. They initially met because Yamakoshi was helping collect speeches for the second edition of *Orations and Essays* and he approached Kuwada to ask her for a copy of her graduation speech. Years later in a 1996 family newsletter, Kuwada wrote about their first encounter, "In 1933 when I was chosen to speak at my grammar school graduation, a man . . . came to me to ask me for a copy of my speech so that he could send it someplace. I had never seen this man before, but I said, 'Okay.' That was the first time I saw and met Frank."

Kuwada went on to Live Oaks High School, graduating in just three years so she could help on her family's farm. Because she had also skipped a grade in grammar school, she was only sixteen when she completed high school in 1936. Yamakoshi had graduated from Gilroy High School four years prior. He also finished high school in just three years to work on the family farm. Both outstanding students deserved higher educations, but familial obligations and lack of money prevented them from going to college. After attending many Buddhist church functions where their friendship deepened, the two were married a year after Kuwada graduated from high school. She was seventeen and Yamakoshi was twenty-two years old. They chose July 3, 1937 for their wedding date since their families and friends would not have to work in the fields on July 4.

Shizue Ohashi, the tomboy from Canoga Park, California, also did not pursue a college education after high school. "I didn't go to college. That was during the Depression so my father decided I'd better have a profession," she explained, "Because there was no work, not even for men." Her father thought barbering was a good vocation and she agreed, so he sent her to a barber's college in Los Angeles. "I did everything my father told me. He had an insight. He told me, 'Shizue, you have a business head so don't go take Latin and all [those types of subjects].'"

After she graduated from barber's school in 1933, an Issei in East Los Angeles asked her to come work at his barbershop. She charged twenty-five cents for a haircut. The barber wanted to sell his equipment and go back to Japan so she took over his shop for $250. She lived in the back of the business by herself until she got

Shizue Ohashi and her husband Hiroshi Naramura in 1934. *Courtesy of Shizue Ohashi.*

married and her husband joined her. In August 1934 Ohashi married Hiroshi Naramura who was nine years her senior and an Issei who had come to the United States at the age of sixteen. They were a dual-income couple: she made about $20 a week cutting hair and he earned $18 a week working at Grand Central Market in the produce department. Ohashi said the income "wasn't bad" during the Depression, a time when Frank Chuman recalled Nisei couples living on as little as $50 per month.

*The world interest of the last century in the Atlantic has been shifting to the Pacific base. Probably in the near future, the Pacific will be the central stage of international drama.*

Yoshiko Higuchi,
Monterey Union High School, 1932

Over sixty years later, the memory of Pearl Harbor is still vivid for some of the students and they relive the pain with each anniversary. Kazuya Sanada, the ex-Boy Scout from San Francisco, remarked, "When December 7th comes around, it kind of hits you. . . . It still hurts."

By 1940, many of the valedictorians were finishing college or had started families. They looked forward to the future with high hopes, but trouble loomed on the international stage. In 1931 Japan had seized and occupied Manchuria, a province of China. During

By 1940 several valedictorians had started families. Kameko Yoshioka with her first born son, David, at a Southern California beach in 1940. *Courtesy of Lisa Sato.*

the rest of the decade, the Japanese military systematically consolidated its hold over much of Asia. In 1937 Japan began a brutal war in China and occupied northern French Indochina (Vietnam) in 1940.

The United States was already worried about the rise of Nazism and conflict in Europe. It turned its attention to the Far East and placed an embargo on raw materials and oil to Japan. This provided the Japanese military an excuse to wage war. The Nisei's world was destroyed on December 7, 1941 when Japan attacked Pearl Harbor and the United States entered World War II. Anyone of Japanese descent, including American citizens, was now the enemy and a walking target for outright abuse.

Sanada had graduated from the University of California, Los Angeles in June 1941. Prior to his graduation, Alexander & Baldwin, one of the big accounting firms in Hawaii, had visited Sanada's campus to recruit bilingual Nisei staff and had offered him a job. To prepare for his move to the islands, he sold everything he owned and bought some new clothes. He said, "I was planning to go as soon as possible, but couldn't get on a ship. Everybody was going to Hawaii for vacation because Europe was at war." In October, as he tried in vain to book passage, an ominous cablegram came from the accounting firm. It read, "Trouble in the Pacific." Sanada didn't mind. He was anxious to start his new life. Then another cablegram followed in November that told him not to come. The company's assets were frozen in Japan, but the firm promised to hold his job for him.

Sanada was still living with his parents in Los Angeles, waiting for instructions from the Hawaii accounting firm, when Pearl Harbor was attacked. That Sunday in December he was working at Von's Supermarket in Santa Monica and noticed some people outside were walking around with guns. All the Japanese Americans at the store who had contact with customers were sent to work in the warehouse to protect them from potentially hostile shoppers. Describing what it felt like to be of Japanese heritage after what Japan had done, Sanada said, "It was kind of embarrassing and it was kind of hurting you, too," he said. "And here I am, born and raised here. I'm a citizen."

Joe Nakanishi shared the same feelings of shame and pain. He had grown up in Martinez, California and was attending California Polytechnic State University, San Luis Obispo. He will never forget December 7, 1941 because it was also his sister's wedding day. The next day he boarded a Greyhound bus and was returning to San Luis

Kazuya Sanada in graduation gown at UCLA in 1941. *Courtesy of Kazuya Sanada.*

Joe M. Nakanishi on a farm in 1940.
*Courtesy of Joe M. Nakanishi.*

Obispo. At Pinole, two sheriff's officers came aboard and took him off the bus. They searched his baggage on the sidewalk. He said, "It was embarrassing to see people watching as if I was a spy or a criminal." He was allowed to continue his trip and on arrival at San Luis Obispo, two more sheriff officers awaited him, searching his luggage again. They let him go and did not bother him after that.

Frank Chuman was at home with his sister and parents when they heard the news of Pearl Harbor over the radio. Immediately, his mother and father set about burning letters and photographs of family members in Japan and anything else that connected them with the old country. They didn't want to appear loyal to Japan in any way. Chuman watched his father destroy two beautiful heirloom swords that he had brought in 1906. His father took the swords outside to the backyard and thrust the naked blades straight into the ground as deep as they would go. Then he covered the handles with dirt so that they couldn't be seen from the surface. As a boy, Chuman had grown up admiring the swords and looked forward to inheriting them someday. "Even today, I still have a sort of ache in my heart, because I would be very proud to display those swords in my home," he said. "I thought to myself, how stupid of Japan to go to war with the United States. I felt that my relationship with Japan as a nation, as a people, maybe even emotionally, would end with the outbreak of the war. This, of course was very naïve thinking, but that's the way I thought."[4]

Despite how much the students in this volume had heard about Japan through their parents, they had very little connection to it. Almost half of them, including Frank Chuman, had never been there. Nine years before the Pearl Harbor attacks, Kameko Yoshioka had written in her speech at Edison Technical High School, "We, whose parents have already taught us the ideals of their homeland, should, as loyal Americans, lose no chance of learning and understanding the ideals of America, *our* country."

"I felt that I was thoroughly Americanized," said Matilde Honda. "We [Nisei] didn't associate ourselves with Japan in any way except through our parents."

About war with Japan, Michiko Naito remarked, "I wasn't happy about the whole situation but never felt any loyalty to Japan as being born and raised in America. My loyalty was only to this country." Pearl Kurokawa had similar feelings saying, "I never felt there was a choice."

The Nisei and their families feared retaliation because they were of Japanese ancestry. They knew the discrimination and hatred against them would only grow worse. December 7th not only opened the war between Japan and the United States, it also sparked the mistreatment of Japanese Americans by their own government. Later that day, Frank Chuman drove to Little Tokyo in Los Angeles to see what was going on. "It was like a ghost town," he said. "I felt very conscious of the fact that I had a Japanese face. I wondered how we would be treated by our non-Japanese friends and neighbors." [5]

## Notes

1   Five other valedictorians (three female and two male) graduated from two-year colleges. Three other female valedictorians went to four-year colleges later in life after World War II.

2   Jere Takahashi, *Nisei/Sansei, Shifting Japanese American Identities and Politics* (Philadelphia: Temple University Press, 1997), 28–29.

3   Yoo, *Growing Up Nisei*, 35. Citing Toyomi Morimoto, "Language and Heritage Maintenance of Immigrants: Japanese Language Schools of California, 1903–1941" (Ph.D. diss., University of California, Los Angeles, 1989), 130–132.

4   John Tateishi, *And Justice for All: An Oral History of the Japanese American Detention Camps* (New York, NY: Random House, 1984), 228–229.

5   Hosokawa, *Nisei: The Quiet Americans*, 233.

During World War II some valedictorians lived in horse stalls. Here, an Issei woman knitting in her horse stall barrack in the Tanforan Assembly Center near San Francisco in July 1942. *Courtesy of the National Archives and Records Administration, WRA Collection (Gretchen Van Tassel).*

# 3. Kiss Freedom Goodbye

*Memories are the priceless treasures of youth, which neither gold nor jewels can buy. No one can rob us of these. In the days to come when we may be flanked with despair and bitterness we can always hold our memories most dear.*

Ayame Ichiyasu
San Francisco High School of Commerce, 1933

"THE WAR came along and it was sort of a fine time to get rid of us," said one valedictorian who wished to remain anonymous. "I felt that way at the time and still feel that was the reason instead of all this scare about being spies. . . . We were all suspected, but why not the Germans and Italians?" The valedictorian continued, "I do not believe that we were evacuated because of military necessity. Economics and politics had a lot to do with it. Certain factions in California wanted the Japanese out, especially the big farmers, who feared that the Japanese were becoming too successful."

The Issei had transformed the California desert into some of the most fertile farmland, of which they owned and leased thousands of acres. They produced almost thirty-five percent of the state's truck crops and by 1941 they had a monopoly on beans, strawberries and celery.[1] With Japanese farmers out of the way, their competition would cease.

For almost fifty years, racist groups wanted to get rid of the Japanese in California. Now that the country was at war with Japan, they saw their chance. They began an intense hate and rumor campaign. Newspapers trumpeted false reports about Japanese Americans living along the West Coast, serving as spies or participating in sabotage against the United States. None of the claims were true but the facts didn't stop the swell of public hysteria against people of Japanese heritage. Anti-Japanese groups and the media, most

Asians in California feared being mistaken for Japanese. Chinese wore buttons that read, "American Chinese." Here, a farmer clearly identified himself as being Filipino. *Courtesy of the National Archives and Records Administration, WRA Collection (Dorothea Lange).*

notoriously the Hearst newspaper chain, urged the government to round up and "evacuate" everyone of Japanese ancestry from California as a precaution.

People of Japanese heritage could not defend themselves against the tidal wave of paranoia, racism and economic greed. They had no political clout, no power in the press, and no well-known public figure to speak out for them. Despite intelligence reports that said they were loyal, despite the Nisei's rights as American-born citizens, President Franklin Roosevelt signed Executive Order 9066 on February 19, 1942. The order gave the U.S. military power to remove anyone of Japanese ancestry from the West Coast.

In March 1942 people of Japanese heritage in California were told to leave the western half of the state and voluntarily move inland. When this was declared, six of the valedictorians in this book left the state. Other students moved to the eastern half of California, complying with the government's command.

Shizu Komae had given birth to her son in Los Angeles just a few weeks prior to the announcement. "Official word was that certain areas were designated as military areas, so if you live in the area,

you are going to be taken away [by the government]," she explained. "Los Angeles was Area A because it is closest to the ocean, but there was also Area B. . . . Since my husband was from the Sacramento area, we moved up there, hoping that we wouldn't have to move [again] because we were in Area B."

During the same time, Pearl Kurokawa's parents tried a similar strategy. Her father was a farmer and thought he could continue growing crops in central California. "He moved to central California because that area was still declared, 'okay.' He was going to start farming there again," Kurokawa said. "So he got rid of his property very cheaply because he wanted to just completely let go of his affairs and start something fresh in central California. But of course as it ended, that didn't work either so he really lost a lot."

Even though some Japanese Americans had relocated inland, the entire state of California and western parts of Washington, Oregon and Arizona were eventually cleared of people of Japanese heritage.[2] Region by region, Japanese aliens (the Issei) and "non aliens" (a euphemism for American citizens) were forced to report for detention in fifteen temporary facilities on the West Coast.

As the Nisei scrambled to prepare for incarceration, there was a flurry of marriages. Many rushed their weddings because of uncertainty about the future. Michiko Naito said, "It didn't make any sense waiting for the end of the war."

Left: Region by region, exclusion orders were posted in the street, directing removal of all persons of Japanese ancestry. This photo was taken in San Francisco on April 11, 1942. *Courtesy of the National Archives and Records Administration, WRA Collection (Dorothea Lange).*

Above: Newspaper headlines in Oakland, California eight days after President Roosevelt signed Executive Order 9066 to remove people of Japanese heritage from the West Coast. *Courtesy of the National Archives and Records Administration, WRA Collection (Dorothea Lange).*

Five valedictorians got married just before being interned. Among them was Doris Fujisawa of Los Angeles who married Peter Fujioka in a wedding ceremony in Hollywood. Fujisawa's sister, Alice, who was then living in nearby Gardena, was not able to attend the wedding because of curfew and travel restrictions placed on Japanese Americans. According to Alice, Fujisawa and her husband "always joked they had honeymooned at Santa Anita," the racetrack where they were incarcerated.

Orphans at the Los Angeles Japanese Orphanage in 1942 were also subject to detention. *Courtesy of the National Archives and Records Administration, WRA Collection.*

*The size and number of packages is limited to that which can be carried by the individual or group.*

Civilian Exclusion Order

Ida Shimanouchi recalled, "In the haste to prepare for evacuation most of our household property—including furniture and a piano, went for a total of $80!" Some Nisei and their families had only as little as two weeks before they reported to the internment camps. They were allowed to bring with them only what they could carry so they left behind homes, farms, businesses, cars, furniture and pets—a lifetime of accumulated property and memories. Their essential belongings and most precious possessions were condensed into bundles and suitcases they could carry into the camps. There was simply not enough time to settle affairs properly. Items were sold in distress to people taking advantage of the Japanese Americans' predicament.

Farmers of Japanese heritage never saw the profit from crops they were forced to leave behind. Norio Yasaki's son wrote, "My grandfather and uncles lost their harvests from their fruit ranches

The detainees prepared their baggage to be transported with them to the Tanforan Assembly Center. This neighborhood in Oakland, California was cleared of people of Japanese heritage under Civilian Exclusion order No. 28. *Courtesy of the National Archives and Records Administration, WRA Collection (Dorothea Lange).*

Many of the valedictorians' parents were farmers. Here, a family near Mission San Jose, California, picking their strawberry crops just a few days before reporting for detention. *Courtesy of the National Archives and Records Administration, WRA Collection (Dorothea Lange).*

since the families left just prior to picking." Michiko Naito's in-laws were lettuce and garlic growers who also had to abandon their fields. Naito said, "It was quite depressing for them because the person who owned the land was my husband's teacher and he kept all the profit. After the war [the landowner] would not sign the paperwork so the family could claim some losses."

Issei who owned businesses and farms suffered financial devastation. Many of the students' parents were in the agricultural industry so they lost leases or disposed of their land at a tremendous loss. Tractors, trucks and farm equipment were hurriedly sold, abandoned or entrusted to non-Japanese.

Many people stored their belongings in friends' basements, barns and Japanese temples, only to have them looted while they were incarcerated. Naito owned a 1930s copy of *Orations and Essays.* It was packed away with the rest of her family's belongings in a barn owned by neighbors who offered to store the items while the family was incarcerated. When Naito and her family came out of the camps, the neighbors claimed the barn burned down.

When Shizue Ohashi, the barber, learned she was to be interned, she sold her barber's chairs for the amount she had paid for them. She took up the U.S. government's offer to store her bedroom

A family waiting for a special train that will take them from their hometown to the Merced Assembly Center, about 125 miles away. Each family member, from eldest to youngest, wore an identification tag with a pre-assigned number on it. *Courtesy of the National Archives and Records Administration, WRA Collection (Dorothea Lange).*

furniture, refrigerator and sofa in the War Department's warehouses and was able to recover them later. While others in desperation let their belongings go for a fraction of the cost, Ohashi trusted the U.S. government to hold her possessions. She said, "At that time a lot of the Japanese were leery of the government. They said they sold [their possessions] for pennies. But I had some faith. . . ."

The 120,000 people incarcerated were never charged with any crime or wrongdoing. Almost two-thirds of them were American-born citizens whose civil liberties were completely violated. The rest were mostly Issei who had lived in the U.S. for twenty to forty years, but were unable to obtain citizenship under current laws.[3]

The people of Japanese heritage were first imprisoned in euphemistically named "assembly centers." Toward the latter part of 1942, they were "evacuated" and sent to "relocation centers," permanent concentration camps built in the interior of the United States.

The assembly centers were primitive camps, hastily constructed on fairgrounds and racetracks. People lived in horse stalls and crudely constructed barracks partitioned into rooms. They were surrounded by barbed wire, under armed guard, fed in prison-like mess halls and slept on straw mattresses. There was no privacy in

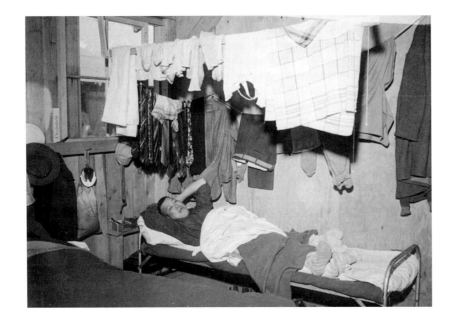

Detainees not assigned to live in horse stalls lived in bare barracks divided into rooms. Here, an Issei man in the camp in Manzanar, California, resting on his cot in his allotted space. Army cots and mattresses were the only items furnished by the government. *Courtesy of the National Archives and Records Administration, WRA Collection (Clem Albers).*

communal areas, or in the cramped space allotted to each family. The strain of incarceration soon led to the disintegration of family life.

Yoshiko Higuchi's daughter, Ellen, wrote, "My mother expressed to me the humiliation of being in camp, and mostly the loss of the basic freedom of privacy." One of the worst aspects of the makeshift camps was the absence of partitions or doors in the communal toilets. "She told me about having to go to the bathroom where everything was completely open, no separate stalls. It made a humiliating experience that much more degrading."

The army was not equipped or prepared to take care of the needs of families, particularly babies. Chizuko Doi had a difficult time keeping her three-week-old infant fed. Baby formula was in scarce supply and the barracks did not have any refrigeration or cooking facilities. Doi, one of three students in this book who married a non-Japanese, was incarcerated with her baby and young daughter for four months at the Fresno Assembly Center in the Central Valley in California. Because her husband was not Japanese, she and her children were released instead of being sent to a permanent camp.

Imprisoned, the valedictorians were in a state of shock over what had transpired in the previous months. Out of fifty students, thirty-five (70%) of them were locked up. At the time, they were between twenty-two and thirty-three years old and several had small children.

Yukiko Sanwo had grown up in Kerman, California and was held with her husband and two children in nearby Fresno. She said, "I kept on feeling, why did this have to happen?"

People incarcerated in the Tanforan Assembly Center, waiting in line to eat in the mess hall in April 1942. The wide road running diagonally across was the former racetrack with newly built barracks in the background. *Courtesy of the National Archives and Records Administration, WRA Collection (Dorothea Lange).*

"I was stunned, being a U.S. citizen by birth, educated in our school system, studied the Constitution," said Joe Nakanishi who was incarcerated in Turlock, California. "There seemed to have been a double standard, one for peace and one for war."

Others understood that the United States government had a war to fight and as Charles Inouye described it, the country was under "abnormal" conditions. "We couldn't ask [the U.S. government] for too much. We thought we would get a fair shake," he said.

Haruko Fujita, who was assigned to the Santa Anita Racetrack near Los Angles, wrote, "The U.S. government was unfair. I was born here and had never seen Japan."

Another valedictorian, Kiyoshi Nobusada, had a successful career before the war, working in Kingsburg, California. He was the chief chemist in complete charge of all production at the Central Winery, Inc. that had a capacity of nine million gallons. He was incarcerated with his wife, son and extended family. Nobusada's wife, Yemi, wrote, "[Kiyoshi] felt *shikataganai*. An order is an order. Do what is best

Families ate meals in mess halls with hundreds of other people with no chance of private interaction. *Courtesy of the National Archives and Records Administration, WRA Collection (Clem Albers).*

for all." *Shikataganai* is a common Japanese saying that means: "It can't be helped." Rather than fighting and becoming angry at the United States, many internees succumbed to a feeling of resignation in order to cope.

"Of course, I felt a great sense of injustice," said Ida Shimanouchi, who was held with her family in the Tanforan Racetrack near San Francisco. "The war brought on our plight. . . . I may have rationalized my position by maintaining a *shikataganai* attitude."

Ayame Ichiyasu was also held at the Tanforan Racetrack. Her brother Kiyoshi, said, "[Ayame] felt the need to make the best of a terrible situation for the sake of the Japanese community—especially the students."

Under Caucasian supervisors, the inmates ran everything in the camps. People organized themselves and worked together, sharing their knowledge and skills. Those with restaurant experience cooked in the kitchens while others washed dishes, collected garbage, cleaned toilets or repaired equipment. Some Nisei organized recreational activities, helped the elderly or worked as clerks in offices.

Adults diligently tried to continue children's educations. Kazuya Sanada, who once had high hopes for Hawaii, ended up at the Santa Anita Racetrack near Los Angeles. He taught American history to twenty-five junior high school students with textbooks he received after writing to one of his old professors at the University of California, Los Angeles. He saw the complete irony of teaching

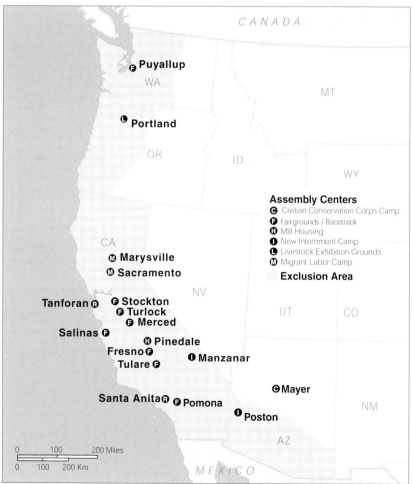

Top: The assembly centers did not have washing machines or laundry facilities. People washed their clothes, towels and sheets by hand in large buckets. Here, a mother in Santa Anita, California with her children after hanging the day's wash out to dry. *Courtesy of the National Archives and Records Administration, WRA Collection (Clem Albers).*

Bottom: In 1942 people of Japanese heritage living in California and western parts of Washington, Oregon and Arizona were incarcerated in temporary concentration camps called "assembly centers." There were fifteen assembly centers and two permanent internment camps, Manzanar and Poston, were also used as assembly centers. The map legend indicates the prior usage of the assembly centers.

American history with all its messages of justice and democracy while, "Here we are interned!" he said.

When Sanada first entered the camp, he didn't think it was so bad. "In Santa Anita we had a nice band. Almost every weekend we had a dance. There was a friendly group of people there." He had just gotten married and he and his bride had their own private quarters away from their families. He was excited to be on his honeymoon. But after a while his "carefree" attitude changed. He started to think, "Why am I here?"

Not only were Japanese Americans stripped of their freedom, rights and possessions, their children's birthdays were spent in meager, pathetic conditions. Just beyond the fences and armed guards, life went on. Shizue Ohashi, the barber, recalled the first birthday her son spent in detention. In August 1942 after four months of confinement, she asked a Caucasian business associate to buy a cake and bring it over to the Santa Anita Racetrack.

The associate bought a big beautiful cake that read, "Happy 4th Birthday Kenny." Ohashi said, "She brought it over to Santa Anita and the guards said, 'We sure hate to stick a knife through that to see if there's anything illegal.' And [the associate] bawled them out and said, 'Don't you dare do that! This is for a four-year-old boy. Why would I put a knife or a pistol in a cake?' And so they let it through." For the first time Ohashi and her family ate cake while imprisoned. The other kids and adults wanted a taste, too. "I had to cut little pieces for *everybody*. Everybody had some," Ohashi said. "That was the birthday my son remembers." For the time being she was happy, but that would soon change. Kenny's next three birthdays were spent in the hot, desolate swamplands of Arkansas.

## NOTES

1 Takahashi, *Nisei/Sansei, Shifting Japanese American Identities and Politics*, 19. Citing Dorothy Swaine Thomas and Richard S. Nishimoto, *The Spoilage* (Berkeley: University of California Press, 1946), 4; Leonard Broom and Ruth Riemer, *Removal and Return: The Scio-Economic Effects of the War on Japanese Americans* (Berkeley: University of California Press, 1949), 82-83; and Masakazu Iwata, "The Japanese Immigrants in California Agriculture," *Agricultural History* 1962; 36: 32–33.

2 By 1940 there were 127,000 people of Japanese heritage in the United States with ninety percent of them living on the West Coast. Seventy-five percent of them were living in California where they were 1.6 percent of the general population of the state. In total, they were less than one-tenth of one percent of the entire United States population. See Harry L. Kitano, *Japanese-Americans: The Evolution of a Sub-Culture*, (Eaglewood Cliffs, N.J.: Prentice Hall, 1969), p. 162.

3 Chuman, *The Bamboo People*, 143.

# 4. Outside the Barbed Wire

*Ah! Soon must we forsake thee*
*Our own, our sheltering home,*
*But we will ne'er forget thee*
*Wherever we may roam.*

Helen Kuwada
San Martin Grammar School, 1933

VALEDICTORIAN Pearl Kurokawa left California in early 1942 when she received a long distance marriage proposal from a Nisei soldier in Illinois. She had met Samuel Kimura while she was in nursing school at the University of California, San Francisco and he was a medical student. After he finished his internship, in August 1941, he volunteered for the army and was sent to Camp Grant for basic training. Following the attack on Pearl Harbor, he proposed to Kurokawa by wire and told her to join him.

"He heard [that] we had to get out of California so he immediately wired me to come to get married," Kurokawa said. "My father had a truck and a family passenger car, so he said, 'We'll give you the passenger car for your wedding gift. You drive that back East.'" Kurokawa had never been outside of California before. "It was really an experience," she said. Including Kurokawa, six valedictorians left the state in early 1942, avoiding internment.

Following the attack on Pearl Harbor, the FBI picked up and imprisoned thousands of Issei community leaders, teachers, priests and newspapermen in Hawaii and on the West Coast. They were confined in special camps on the mainland run by the U.S. Department of Justice. Kozue Fujikawa's father was one of those taken because he was on the Japanese language school board and Judo board in California's San Fernando Valley. He had a brother living out of the state, so Fujikawa and her family left for her uncle's

Pearl Kurokawa married Dr. Samuel Kimura in Illinois in 1942. Kimura served as a medical officer in the 522d Field Artillery, a unit of the 442d Regimental Combat Team. *Courtesy of Pearl Kurokawa.*

home in Honeyville, Utah on the last day voluntary departure was possible. Fujikawa's older sister said Fujikawa was "in a state of shock." After spending time in the Department of Justice internment camps in New Mexico and Montana, Fujikawa's father was released and reunited with the family in Utah.

Katsumi Yoshizumi also chose to go to Utah because he had relatives there. He had grown up in the San Pedro area in California and had attended Compton Junior College, majoring in accounting. After graduation he worked for the Mutual Fish Company in San Pedro. At the outbreak of the war, he married his high school sweetheart, Yoneko Marumoto. Complying with the government's orders, they left the West Coast for Utah where they farmed during the war.

Another valedictorian who left California was George Inagaki from Sacramento. He was very active within the Japanese American Citizens League (JACL), the national Japanese American organization founded in 1929 to fight for civil rights.[1] With the war against Japan, Inagaki realized that discrimination toward Japanese Americans would only increase so he worked tirelessly as a JACL leader. His son Chris said, "I believe [my father] understood the fears of America. He was determined to show the country that Japanese Americans were loyal."

After the war began, JACL moved its headquarters from San Francisco to Salt Lake City, Utah, safely out of the military zones forbidden to persons of Japanese heritage. In the early summer of 1942, the organization sent Mike Masaoka, the national secretary, to find influential people and organizations to help the JACL improve the plight of the imprisoned Japanese Americans. Masaoka chose Inagaki as his partner to go with him on the trip across the country. Inagaki said goodbye to his wife, Yukie Yagi. While she stayed in the camp in Poston, Arizona, Inagaki left with Masaoka.[2]

The pair traveled from Salt Lake City to Cleveland, Ohio and on to New Orleans. They ended their journey in Washington D.C. Several times along the way, they were harassed and jailed by local police who thought they were spies.[3] Inagaki's friend and army colleague, Hiro Takahashi, described one incident Inagaki told him about: "Mike Masaoka and George stopped over one place [in the South]. Then the local police caught them and put them in the jail or a cage. Townspeople came and cussed at them and even spat at them."

As the JACL's representatives, Inagaki and Masaoka stayed on the East Coast to keep in close contact with government leaders and lobby for better conditions for Japanese Americans. The JACL

Top: Katsumi Yoshizumi relocated to Utah during World War II and farmed with relatives. *Courtesy of Betty Kobata.*

Bottom: Mike Masaoka, the JACL national secretary, traveled across the country with valedictorian George Inagaki. *Courtesy of Chris Inagaki.*

After helping represent the JACL in Washington D.C., George Inagaki volunteered for the U.S. Army when Nisei men were re-admitted in 1943. Inagaki was assigned to the Military Intelligence Service. *Courtesy of Chris Inagaki. Photographer, Toyo Miyatake.*

proposed that the U.S. military re-admit Nisei men into the army and also petitioned President Roosevelt to reinstate the draft for Japanese Americans so they could prove their loyalty to the U.S.[4]

In January 1943 the U.S. Army allowed Nisei back into their ranks on a voluntary basis. Inagaki signed up immediately. He went on to serve in the Military Intelligence Service branch of the army.

To avoid internment, Matilde Honda, a public health nurse, left Brawley, California and headed for Colorado by train in the middle of the night. A nursing position with a Seventh Day Adventist hospital was waiting for her in Denver. Her Caucasian family doctor from her hometown urged her to leave and had lined up the job for her.

"The overwhelming feeling was to cooperate with the government's orders rather than right the wrong at the moment," Honda said. "I felt I was cooperating with the United States government's orders. I felt *no* bitterness [or] anger at the time." In Colorado, she didn't experience any hostility. "Governor Carr of Colorado set the tone by publicly welcoming us to his state."

In Denver, Honda's sister, Viola, and brother-in-law, Roku Sugahara, soon joined her. Roku Sugahara had graduated from Manual Arts High School in Los Angeles in 1930 and is a valedictorian also included in this book.

Sugahara was born in 1912 in Los Angeles into a family of five children with two boys and three girls. While Sugahara was still very young, his parents died and the Japanese Methodist Church in Los Angeles looked after the five orphans. His sister, Masa, wrote, "When my parents passed, we girls were placed in a home for girls. My younger sister and I were babies. . . . My brothers lived in a home for male college students. I saw my brothers about once a month at church when we were old enough to go. . . . Being male, my brothers were on their own."

From the age of nine, Sugahara earned money delivering the *Rafu Shimpo* newspaper on his bicycle.[5] He inherited funds for college tuition and attended the University of California, Los Angeles, majoring in economics. While attending UCLA, he met Viola Honda during his senior year. They married after graduation, a year before the war started.

Sugahara suffered from what he thought were ulcers but was later diagnosed as stomach cancer. He didn't want to be interned because he knew the government camps would have poor medical facilities. When the order to leave California came, an Issei wanted his car driven to Colorado, so Sugahara and Viola packed the vehicle with their belongings and left the state. Viola said it was scary being on the road. When they stopped to buy food, Sugahara told her, "You go in [to the store] by yourself. They won't attack a girl." In Denver the couple supported themselves by working as domestics.

Two valedictorians, Ayami Onaka and Charlotte Shimidzu, were living in Hawaii when Pearl Harbor was attacked.[6] Because Hawaii was 3,000 miles closer to the enemy and about one-third of the

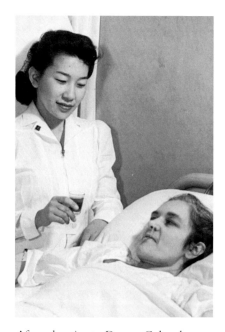

After relocating to Denver, Colorado, Matilde Honda (left) worked as a staff nurse at Colorado General Hospital. *Courtesy of the National Archives and Records Administration, WRA Collection (Hikaru Iwasaki).*

Roku Sugahara and his wife, Viola, in swimming attire in Grand Isle, Louisiana in 1949. *Courtesy of Setsuko Asano.*

population was of Japanese ancestry, it was far more vulnerable to sabotage and invasion. Yet, Ayami Onaka wrote, "Japanese Americans living in Hawaii were not restricted. Japanese American citizens were treated like all other ethnic groups—food rationing, gas rationing, curfews to obey—regulations were for all people." Only prominent Issei community leaders were sent to internment camps on the mainland.

During the same time, five valedictorians were in Asia. All of them had left the U.S. before World War II began. Their experiences were completely different from those of Japanese Americans in the United States.

Since 1934 Goro Murata had been in Tokyo working for the *Japan Times*, an English language newspaper. He contributed to a "Nisei Page" of the publication and sent articles from Tokyo to the *Rafu Shimpo* newspaper in Los Angeles. During the war he was active with an organization called the "Nisei in Japan Federation" and when the war ended he gained the trust of United States Occupation officials and continued to work for the *Japan Times*.

In the late 1930s, Kiyoshi Murakami was studying jurisprudence in Japan at the Chuo University Law School. Because of the war, his graduation was accelerated a few months earlier and he was drafted into the Japanese Army.[7] Since he knew English and was well educated, he became a platoon officer and was sent overseas near Java (Indonesia). He served in the transportation branch of the army. Later, he was wounded and sent to a hospital in Singapore where he remained for seven months. After he recovered, he was discharged and returned to Japan in 1946.

Another valedictorian, Toshio Yamagata, had left the U.S. for Japan in 1940 after graduating from the University of California, Berkeley. When he first arrived, he worked as an office clerk in Nagoya and later took a job in Harbin, Manchuria. During the war he translated books and printed matter for the Japanese Army.

Michiko Yoshihashi was also in Japanese-occupied Manchuria. Born in Los Angeles in 1918, Yoshihashi went to Japan in 1937 after graduating from high school and working at a photo company in Southern California. She went to her parent's homeland to meet a potential husband and planned to return to the United States if the "match" did not work out. Their relationship developed and in 1938 she married Yoshio Kawae. The same year, they moved to Manchuria and remained there during World War II, returning to Japan in 1946.

Jimmie Hamasaki from Santa Maria, California went to Japan in 1935 to attend college. He was admitted to Meiji University in Tokyo and in early 1941 graduated with a law degree. In July 1941 he accepted a job with the U.S. Consulate in Formosa (Taiwan) and married his wife, Clara Yamagishi, a Nisei born in Gardena, California. Following the wedding ceremony, the couple traveled to Formosa which had been under Japan's control since 1895. They moved into the United States Consulate where Vice-Consul Glen Bruner was already living in the upstairs quarters.

Almost five months after the Hamasakis arrived, on December 7, 1941, they learned that the Japanese had bombed Pearl Harbor. The Vice-Consul and Hamasaki spent the day burning documents and were ready for the Japanese authorities when they arrived in the afternoon. The Japanese confined them to their quarters. By the end of the year they were taken to the United States Embassy in Tokyo. The Japanese planned to trade the Americans for Japanese diplomats being held by the United States government.

The situation was extremely distressing because Clara was pregnant and close to having her baby. By April 1942, the group was still

During World War II Toshio Yamagata translated documents as a civilian employee for the Japanese Army occupying Manchuria in China. *Courtesy of Jeannette Sanderson.*

Left: In Tokyo in July 1941, Jimmie Hamasaki married Clara Yamagishi who wore a wedding dress she sewed herself. One week after the ceremony they relocated to the U.S. Consulate in Formosa (Taiwan) where Hamasaki was to be employed. *Courtesy of Clara Hamasaki.*

Above: Jimmie Hamasaki and his wife, Clara, with their son, Jim, in front of their first apartment in Arlington, Virginia, in late 1942 after being part of the first diplomatic exchange between the U.S. and Japan during World War II. The family's apartment was government housing built for federal employees. *Courtesy of Clara Hamasaki.*

being held in Tokyo and Clara was told she had better go to the hospital to have the baby induced because they were to leave soon. Their son was born that month but the group did not leave until June. After boarding a ship and traveling to East Africa, on July 23, 1942, the Hamasakis were part of the first exchange of diplomats between Japan and the United States in Lourenço Marques.

When the Hamasakis arrived back in America, they were treated with suspicion by the United States government. Ironically, while the Japanese held them as prisoners of war for almost eight months, the United States government had incarcerated the Hamasakis' families in California. Clara said, "When we arrived in New York, those of us with Japanese faces were taken to Ellis Island in order for United States officials to 'check us out.' Vice-Consul Bruner went to bat for us in Washington but it still took six weeks for us to be released. We lived in prison-like rooms. There, we learned for the first time that thousands of Nisei and Issei were in concentration camps."

By the time the couple and their baby got off Ellis Island, Hamasaki was assigned to a civilian employee position with the War Department to do intelligence work in foreign weapons technology at the Pentagon. He tried to visit his parents in Gila River, Arizona but permission was denied and he never saw them during the war.

> *Let us be good citizens! The future of our country depends solely on the step we take. The country is crying to find men and women who are willing to sacrifice their selfish desires for the good and welfare of the community and country.*
>
> Pearl Kurokawa<br>Arroyo Grande Union High School, 1932

Valedictorian John Aiso was performing an invaluable service to his country in secret before World War II began. After graduating *cum laude* from Brown University and being named valedictorian, in 1934 he became the first Nisei from the continental United States to graduate from Harvard Law School.[8] He practiced law in New York and then worked in Japanese-occupied Manchuria as head of the legal department of a subsidiary of the British-American Tobacco Company. After nearly three years in China, Aiso returned to the United States and attended the University of Southern California Law School where he crossed paths with Frank Chuman who was also studying law. Aiso went to the university to access its law library to prepare for the California bar exam, which he passed, in January 1941. He practiced law in Southern California until he was drafted, reporting for duty in April 1941.

The thirty-one-year-old attorney became a buck private. He was sent to Camp Haan in Riverside, California where he was assigned to work in a company that was responsible for repairing trucks. After a few months he looked forward to being discharged because the army had decided to release draftees over twenty-eight years of age. Instead, because of his Japanese language ability, Aiso was sent to the Presidio of San Francisco.[9]

A small handful of army intelligence specialists knew war with Japan was inevitable and wanted to train Japanese language interpreters and translators. At the Presidio, Lt. Col. John Weckerling laid out the plan to start a Japanese language school for military intelligence training. The Colonel convinced Aiso to commit to the project by saying, "John, your country is in need of you!" Aiso had never heard a high ranking official say to him, "Your country" and was moved. To the Colonel and his plan Aiso responded, "Okay, sir!"[10]

Because there was such a shortage of qualified teachers, Aiso was appointed head instructor. He and two civilian Nisei teachers hastily prepared materials and opened the school on November 1, 1941, five weeks before the Pearl Harbor attacks.

The school was so underfunded and assembled in such a hurry that the instructors used apple boxes and orange crates until they were able to secure furniture. After the U.S. entered World War II, the army reclassified Nisei men as 4-C, "enemy aliens" and ineligible for the draft. The intelligence section, however, struggled to find Nisei with Japanese language skills advanced enough for the program. So great was the need for linguists, Selective Service rules were ignored to induct qualified men.

The first class of about sixty handpicked Nisei advanced through the school's curriculum of Japanese reading, writing, military vocabulary, interrogation and translation at an intensive, relentless pace. Eight hours a day, they learned Japanese geography, map reading and how to analyze captured documents. Even after "lights out" in the barracks, they went to the bathroom facilities to continue their studies. The pupils crammed late into the night and in every spare moment. Weekends were devoted to military training because they were expected to be soldiers as well as linguists.

By May 1942, the first class of Military Intelligence Service (MIS) students had graduated and were assigned to outfits in Guadalcanal and the Aleutian Islands, becoming the "eyes and ears" of the Allied Forces in the Pacific. Although Japanese Americans could have used the publicity about their loyalty and contribution to the war effort, the secret nature of their work was not revealed and the information did not become declassified until 1973.[11]

In May 1942 the school was transferred to Camp Savage in Minnesota because Executive Order 9066 prevented its Japanese

American soldiers and instructors from staying in California. Upon its move, the school was reorganized as the Military Intelligence Service Language School under the War Department. New courses were added and the second class of 200 MIS students began their rigorous studies in June 1942. By then reports started coming back from the Pacific Theater about how valuable the Nisei were.

In January 1943 the U.S. military publicly re-admitted Nisei into the army on a voluntary basis and valedictorian George Inagaki signed up immediately. Because he knew the Japanese language well, he was assigned to the MIS. He went to Camp Savage and began attending the language school in July 1943.

Hiro Takahashi, a Kibei (a Nisei educated in Japan), attended the MIS school at the same time. He said, "When a bunch of us Kibei were [shooting the breeze], one large rookie, a very friendly guy, started talking to us in plain California Japanese as soon as he came in the barrack."[12] That was the first time Takahashi met Inagaki. "We did not know George was such an elite member of the JACL group until later. He was very nice and friendly. He melted in among us Kibei and we got along real good. I felt I was fortunate to know and associate with him."

George Inagaki (foreground) with Japanese children and elderly civilians. As a Military Intelligence Service soldier, Inagaki served as a translator and interpreter in the Pacific Theatre. He also interrogated captured Japanese prisoners and translated documents. *Courtesy of Chris Inagaki.*

Mas Abe was also in the same class as Inagaki and said Inagaki was "down to earth" and "a real good guy." He especially praised Inagaki's Japanese speaking ability.

In early 1944 after the MIS school graduation, Inagaki and his cohorts were sent to Camp Blanding in Florida for two months of basic and jungle infantry training. They worked very hard and had a great sense of camaraderie and fun. Takahashi said, "We, among our close buddies . . . [Inagaki, Abe and others] made an agreement beforehand. The two of us who got the poorest scores on rifle target practice would have to treat the winners to Chinese dinners after we returned to Minneapolis." The target distances were from

During World War II, four valedictorians were civilians in Asia. Goro Murata was in Japan, Toshio Yamagata and Michiko Yoshihashi were in Manchuria, and Jimmie Hamasaki was in Formosa (Taiwan). Three other valedictorians were in the military during the war. Kiyoshi Murakami was in the Java area, serving in the Japanese Army; George Nishida was in the U.S. Military Intelligence Service (MIS) in Guam and Japan; and George Inagaki fought in the U.S. MIS in Saipan, Tinian, Iwo Jima and in Okinawa.

100, 200, 300 and 500 yards away and the shooting positions were standing, prone and kneeling. Takahashi didn't fare well in the contest. "Mas Abe and I had to dish out our money," he said.

When Inagaki and his MIS classmates had some time off, they visited a resort in Silver Springs near Ocala, Florida. Takahashi recalled, "George bought his wife an alligator handbag that cost $60." The other privates could not afford such an expensive item when the army pay was about $25 per month. "We lightly teased him by saying that he was a different species after all."

After their training in Florida, the group returned to Camp Savage. They had a two-week furlough before being shipped out to combat. Inagaki asked Abe where he was going for his time off. Abe said he was staying at the base because he was low on funds. So Inagaki offered to lend him $100. Abe said, "I told [Inagaki] what if I go overseas and kick the bucket? I want to pay you back." Inagaki insisted so Abe took the loan and went to visit his aunt in the Poston, Arizona camp and looked in on Inagaki's mother who was also being held there.

Inagaki was appointed the leader of nine other MIS soldiers and sent to the Joint Intelligence Center, Pacific Ocean Area (JICPOA) in Hawaii. From there, he was detached to different U.S. Marine units and sent on missions.

He took part in the Saipan Campaign in June 1944 and in July fought in the Tinian battle in the Mariana Islands. During his missions he translated documents and interrogated captured Japanese soldiers. He returned to JICPOA for R and R (rest and recuperation) and had a chance to catch up with his MIS colleagues. Takahashi said, "He visited us with plenty of Hawaiian goodies and told us about his horrible battle experience on the front." In the spring of 1945 Inagaki participated in the Iwo Jima campaign, followed by the battle of Okinawa that ended in June 1945.[13]

Although trained as linguists, the MIS officers and Nisei intelligence men fought in every landing through New Guinea, the Marianas, the Philippines and Okinawa. They translated captured battle plans, intercepted messages and interrogated Japanese POWs. Douglas MacArthur's Chief of Intelligence, General Charles Willoughby, remarked, "Never before in history did any army know so much concerning its enemy, prior to actual engagement, as did the American army during most of the Pacific campaigns."[14] He also said the Nisei "shortened the Pacific war by two years."[15]

Ironically, being killed by their own side was one of the greatest dangers the MIS Nisei faced. John Aiso said, "We were probably the first soldiers in history with bodyguards so as not to be mistaken for an enemy by our troops."[16]

The school at Camp Savage grew so much that in 1944 it was moved to Fort Snelling, several miles away. Throughout the war, Aiso continued to instruct and oversee the program that trained 6,000 MIS students who helped save thousands of American lives.[17] Even after World War II ended, the linguists' indispensable translation and intelligence work continued for years. They served in both military and civilian roles in almost every aspect of the Allied Occupation of Japan, bridging the language gap between Japanese and English.[18]

## NOTES

1   JACL website. http://www.jacl.org/about.html

2   Hosokawa, *Nisei: The Quiet Americans*, 379.

3   Ibid., 380–381.

4   Ibid., 360–363.

5   Sugahara later gave his paper route to another valedictorian in this book, Kazuya Sanada of University High School.

6   Hawaii was a U.S. territory in 1941 and became the fiftieth state of the U.S. in 1959.

7   Murakami was a dual citizen of the U.S. and Japan. Before 1924, Japanese citizenship was automatically extended to children of Japanese nationals, regardless of their country of birth, and males were required to serve in the Japanese military. See Takahashi, *Nisei/Sansei*, 25-26.

8   Ichinokuchi, *John Aiso and the MIS*, 10.

9   Ibid, 15.

10  Ibid.

11  Ibid., 19.

12  The leader of Inagaki's barrack was Jim Fujisaka, who later married Mary Miyamoto who is featured in this book.

13  Joseph Harrington, *Yankee Samurai: The Secret Role of Nisei in America's Pacific Victory*, (Detroit, MI: Pettigrew Enterprises, 1979), 25, 211, 277, 315, 336, 341.

14  Hosokawa, *Nisei: The Quiet Americans*, 398.

15  Ichinokuchi, *John Aiso and the MIS*, 19.

16  Ibid.

17  Ibid.

18  Ibid., 81.

Several valedictorians in this volume taught high school students in the internment camps. Here, teenagers with books walking through the Manzanar Relocation Center in 1943. *Courtesy of the Library of Congress, Prints & Photographs Division. Photographer, Ansel Adams [LC-DIG-ppprs-00354].*

# 5. Exiled to Nowhere

*We must have the quality of character which makes us dig in and fight against overwhelming odds. We must have that unquenchable will, the will to come up with a smile, no matter how badly we may be beaten.*

Frank Chuman
Los Angeles High School, 1934

IN SEPTEMBER 1943 valedictorian Shizue Ohashi, the barber, and her husband and children were assigned to a permanent concentration camp in Rohwer, Arkansas while her father and sisters were sent to Manzanar, California. Her father requested that Ohashi be assigned to the same facility as the rest of the family but permission was not granted until the very day Ohashi was to leave for Arkansas. With all her belongings already packed on a train bound for Arkansas, Ohashi faced the nerve-wracking decision of whether to go to Manzanar and have her possessions rerouted, or go to Rohwer and be separated from her extended family. Ohashi's second son was only three months old. She had bought a lot of baby clothing, formula and a baby bed for the child and everything was packed on the train for Rohwer. In the end, practicality won out. "I think we'd better go to Arkansas," she told her husband. He agreed.

Of the long tedious trip under guard on an old train, Ohashi said, "My husband and older boy (Kenny) slept on that straight wooden chair. Straight. No cushion or anything." In contrast, she and her baby slept in the Pullman™ with air conditioning. "It took *days*. Five days to go to Arkansas . . . They made us pull the shades down so we didn't know where we were."

By mid-1942, most of the people of Japanese ancestry on the West Coast had been incarcerated for several months in temporary assembly centers near their hometowns. After the Battle of Midway

Left: Of the thirty-four valedictorians interned, only one, Haruko Fujita, was sent to the Amache camp in Colorado, officially named the Granada Relocation Center. *Courtesy of the National Archives and Records Administration, WRA Collection (Joe McClelland).*

Bottom: In 1942 people of Japanese heritage were taken from the assembly centers and sent to ten permanent concentration camps built in barren and remote areas. The map also indicates many of the cities the valedictorians relocated to during and after World War II.

in early June, the West Coast was no longer in danger of being invaded by Japan. Despite this, the United States government continued to build ten permanent concentration camps in desolate areas of Arizona, Arkansas, California, Colorado, Idaho, Utah and Wyoming. In June 1942 the government began shipping detainees inland even though the centers were not complete. Thirty-four students in this volume and their families were sent to nine of the facilities.[1]

By the end of 1942 the last internees had been transferred from the temporary assembly centers to isolated "relocation centers" in the middle of deserts or swamplands. Surrounded by barbed wire fences and guard towers, each concentration camp was made up of thirty-six or more "blocks." Each block housed about 300 people and was composed of twelve barracks, a mess hall, latrines, shower and laundry facilities, and a recreation hall.

The barracks were divided into rooms of about twenty by twenty feet that sheltered a family or group of individuals. Each bare unit had only a potbelly stove, a light hanging from the ceiling, army cots and mattresses. The people used blankets and rope to divide up the space for individual privacy. It was up to the detainees to make their own furniture and shelves with whatever scraps of lumber they could scrounge up within the camp.

The primitive conditions of the living quarters were matched by the harsh climate. Camps experienced severe temperatures, dust storms, and serious drainage problems. Kazuya Sanada who was incarcerated in Rohwer, Arkansas said, "We had no heat. We had to burn coal or wood and so [the fire] would die down in the middle of the night. . . . The young ones sound asleep would freeze in the morning. It snowed there, too, in the wintertime."

Haruko Fujita who was held in the Amache camp in Colorado wrote, "The barracks had gaps between the boards and the wind blew through. . . . The winters were terribly cold and summers unbearably hot. Good thing I was young." Since the valedictorians were incarcerated in their early twenties and thirties during the physical prime of their adulthood, they were better able to cope with the substandard living conditions and extreme climate. Life in the camps was hardest on the elderly Issei, especially those in poor health. For the students the psychological stress was even more difficult than the physical discomfort. Hidemitsu Ginoza who was in Heart Mountain, Wyoming said, "The awful anxiety—thinking about the future," was what he remembered most about being in the camps. The people had no idea when they would be released or what the government would do to them next.

In spite of the uncertainty, life went on. The Nisei who wanted to work were able to do a wide variety of jobs under the better-paid Caucasian supervisors who lived in special quarters. At the permanent camps the Japanese Americans earned $12–$19 per month.

Kazuya Sanada was the manager of Block 6 in Rohwer, Arkansas but stayed in the position only a few months. One of the most demanding jobs in camp, the manager had the responsibility of informing the 300 people in the block of regulations and instructions from the Caucasian administration that oversaw the detention center. The manager also listened to complaints and tried to solve problems. Sanada was not able to speak Japanese so communicating with the many Issei in his block became too difficult and frustrating. He took a job with the Social Welfare Department instead, handing out clothing and helping those in need such as the elderly and widows.

Several students worked as teachers. Helen Hirata from San Bernardino, California was incarcerated in the camp in Poston, Arizona which was on an Indian Reservation.[2] She taught high school Latin and Spanish as well as typing and shorthand. She was also the high school's senior class advisor. Pupils in the same camp had the opportunity to learn shorthand for one year from valedictorian George Nishida from Dinuba, California. Mary Asada also taught shorthand during her time in the camp in Gila River, Arizona, which was also on Indian tribal land.[3]

James Hashimoto from Long Beach, California worked in the offices at the camp in Jerome, Arkansas. He also participated in many baseball games and entertained internees by playing the guitar and ukulele. Joe Nakanishi was a grounds supervisor in Gila River. He said, "I saw to it that all garbage was collected from all the mess halls. We had three trucks. We also picked up flowers and plants from the camp nursery and distributed them to each block."

At the same relocation center in Gila River, Kiyoshi Nobusada designed a vegetable dehydration plant for the War Relocation Authority, the government agency that managed the internment camps. With a major in food chemistry from the University of California, Berkeley, Nobusada had taken classes in bacteriology, soil science and agricultural production. He had also gained extensive experience in wine production before the war. As head of the farming division of the camp, he supervised the personnel, the

Top: Helen Hirata taught high school Latin, Spanish, typing and shorthand in Poston, Arizona. *Courtesy of Phyllis Mizuhara.*

Bottom: Because she was a registered nurse, Mary Miyamoto was separated from her family and sent to the Jerome Relocation Center in Arkansas. *Courtesy of Ann Gorai.*

mixing of insecticides and soil analysis for the agricultural division. The camp grew food for its own mess halls as well as for other camps.[4] In his spare time he also organized cooperative enterprises and ran educational programs.

Because she was a registered nurse and Japanese American professional health workers were scarce, Mary Miyamoto was assigned to Jerome, Arkansas while her family was sent to Poston, Arizona. Before the war started, Miyamoto had been the head nurse at the University of California San Francisco Hospital. In Jerome she worked in the camp hospital. Miyamoto's son, Steve, wrote that other than the "degrading physical facilities" his mother "didn't complain about too many things" regarding her camp experience. However, he did mention, "My mother commented some of the older men were 'poor patients'—demanding and unappreciative."

Frank Chuman was the administrator of the 250-bed hospital in Manzanar, California. In 1942, shortly after the Pearl Harbor attacks, the United States Public Health Service appointed him to the position. Instead of being sent to a temporary assembly center, he went

Two valedictorians were sent to the Manzanar Relocation Center in California. Here, people walking in the snow past a handmade wooden fence after leaving the camp's Buddhist church in 1943. *Courtesy of the Library of Congress, Prints & Photographs Division. Photographer, Ansel Adams [LC-DIG-ppprs-00358].*

Frank Chuman (third from left, wearing glasses) was appointed the administrator of the Manzanar Relocation Center hospital by Lt. Commander John Bowden of the U.S. Navy (right). A team of Nisei volunteers including a registered nurse, Fumiko Gohata (left), prepared the camp's medical facilities in 1942. *Courtesy of the Los Angeles Public Library Archives.*

directly to camp in Manzanar, California in March 1942. At the same time, his sister volunteered with sixty other Nisei to enter the camp early and help prepare it for the 10,000 detainees, including Chuman's parents who were incarcerated there.

Chuman said it was sometimes hard to get basic fixtures for the hospital facilities. "Food was also at times difficult to purchase for special types of patients. Shelves, ramps and storage spaces were made of discarded building material gathered from throughout the camp," he said. Other problems arose because the building was designed as an army base hospital to serve men, not pregnant women, small children, newborn babies and the aged.

Chuman was "angry, angry, angry" about internment but directed his energy at the tremendous amount of work to be done. "Everybody put aside, for the time being, what made them angry to be in that spot and said, 'We've got to help the people,'" he said.

The women in this volume, especially those married with children, displayed tremendous resilience and fortitude. While incarcerated, they still bore the traditional caregiver roles of wife, mother and daughter. As best they could, they held their families together in abnormal living conditions. Sandwiched between generations, they took care of their children as well as their parents and in-laws.

Helen Kuwada and Frank Yamakoshi, the young married couple, had a very difficult time in Poston, Arizona. Yamakoshi contracted tuberculosis and spent most of his detention in a hospital in Phoenix, Arizona. Kuwada's daughter, Agnes, said her mother "was in despair" because Yamakoshi was ill and Kuwada was left with in-laws and two small children to care for. Eventually, Yamakoshi made a full recovery.

Another valedictorian's husband also became ill with tuberculosis in the same camp. Because her husband was in the hospital, the student needed to get a job that allowed her to keep her children by her side. She cleaned the women's toilets every morning seven days a week with her two-year-old and four-year-old next to her. She said, "I needed the $12 or $16 [the camp administration] could give me."

Michiko Naito said she was "not the healthiest" after the birth of her daughter in Poston. When her husband was released to work

Left: Eight valedictorians and their families were incarcerated at the camp in Poston, Arizona, officially named the Colorado River Relocation Center. Here, Mitsue Matsumune in front of her barrack in Poston II in 1944. Three divisions, Poston I, II and III, three miles apart from each other, comprised the relocation center. *Courtesy of Marion Hayashi.*

Above: Mitsue Matsumune (standing) with a good friend she made in camp, Marion Lind. A teacher overseeing the preschools in Poston, Lind also met her future husband, Nisei Shuki Hayashi, while working in the relocation center in 1943–1944. *Courtesy of Marion Hayashi.*

A typical wood cutting scene in the northern part of the Rohwer Relocation Center in Arkansas. Seven valedictorians were sent to this camp. *Courtesy of the National Archives and Records Administration, WRA Collection (Tom McGehee).*

in New Jersey, she had to get a job in camp so she could earn $3.50 each month for the family's clothing allowance.

Being sick or pregnant was risky due to poor medical facilities, but seven female valedictorians gave birth while incarcerated. By the time Japanese Americans left the detention centers at the end of 1945, almost 6,000 babies had been born in the camps.[5]

Kazuya Sanada almost lost his wife when she gave birth to their first child. The camp hospital in Rohwer, Arkansas was just being built and there were not enough doctors. He said, "[My wife weighed] about 125 pounds. . . . She ballooned up to 160–170 pounds because there was no prenatal care. Then when she gave birth she had a hemorrhage and lost blood. My son was the first child born in Rohwer at the time."

In camp, taking young male children to use the toilets and showers was an issue for some mothers. Shizue Ohashi recalled one time when the men in the Rohwer camp could work temporarily in the fields for local farmers. It was a good opportunity to make some money, but Ohashi told her husband, "You bend down and it's crouch work. You could never last that long. Besides, how can I have you going out into the fields when I have two boys." She needed him to take their young sons to the men's lavatory. For her, "it wasn't worth it." She said to him, "I don't want you to go there to try to make some money and wear yourself out."

*Let us make loyalty our controlling spirit. . . . Let us prove that we are the stuff of which the best citizens are made.*

Jimmie Hamasaki
Santa Maria Union High School, 1934

For several valedictorians, the worst experience in camp was the turmoil they experienced in February 1943 when they filled out a "loyalty questionnaire." The War Relocation Authority, the government agency in charge of running the camps, gave the form to all the detainees and wanted to use it to separate "loyal" Japanese Americans from those "disloyal" to the United States.[6] The government planned to segregate the "disloyal," putting them in a different camp and eventually deporting them to Japan.

The title of the form, "Application for Leave Clearance," caused confusion and distress. Many Issei did not want to leave the camps because they had nowhere to go and were afraid of the hostility they might face if they left.

The content and wording of the questions further provoked the detainees, throwing the camps into turmoil. Question 27 of the form caused problems by asking, "Are you willing to serve in the armed forces of the United States on combat duty, wherever ordered?" The question tried to determine who would be eligible for eventual military duty. It should have been given only to the Nisei men, but it was also given to the women and the Issei.

Question 28 was a trick question because there was no right answer. It asked, "Will you swear unqualified allegiance to the United States of America and faithfully defend the United States from any or all attack by foreign or domestic forces, and foreswear any form of allegiance or obedience to the Japanese emperor, to any other foreign government, power or organization?" To answer yes, implied the Japanese Americans were admitting to having a prior allegiance. To answer no, meant they would not swear loyalty to the United States.

Frank Chuman was so mad at the mistreatment by the United States government that he answered "no, no," to questions 27 and 28. He said, "So out of a feeling of anger and disappointment in the United States government's attitude towards us and their unwarranted suspicion, and the way they treated us. . . . It made me so goddamned angry that for the record I wanted the government to know that I was angry. So I said, 'No, no just shove it up your ass'."[7]

The detainees were outraged. The United States government expected Nisei men and boys to fight and die for the country yet incarcerated them in concentration camps. To compound the injustice, before the Pearl Harbor attacks, the United States Navy and Marines had a policy of not accepting Japanese Americans because of their ethnicity.[8] Immediately after the attack on Pearl Harbor, the army classified Nisei men as 4-C, "enemy alien" and removed many Japanese Americans already serving in their ranks.

Some Nisei children answered "no, no" in order stay with their Issei parents, even if it meant deportation to Japan. Kazuya Sanada said, "Some of my friends were born here, but their [parents] wanted them to go back with them to the old country." He was angry

The "loyalty questionnaire" caused such an uproar, valedictorian Norio Yasaki was transferred from Tule Lake, California for his safety. Here, at the Tule Lake Relocation Center, segregated detainees from Topaz, Utah waiting to be inducted into the camp. *Courtesy of the National Archives and Records Administration, WRA Collection (Charles Mace).*

seeing his American-born friends segregated and sent to the camp for "disloyals." He said, "I couldn't understand it." He was so upset, he wrote a letter to President Roosevelt that said, "We're being taken into the army, but our [parents] are in here. What are you going to do with us? You know, we're citizens!"

Joe Nakanishi who eventually served in the Military Intelligence Service said, "I was a 'yes, yes' boy. There was bitterness in my heart." Chizuko Doi felt "very bitter" because her brothers, who were incarcerated, were drafted and had to fight in the war. Another valedictorian pointed out, "We were all interned because we might be aiding the Japanese. However, they did not hesitate to draft the boys out of camp to fight *for* the *USA*."

Shizue Ohashi, the barber, filled out the questionnaire for her husband who was an Issei. She said, "My husband was an alien and when I answered [question 27] for him. . . . I wrote, 'No [I will not serve in the military because] I am not allowed to be a citizen of the U.S.'" Even though Ohashi's husband had been in America since he was sixteen, he could not become naturalized under the laws of that time. She went on to explain that the U.S. government was especially interested in the loyalty response of the Kibei. "They were the ones, even though they were American-born, they were educated in Japan. They were usually raised by their grandfathers or relatives. . . . They're the ones that said, 'no, no' and they got sent to Tule Lake."

Tule Lake, a camp in California near the Oregon border, was chosen to house the "disloyals" because it was a large camp and because many dissidents, pro-Japanese and Kibei were already living there. Some Nisei labeled "disloyal" were not truly against the United States, but answered "no, no" or refused to fill out the form to protest their mistreatment by the United States.[9] Others were militant pro-Japanese thugs looking for trouble. In Tule Lake the bullies and enraged protesters prowled around looking to intimidate other people. Declaring loyalty to America would put any detainee there in physical danger.[10]

The Tule Lake camp fell victim to strikes, protests and violence. Valedictorian Norio Yasaki, who before the war had been a Methodist student minister in Loomis, California, was originally assigned to the camp but was later moved. Yasaki's son, Frederick, said, "The situation was not easy for my parents at Tule Lake." After signing, "yes, yes," pledging loyalty to the United States, Yasaki, his wife and newly born daughter were transferred to the Amache camp in Colorado. "My dad and mother were ostracized by some for their loyalty to the U.S. Apparently, my father was thought by some to be an 'internal informant' to camp officials since he was a block leader loyal to the U.S."

## NOTES

1   No valedictorians were sent to the camp in Minidoka, Idaho which held detainees from Oregon, Washington and Alaska.

2   Jeffery Burton and others, *Confinement and Ethnicity, An Overview of World War II Japanese American Relocation Sites*, vol. 74 of *Publications in Anthropology* (Tucson, Arizona: Western Archeological and Conservation Center, 2000), 38–39.

3   Ibid.

4   Ibid., 68.

5   Ibid., 47 (table).

6   Hosokawa, *Nisei: The Quiet Americans*, 363–365.

7   Tateishi, *And Justice for All*, 231.

8   Hosokawa, *Nisei: The Quiet Americans*, 360.

9   Ibid., 365.

10  Ibid.

# 6. Early Farewells

*We should never stoop so low in our speech or action, as to besmirch and defile the noble name of America. Rather, we should exert our energy, our time, our money, and if necessary our very lives, to do all that is a credit and honor to our nation.*

Frank Chuman
Los Angeles High School, 1934

VALEDICTORIAN Ida Shimanouchi was incarcerated with her parents and two younger sisters at the Tanforan Racetrack south of San Francisco and then sent to Topaz, Utah in 1942. In Topaz, she helped set up the camp library. After a month and a half, the opportunity for freedom came. Mills College, where she had received her B.A., helped arrange a fellowship for Shimanouchi's graduate work in English at Smith College in Massachusetts.

Although only in Topaz for a short time, she experienced the harsh lifestyle the detainees endured. "The difficulties were mainly physical ones," she said. "The dust storms affected my eyes abnormally. I had conjunctivitis. The lack of privacy in the latrines proved to be problematic, to say the least! Camp life was hardest on my father who was already suffering from a stroke."

When the news came that Shimanouchi had a chance to further her education, her family urged her to go, especially her father. She was happy to leave, yet concerned for her parents and sisters left behind.

At Smith College, she was treated well, although some townspeople were against her and other Nisei students' presence. "I experienced no discrimination at the college. In fact, the faculty and [my] fellow students were warm and friendly," she said. "There already had existed conflicts between town and gown, however, when some of the townsfolk, including a very vocal jeweler on

Some valedictorians in this volume left the camps to continue their postgraduate education. Here, a large group of detainees at Tule Lake, California bid farewell to several Nisei leaving for schools outside of the West Coast. *Courtesy of the National Archives and Records Administration, WRA Collection (Francis Newell).*

Main Street, learned that a group of Nisei were attending Smith and that a Canadian Nisei was appointed to the physics faculty. The *Hampshire Gazette* covered the news, citing the jeweler, who called for the resignation of the college president."

Nothing became of the incident, but Shimanouchi remembered it vividly. After leaving camp, she returned to Topaz about a year and a half later to attend her father's funeral. "Yes, he died in camp—a bitter experience for all of us."

In May 1942 an organization called the National Student Relocation Council was formed. Largely organized by Quakers, the group was created to help Japanese American students find suitable schools to attend outside of the West Coast. The Nisei were granted permission to leave the camps if the applicant had a place to go, financial support and no derogatory information in FBI and intelligence records.

Valedictorian Frank Chuman decided he wanted to finish his interrupted law studies after working for a year and a half as administrator for the hospital in Manzanar, California. Representatives of the National Student Relocation Council had visited the camp and had given a talk. "They said they would find suitable schools for us; they would arrange for the sending of transcripts . . . and that they would try to find funds for us and they would try to find friendly neighborhoods for us to live in," Chuman said.

The offer sounded great, but he regretted the way he had answered the "loyalty questionnaire." He was completely unaware of the negative consequences of his answer and said, "I thought to myself, this 'no, no' bothers me because I said that as a manifestation of my objection to what the government did to us, but I don't really have any feeling of disloyalty to the United States. This is my country. I just said that because I was angry."

So Chuman went to Ralph Merritt, Manzanar's project director, and told him he wanted to change his answer. Merritt agreed that Chuman hadn't meant "no, no," and made it a personal crusade to argue for Chuman in Washington D.C. After many attempts, Merritt was finally able to persuade the U.S. military and government officials that Chuman had said "no, no" out of anger and disappointment rather than real feelings of hostility or disloyalty. "So they changed me back to 'yes, yes,'" Chuman said.[1]

With his "loyal" status restored, Chuman received permission to leave Manzanar and with the help of the National Student Relocation Council he attended the University of Toledo Law School in Ohio. His parents, who had owned a dry cleaning business before the war, encouraged him to continue his studies. "Father literally digs under the mattress and he pulls out a sock with $150 in cash. He gave it to me. He said, 'This is all we have. We lost everything, but it's okay, don't worry about us.'"

Chuman left Manzanar in September 1943 and was warmly welcomed at the University of Toledo. Toward the end of November his dorm roommate, Bevan Alt, delivered some heartbreaking news: Alt's brother who was in the U.S. Marines Corps was killed in action on Tarawa in the Gilbert Islands.

Alt did not blame his loss on Chuman who said, "[Alt] never, never, never expressed any antagonism to me because I was a Japanese American. He didn't identify me with the Japanese enemy. He never did that."

A few days later, to Chuman's surprise, Alt's parents invited him to their home to spend Thanksgiving with them. He recalled, "The family did not say anything at all which indicated that they [blamed] me [for their son's death] because I was of Japanese ancestry. I was separate from their son dying in battle." Chuman had a wonderful home cooked Thanksgiving meal and spent time with the family. "We went ice skating. We went pheasant hunting. . . . There was a girl there that I skated with. She didn't think I was a freak."

In 1944 Chuman transferred to the University of Maryland to study Admiralty Law. The students there were especially curious about him because they had never met an Asian American before. Chuman's classmates gathered around him in the student union to hear stories about the incarceration of Japanese Americans on the West Coast. During his time in law school he also gave talks at churches and civic clubs about the internment camps. He said, "They didn't even know the Japanese Americans were evacuated and incarcerated." After he gave his talks, people would say to him, "What! You're an American citizen! You've been evacuated and you lost everything? How can this happen in America?"

In November 1942, almost one year after Japan attacked Pearl Harbor, Mike Masaoka, the JACL national secretary, warned the Nisei, "There are politicians even now who are trying to pass laws in Congress to strip us of citizenship and ship us to Japan when the war is over. The most effective weapon against this kind of persecution is a record of having fought valiantly for our country . . . "[2]

In January 1943, the United States allowed Japanese American men back into the army. About 2,500 Nisei men volunteered to join the institution that had uprooted and imprisoned them. They formed a segregated, all Japanese American Regimental Combat Team—the 442d—that merged with 100th Battalion from Hawaii.[3]

Many of the volunteers left the detention centers while their families were still incarcerated. Valedictorian George Nishida signed up to serve while he and his whole family were interned in Poston, Arizona. He had been born and raised in Dinuba, California and had graduated from Woodbury College before the war. Because he knew the Japanese language, he was assigned to the Military Intelligence Service. He was inducted in May 1943 and after attending the Military Intelligence Service Language School in Minnesota, he served in Guam in 1944 and in Japan in 1945.

Pearl Kurokawa's husband, Dr. Samuel Kimura, whom she had married at Camp Grant, was shipped out in 1943 with the 522d Field Artillery, a unit of the 442d Regimental Combat Team. Her husband was a platoon leader in charge of about forty men. While he was overseas fighting in Italy, Kurokawa moved to St. Louis and lived with her sister-in-law who had received permission to leave the camp in Topaz, Utah to attend Washington University.

When Kurokawa visited her family in camp in Poston, Arizona, she was "shocked to see the situation with barbed wire fences and their meager living conditions." She was "frustrated and disappointed"

While still held in Poston, Arizona, George Nishida volunteered for the U.S. Army and served in the Military Intelligence Service. *Courtesy of Agnes Nakamura.*

with the U.S. government. "[My husband] was being accepted [by the U.S. military] on the one hand and on the other, seeing my parents [in camp], I was really divided. But I never felt that I would forego the United States then. This is my country. This is the only country I knew," she said.

In 1941 before the Pearl Harbor attacks, valedictorian Kazuya Sanada received his first draft notice while he was a student at the University of California, Los Angeles. Soon after graduation, he reported to Camp Roberts near Paso Robles, California. Less than a week after his arrival, the authorities told all the Nisei they had been reclassified and sent the men home. Almost three years later, in January 1944, the draft was reinstated for Japanese Americans and the Selective Service System began inducting them even though many were still imprisoned in the camps. Sanada, then a twenty-eight-year-old father interned at Rohwer, Arkansas, received his second draft notice in early 1944. He wasn't the only one. "All these young kids, eighteen, just high school graduates. They got their draft notice," he said.

"[The camp administration] asked me to take all these kids on a bus to Little Rock for a physical. And since I was the oldest, they gave me all the files." Sanada failed the medical examination. He had a rash of poison ivy, high blood pressure and was underweight from having to constantly chop firewood for fuel.

He later learned that the Nisei boys in his group passed their physicals. They ended up in the 442d Regimental Combat Team,

A company of infantry, standing at attention during training at Camp Shelby in Mississippi. The all Japanese American 442d Regimental Combat Team became the most decorated unit of its size and length of service. *Courtesy of the National Archives and Records Administration, WRA Collection (Charles Mace).*

taking part in the rescue of the Texas "Lost Battalion" in the Vosges Mountains in Northeastern France near the German border. Through its heroism and bravery in the European Theater, the 442d Regimental Combat Team eventually became the most decorated American unit of its size and length of service in United States military history. The outfit also held the record for never having a single soldier desert the ranks.[4]

Nisei students and single males who joined the military were the earliest to leave the internment camps. As time went by, others applied to leave. One of them was Lincoln Shimidzu whose sister Charlotte, another Nisei in this book, was in Hawaii during the war.

In April 1943 while Shimidzu was held in Rohwer, Arkansas, he married Mary Fujita. Shimidzu's other sister, Marie, wrote, "[Lincoln] left camp as soon as possible to find work and bring his bride out of camp." Shimidzu was released in October and relocated to Chicago, but had a difficult time finding housing. He was finally able to rent an apartment near the University of Chicago and found work at a wholesale drug chain.

Mary Asada, who had been in Gila River, Arizona since October 1942 also relocated to Chicago. A gentleman had come to her camp to recruit workers for his company so she applied for a job. She was hired to do office work and bookkeeping. She said, "I didn't mingle

Left: Lincoln Shimidzu (standing, center) and older sister, Charlotte Shimidzu (seated, second from right), in a family portrait taken circa 1937 to celebrate their parent's twenty-fifth wedding anniversary. *Courtesy of Marie Nakamura. Photographer, Toyo Miyatake.*

Above: Lincoln Shimidzu married Mary Fujita in the Rohwer Relocation Center in April 1943. *Courtesy of Marie Nakamura.*

too much with other people [in Chicago] but when the girls in our office entertained, I was invited to their parties."

Valedictorian Joe Nakanishi also left Gila River during the war. He relocated to Cleveland, Ohio to work in a defense plant. "People [in Cleveland] were very friendly," he commented. Nakanishi and about ten other Nisei males who had left camp lived in a boarding house. "Every Sunday a minister would drop by to see if any of us boys would like to attend church services."

In 1944 Kiyoshi Nobusada left Gila River and relocated to Denver, Colorado. He became a consultant to the Ambrose Wine Company and worked for the firm until 1945. The company produced preserves and essential foods for the U.S. Navy during the war. Nobusada had very little money but together with a friend from camp, he started a business called Dehydro Products. The venture was a food processing plant that specialized in dehydrated Japanese food products for export to Hawaii. In 1945 after Japanese Americans were allowed to return to California, he and a new partner moved to the Monterey Peninsula and established the Sea Products Company, producing dehydrated seafood. Several decades later, they formed Consolidated Factors that grew to become one of the world's largest processors and distributors of seafood and agricultural products.[5]

Valedictorian Kazuya Sanada temporarily left Rohwer, Arkansas on "seasonal leave" in 1943 to work as a field hand because so many farm youth were serving in the military. "They needed workers in Illinois to harvest tomatoes and vegetables. . . . So about a dozen of us went to Illinois—a place called Stockton, Illinois. And then we picked tomatoes, string beans. All that stuff went to Camp Grant, nearby." He and the other Nisei workers were given a mixed reception. "The town of Stockton was divided," Sanada said. "Half of them didn't like us. They even burned a cross in front of the building that we were staying at. The other half were religious people. They wanted to help."

After Sanada's stint working in the fields, he returned to Rohwer. In 1944 he decided to get out of the camp for good. When he received his "permanent leave," he decided to go to the nearest large city, Chicago, where many Nisei had gone after being released from the camps. Sanada left his wife and baby son behind so he could get settled first. The WRA gave him $50 to start his new life. "I had no winter clothes. It was March, cold, snowy and I got on a train, went

Valedictorian Kazuya Sanada left camp on "seasonal leave" to work for Midwest farmers. Here, former Los Angeles residents topping beets on a farm in Johnstown, Colorado. *Courtesy of the National Archives and Records Administration, WRA Collection (Tom Parker).*

up there [to Chicago]. Had nowhere to go. I went to the YMCA for a dollar a night." Sanada was able to find some fellow ex-detainees who had left Rohwer before him. "By that time I only had about $15 left in my pocket. So I stayed with some of my friends and we pooled our money and then I found a job." About six months later he had saved enough and sent for his wife and son to join him.

## NOTES

1   Tateishi, *And Justice for All*, 233.

2   Hosokawa, *Nisei: The Quiet Americans*, 361.

3   Ibid., 402–403.

4   Chuman, *The Bamboo People*, 179.

5   David Yamada, *The Japanese of the Monterey Peninsula: Their History and Legacy,* (Monterey Peninsula Japanese American Citizens League, 1995), 100.

# 7. The Long Road Home

*Wars now have no real causes—they have only petty excuses and go on because nations have the habit and move by the precedent. Wars cannot settle anything. . . . The strong nation, not the right nation, wins.*

Kiyoshi Nobusada
Hanford Union High School, 1934

IN MID 1944, commencement speakers Shizu Komae and Yukiko Sanwo who were being held in Jerome, Arkansas had to relocate. Komae said, "I was pregnant with my daughter when we moved to Rohwer in June." Her baby was born just a few months later in August. So many people had left the Jerome Relocation Center that the 5,000 remaining internees were sent to Rohwer Relocation Center, the other Arkansas camp. The Jerome facility was then converted to a prisoner of war camp for Germans.[1]

By the end of 1944, the United States and the Allied forces had been getting the upper hand in the war in Europe with troops penetrating Germany. Meanwhile, in the Pacific Theatre U.S. troops continued their island-hopping march across the ocean toward Japan.

On December 18, 1944, the U.S. Supreme Court declared that the War Relocation Authority (WRA) could no longer detain "loyal" Japanese American citizens. In anticipation of the negative ruling, the U.S. War Department had announced one day earlier that the exclusion order against people of Japanese ancestry on the West Coast would be lifted effective January 2, 1945. Overnight, people who had been confined in concentration camps for almost three years were told they were free to return "home."

World War II ended in September 1945 but many internees still remained in the concentration camps. For them, homes and businesses

Reversing the scene of three years prior, detainees boarding trains to leave Heart Mountain, Wyoming in July 1945. *Courtesy of the National Archives and Records Administration, WRA Collection (Yone Kubo).*

had been lost and life savings wiped out. They had nowhere to go and stayed in the camps until the facilities were closed. Except for the centers in Jerome, Arkansas and Tule Lake, California, all the camps were shut down in October and November 1945.[2]

Komae and her family left Rohwer when the center closed in November. "Here's $25 and choose your place where you want to go and we'll pay your way there," she was told by the WRA. She and her husband decided to relocate to Indian Mills, New Jersey because her husband, Henry, received a job offer on a farm. Komae said, "Mr. Sharp [the farm owner] had placed an ad at Rohwer after he found out Japanese Americans were leaving the camp for employment."

The closure of the camps put another valedictorian who prefers not to be named, in a desperate situation. She had cleaned latrines in Poston, Arizona while her husband was ill with tuberculosis and he was still very sick. Because the camp in Poston, Arizona was closing in November, the valedictorian and her daughters needed to leave but had nowhere to go. The student said, "I came out [to California] about a month before to find a place to rent. But you know

After World War II ended, many valedictorians returned to their former hometowns. Katsumi Yoshizumi and his wife, Yoneko, left Utah where they had spent the war and returned to San Pedro, California. In 1953 they took this picture with their three children, Betty, Phillip and Gordon (baby). *Courtesy of Betty Kobata.*

there wasn't anything . . . unless you paid an awful lot of money which I couldn't afford. I went back without finding anything."

On November 12, 1945 the government sent her and some remaining detainees from Poston back to California. They were deposited at a mobile home park near an airstrip in Lomita, near San Pedro, California. "And we were all put in there and we paid $25 a month rent to the government. We were there until we could find a place to go. . . . It was kept up by the government until we could all disperse."

The valedictorian and her family stayed in the mobile home park and she cleaned homes to survive financially. Two years later, her husband passed away. She moved with her children to a large ranch where her Issei parents were employed. She saw how hard it was for her father to adjust and rebuild his life. "When the war broke out, he was leasing land and farming it but then that was all left [behind]. You just leave and go. So when he came back, he had nothing to start again so he had to work for somebody else. I think that was pretty rough for him," she said.

When Pearl Kurokawa's in-laws were released from Topaz, Utah, Kurokawa and her husband brought them back to California and took care of them. Kurokawa said, "We came back to Berkeley because the Kimura family kept their home. . . . My in-laws had packed all their silver and linen and put everything in the basement. But of course, when we came back nothing was left." She added laughing, "The house itself was still there."

Norio Yasaki, the Methodist minister, returned to Loomis, California and resumed his work at the Loomis Methodist Church. Yasaki's son Frederick wrote, "Upon my parents' return to their home in the church parsonage, they found the house was completely stripped of all furniture, sinks and appliances. It was thought nearby neighbors may have emptied the house." He added, "My great grandmother's home was burned to the ground."

In San Francisco, Ayame Ichiyasu's family found their residence had become a house of prostitution. When World War II ended, Ichiyasu was working in Boston at Harvard University as a law librarian and her brother, Kiyoshi, was serving in the Military Intelligence Service. When Japanese Americans were allowed to return to the West Coast, Kiyoshi received an emergency one-month furlough to bring his parents from the Manzanar Relocation Center back to San Francisco. Although a bank had been left in charge of the family home during the war, the tenants had turned it into a brothel. They had to be evicted before Ichiyasu's parents could move in.

Frank Yamakoshi and his wife Helen Kuwada had lost their farm. When they left Poston, Arizona, they relocated to the town of Reedley, California. Yamakoshi's daughter, Agnes, said her aunt and uncle "had a farm that some wonderful Armenian neighbors kept for them." Upon his return to California, Yamakoshi worked as a gardener and Kuwada cleaned homes. Eventually, the couple was able to buy their own home but even after the war, the anti-Japanese hostility remained. The family found bullets shot into the side of their house and the local car dealership still had a sign that read, "No Japs Allowed!"

Helen Kuwada and Frank Yamakoshi in front of the first home they bought in Reedley, California after the war. *Courtesy of Agnes Sasaki.*

Even though the U.S. government allowed Japanese Americans to come back to the West Coast, communities were hostile. Returning to her hometown of Kerman, California where she had lived almost all her life, Yukiko Sanwo was asked "why she had returned to California" and "hurtful words" were hurled at her.

Helen Hirata who had left Poston, Arizona relocated to Los Angeles and tried to help the Nisei resettle. She worked for the WRA who had hired her to assist detainees returning to Southern California find jobs and housing. As in the years before the war, discrimination against people of Japanese heritage persisted, especially when it came to finding housing.

Yoshiko Higuchi's daughter, Ellen, said, "Mother told me about how hard it was to rent a house in San Jose. They were turned down repeatedly before finding a place to stay."

"A year after the war ended, my wife and I decided to buy a home," said Joe Nakanishi. "We had two homes in mind in San Francisco. The real estate agent told us the neighbors didn't want any Japs in their neighborhood."

According to Kameko Yoshioka's granddaughter, Lisa, when Yoshioka and her husband attempted to purchase property three years after the war, neighbors in Montebello, California petitioned unsuccessfully to keep them out.

Frank Chuman went through similar encounters. He said, "I experienced discrimination in trying to purchase a piece of property to build a home for my parents and myself or to purchase a home in Southern California."

Toward the end of 1945 Chuman had graduated from the University of Maryland, passed the state's bar exam and received multiple job offers. He declined them all because the camp in Manzanar, California was closing in November. "My parents had been in Manzanar for three years. They had nothing. They had to get the hell out," he recalled. "So they had no place to go, no money. My brother was in the United States Army, my sister was in Washington D.C. with a good government job. So I decided I was going to take care of my parents instead of going off somewhere all by myself."

When Chuman returned to Los Angeles, his old job at the Los Angeles County Probations Department was still waiting for him. In 1942 after the Pearl Harbor attacks, the state of California fired all Japanese Americans in state civil service positions. Chuman said, "The chief probation officer [had] told me, 'I'm supposed to

After serving in the Military Intelligence Service, George Inagaki returned to California. He and his wife, Yukie, in Southern California in 1950. *Courtesy of Chris Inagaki.*

Four valedictorians permanently resettled in Chicago from the camps. Here, Haruko Fujita in a family portrait with her husband, Harry Tademaru, and her four children, (from left to right) Roy, Sharon, Eugene and Helen in 1946. *Courtesy of Haruko Fujita. Photographer, Fred Yamaguchi.*

terminate your job but I'm not going to do that. You have not given me any cause to fire you. I will put you on a leave of absence.'"

During the war, while Chuman was incarcerated and attending law school, all promotions and raises were applied to his position at the probations department. When he returned to Los Angeles, he was "glad to hear that the job was open" but instead, entered the law firm of Wirin, Rissman & Okrand, special counsel to the Japanese American Citizens League. Chuman was assigned Japanese American cases including ones concerning the Alien Land Law, Commercial Fishing, Restoration of U.S. Citizenship, G.I. War Brides from Japan, and a variety of immigration and deportation cases involving Japanese aliens. He would later author a book, *The Bamboo People: The Law and Japanese-Americans*, based on those cases. In 1947 he was admitted to the California Bar and in 1950 formed a law firm with valedictorian John Aiso and a third partner, David McKibbin.

In August 1945 Shizue Ohashi, the barber, left Rohwer, Arkansas with her family. She was on the train bound for California when she heard Japan had surrendered. She didn't know what to expect from the community when she returned to Los Angeles. The news she had heard was not good. "We had friends who had come to West Los Angeles from camp [earlier] and said they went to the stores and were told, 'No Japs allowed!' And they felt the discrimination," she said.

In spite of what she had been told, Ohashi was determined to return to her hometown. She explained, "We had to go to West Los Angeles. Our property was there." Her Issei father owned several houses under his American-born children's names, since the Alien Land Law prevented him from owning real estate. Ohashi gave her father "a lot of credit" for leaving the properties in the hands of a licensed realtor who was bound to be more ethical than friends or neighbors. "Luckily we had a realtor take care of all the property. . . . He'd collect the rent and put it in our Security Bank account and Security would take our loans from there. So our houses were still intact."

"After we came back, we tried to find that fellow that was running the hotel." While she had been locked up, the manager who took care of her husband's hotel business had siphoned all the profits. "He'd gone to Mexico. He made millions because there were a lot of Japanese on Main Street and 5th Street who were running hotels like that."

Although the political climate in the Los Angeles community was hostile when Ohashi returned, attitudes slowly changed. She recalled, "As more [ex-detainees] came, the government said [to communities] 'You have to accept them.'" She also attributed the improvement of the Japanese Americans' image to the decorated Nisei soldiers who had fought for the United States. "They helped us. Because of them we could come back to our place again. . . . So it's all because of the 442d and their heroism. They caused us to be accepted by the community."

When the war ended, Michiko Naito had already left the camp in Poston, Arizona and was in New Jersey, working at Seabrook Farms, a huge frozen food company. She decided to go back to California in 1948. "In fact, the bosses were so kind they told me to come back [to New Jersey] if California was unsafe," she said. When Naito moved to Reedley, California she faced racism even though the war had been over for several years. "I was offered a job at the local doctor's office but when he told me I might come across some unpleasant patients, I decided not to take the job." Instead, she took a position with an auto dealer and learned she was the first Japanese American to work in town after the war.

Shizu Komae also returned to California after over two and a half years in New Jersey. She said, "We saw no future in New Jersey and things had quieted down in California." In August 1948 she and her family crossed the U.S. in a Ford™ truck they bought for the journey.

Some valedictorians returned to California many years after the war. Some stayed away for good. Of the thirty-four students who had been interned, eight never returned to the state. Four students permanently resettled in Chicago and the others relocated to Utah, Ohio, Michigan and New York.

At his wife's prompting, Kazuya Sanada came back to California fourteen years after the war had ended. When he left the camp in Rohwer, Arkansas in 1944 he relocated to Chicago. Sanada loved the city and because there was no hostility toward Japanese Americans. "[Chicago] was wide open because the Chicago make-up is Polish, Swedish, Irish. There was a conglomeration of Europeans," he said. He remembered all the times in California when he wasn't allowed to go to dance halls or other public places. But in Chicago, even while the war was going on, no one bothered him about his heritage. "We used to go public dancing with no problem and we'd go up to Wisconsin for fishing. You could just walk around, go into any restaurant. . . . That's the reason I didn't come back [to California] for a long time."

When World War II ended, five valedictorians were still in Japan and China. Goro Murata, the newspaperman, was in Tokyo. He had been there since 1934 and worked for the *Japan Times* newspaper. After Japan surrendered, he continued to work for the publication and remained in Tokyo.

George Nishida, a Nisei volunteer from an internment camp in Poston, Arizona, was in the Military Intelligence Service when the war ended. In 1945 he was sent to Japan and in March of the following year he was honorably discharged in Tokyo. For the next fourteen years he stayed in Tokyo and pursued an import/export business in postwar Japan. His sister, Agnes, wrote, "George traveled extensively, dealing with countries such as Iran and Korea (evidence from his old passports). He became prosperous, helping relatives in Japan recover from devastation after the war."

Nishida experienced several "bad business deals" in which some foreign governments reneged on their debts and he returned to the U.S. After "dabbling in a variety of things," he worked for the U.S. Postal Service and later, the *Los Angeles Times*.

Kiyoshi Murakami, the valedictorian who was drafted into the Japanese Army after finishing Chuo University Law School, spent seven months recovering in a hospital in Singapore before returning to Japan in 1946. Murakami's sister, Irene, who survived the atomic bomb in Hiroshima, recalled, "He went back to Hiroshima, to our

Kiyoshi Murakami in Hiroshima after World War II. *Courtesy of Irene Yamaguchi.*

grandparents' home. Of course, he found nothing. Their home was completely destroyed."

Murakami remained in Hiroshima which was occupied by the Australian Army at the time, working for city hall as a translator and interpreter. Later he worked for Nippon Suisan Kaisha, a large seafood products company, as a specialist in the foreign trade department. He traveled all over the world as a "company diplomat." Murakami would remain in Japan for the rest of his life.

Two valedictorians were in Manchuria when Japan surrendered on August 14, 1945. One was Michiko Yoshihashi from Los Angeles who had gone to Japan after high school to meet her future husband. In 1938 she married and moved to Manchuria. Throughout the war she stayed in China and in 1946 returned to Japan where she still lives.

The other valedictorian was Toshio Yamagata, originally from Fowler, California. He had gone to Japan in 1940 after attending the University of California, Berkeley. Before and during the war he was employed as a civilian translator for the Japanese military and

Left: After surviving as a prisoner of war in Siberia for four years and losing his American citizenship, Toshio Yamagata returned to the U.S. in 1958 as the spouse of an American citizen. *Courtesy of Jeannette Sanderson.*

Above: Toshio Yamagata's wife, Mary, and her two daughters, Nancy Sachiko (left) and Jeannette Kyoko, in 1959 at their home in Harajuku in Tokyo. The photo was taken just before they relocated to the United States and joined Yamagata. *Courtesy of Jeannette Sanderson.*

because of this, when World War II ended, he lost his U.S. citizenship. The Russian Red Army took him as a prisoner of war and held him in Siberia for four years.

His daughter, Jeannette, said, "My father did not talk very much about his experiences as a POW except [to say] that it was extremely cold in Siberia where he worked in the coal mines." She added, "He took a somewhat perverse pride in the fact that he actually traveled on the Trans-Siberian Railroad." On another occasion Yamagata described being driven around by Russian guards in a brand-new, American-made Ford™ truck. "It struck him as ironic that he—American-born and a graduate of a top American university—was a prisoner of the Allied forces."

While Yamagata was a Russian POW, his American-born Nisei wife, Mary Muroya, suffered the fate of many civilian women waiting for repatriation to Japan. She worked at menial jobs and taught English, and was once almost raped. Her first-born daughter died of malnutrition.[3] Yamagata was eventually freed in 1949 and was reunited with his wife in Japan. They had two more daughters before deciding to move back to California. In 1958 Yamagata returned to America as an immigrant and spouse of a United States citizen.

In the 1960s he regained his citizenship through naturalization. "When my sister and I knew our father, he was USA all the way," Jeannette remarked. "He was very patriotic, and was very critical of those who did not appreciate the rights, privileges and opportunities enjoyed by Americans."

## NOTES

1   Jeffery Burton and others, *Confinement and Ethnicity,* 40.

2   Ibid., 49.

3   See the appendix for a letter in which valedictorian Toshio Yamagata's wife, Mary, describes her experience in postwar Manchuria.

# Epilogue

*Debt of the present to the past is great. Just as we can repay our parents for their care only by giving equally good care to the generation that follows us. . . . We can repay this debt we owe to all who have come before us only by trying to leave an added contribution to civilization.*

Joe Nakanishi
Alhambra Union High School, June 1939

IN THE DECADES following the war and internment, the students slowly settled down into their previously interrupted lives. Many led unassuming ordinary lives, the kind they had aspired to before the war had turned their world upside down. A few valedictorians led lives of distinction. But each in his or her own way fulfilled the youthful promise displayed in their graduation speeches.

Shizue Ohashi returned to cutting hair. At the same time she juggled the demands of being a wife and raising three kids while attending night school to study real estate. She earned a broker's license in 1948, and she has retained her license into her eighties.

In her early years in real estate, she faced discrimination and she had "a hard time" because male brokers wouldn't work with her. If she won a listing, they tried to take it away from her. If she wanted to make a purchase for her client, they wouldn't sell. Eventually, if the broker wanted to deal with her, she would say to him, "You had a house and I wanted to cooperate with you to sell it to a Japanese family and you wouldn't let me do it. Now do you expect me to cooperate with you?"

"I had it tough. I had to stand up for my rights," she said. Not only did she fight racism, she faced the added burden of her gender. "Because there weren't very many women brokers at that time or business women. . . . There were times when I had to share a commission which I knew I didn't have to, but I didn't want to fight it."

By 1968 Shizue Ohashi had achieved success as a businesswoman and president of the Southern District Adult Buddhist Association, a league of Buddhist temples in Southern California. *Courtesy of Shizue Ohashi.*

Another valedictorian, a single mother, obtained a clerical position five years after the war, but found out later that she almost wasn't offered the job because of her ancestry. "One of the girls in the office told me that the boss went around asking if they minded working with a Japanese," she recalled. "I guess they all must have said no, they didn't mind, because I was hired." She eventually was able to put two daughters through college.

For the generation of students featured in this book, sending their children to college was a priority. Almost all of them accomplished that even though they had to forego higher education for themselves. Valedictorian Helen Kuwada had to give up her dream of being a business major, so she was determined to make sure all five of her daughters went to college, and they did.

Haruko Fujita from Arcadia, California also never fulfilled her dream of higher education. She was valedictorian of her junior high as well as high school but because of life circumstances, she was never able to attend college. Fujita's greatest pride was seeing her children earn their college degrees. In 1958 when Fujita's eldest daughter, Helen, wanted to mention the internment camps in her valedictorian address, the high school administration in Chicago would not allow it.

With perseverance, three other female valedictorians attained their college degrees later in their lives. In the 1930s Shizu Komae was admitted to the University of California, Los Angeles after she graduated from high school. She enrolled but did not attend classes. Her mother fell ill and Komae was needed to help the family. Decades later at the age of forty-two, when Komae's daughter, Kay, started attending junior college, Komae also enrolled. Two years later Komae transferred to the University of California, Los Angeles and graduated as a Japanese major in 1966.

After World War II ended, Yoshimi Nagayama worked as a seamstress sewing wedding gowns and became a part-time dental assistant. She decided to study dental hygiene at the University of Southern California while managing the responsibilities of being a working wife and mother. In 1952 at the age of thirty-seven, Nagayama received a B.S. in dental hygiene and her teaching credentials. After years of hard work and sacrifice, she embarked on a successful career as a dental hygienist and taught dental nutrition at Los Angeles City College.

Salutatorian Mitsue Matsumune's eyesight deteriorated during her youth. Shortly after the war ended she completely lost her

vision. Despite this, after attending a school for the blind in Oakland, she went to the University of California, Berkeley and attended classes with the help of a reader. She did not elect to specialize in a major, but studied general education. In 1955 she graduated as a Phi Beta Kappa. The following year she married her reader, Robert Rottman. She and her husband went on to have a daughter and a long and happy marriage.

Valedictorian John Aiso was perhaps the most distinguished of the students contained in this book. Under his leadership in the U.S. Army, thousands of linguists graduated from the Military Intelligence Service Language School between 1942 and 1946. Aiso retired from the military with the rank of colonel, making him the highest-ranking Japanese American at that time.

After World War II, Aiso resumed his law practice in Southern California and founded a firm, Aiso, Chuman & McKibbin with valedictorian Frank Chuman in 1950. In 1953 Aiso became the first Japanese American, as well as Asian American, judge in the continental U.S. when he was appointed to the Los Angeles Municipal Court. Ironically, Governor Earl Warren, who had advocated the internment of the people of Japanese heritage at the start of World War II, appointed Aiso. Four years later, Aiso was elevated to the Superior Court of Los Angeles County. In 1972 he retired from the bench and became special counsel for O'Melveny & Meyers. In 1987, several years after his final retirement, Aiso tragically died from injuries sustained in a mugging at a gas station. In his honor,

Left: Mary Miyamoto in her garden in 1991 in Fresno, California. *Courtesy of Ann Gorai.*

Above: In 1984 the Japanese government awarded John Aiso the prestigious Third Class Order of the Rising Sun for his service in the occupation of Japan after World War II and for furthering the understanding and goodwill between the people of Japan and the U.S. Aiso was seventy-four when he received the Third Order of the Chrysanthemum Medal of Merit from the Emperor of Japan. *Courtesy of Arthur Kamii.*

North San Pedro Street inside Little Tokyo in downtown Los Angeles was renamed Judge John Aiso Street.

The most consistent legacy of the internment for the Nisei generation, including the valedictorians, is their reluctance to speak about their time behind barbed wire. Mary Miyamoto's son, Steve, said he believed his mother "felt a lot of humiliation and shame about the internment" and "would not want to answer" his brother's questions about the camp experience. "Mother probably felt the federal government acquiesced to California political pressure and hysteria." Still, he added, "She would not make direct negative statements."

As a parent, another valedictorian reacted similarly and would not talk about the internment. One day after her young daughter had asked her, "Our government did all that to you?" the valedictorian decided, "Well, that's it. I'm not going to say another word. I never talked about it in front of the kids because I didn't want them to feel that their government was in any way bad. And so they grew up without any notion of what we went through."

She was more willing to describe her experiences when her daughters had grown up. "By that time I was ready to discuss a lot of stuff, all that happened, the why and the wherefore and how I felt about it. . . . I didn't think they needed to know until they grew up and could think for themselves. I think a lot of us were that way. We didn't talk about it much. It was not a good time in our lives, you know. Bad time. Maybe we just put that all behind us and in the background."

Helen Kuwada and Frank Yamakoshi (seated) with their five daughters (from left to right) Carol, Lois, Shirley, Esther and Agnes in 1987. *Courtesy of Agnes Sasaki.*

Others reacted to their wartime experiences by repressing their Japanese heritage and emphasizing American culture to their children. Many did not press their children to learn the Japanese language. "Somewhere along the way, my mother decided to be very American," said Kozue Fujikawa's daughter, Christine. "I took baton twirling lessons instead of Saturday Japanese [language] school, so I could march in loyalty day parades. My mother remained proud of her Japanese heritage but it was a quiet pride. Her choice after the war was to be, and to raise her children to be, *very* American."

Frank Yamakoshi and Helen Kuwada's grandchildren wrote school papers about the internment and interviewed their grandparents about their experience. But the couple didn't talk much about the camps to their daughters. "We know how bitter Dad must have felt—losing his farm and equipment, then having to find a new occupation," said Agnes, their eldest child. "Just like our dad, Mom didn't talk too much about camp life. But we could tell there was bitterness."

"And yet," she continued, "growing up, we were brought up to be extremely loyal to America. Dad had a large American flag and on appropriate occasions would proudly fly it in front of our home. He was careful not to let it touch the ground as it would have to be burned." She added, "Our parents impressed upon us the importance of community service and volunteerism. They made us believe that we could accomplish anything—to us there was no barrier or glass ceiling."

Like many others who had been interned, Yamakoshi and Kuwada were determined to show their patriotism in every way possible. "For many years, they always bought American cars because they wanted to show their loyalty to America," said Agnes. "One of the local car dealerships had a sign that read, 'No Japs Allowed!' Ironically, years later, this dealership loved to do business with Japanese Americans! Even our parents bought cars from them. Dad and Mom were very forgiving individuals."

Valedictorian George Inagaki's son, Chris, said, "I believe the post-war experience was easier because of [the Niseis'] show of loyalty to the U.S. However, in most parts of the country, acceptance was difficult so my father became more active in the JACL to overcome these situations."

An outgoing, friendly leader, Inagaki was active in the Japanese American Citizens League (JACL) for more than thirty years and became very successful in business and banking. "His goals were to

George Inagaki (left) and his son, Chris, in San Francisco in 1972. *Courtesy of Chris Inagaki.*

help as many Nisei as he could get back on their feet so that they could pursue the American Dream," Chris remarked. "I believe my father was a simple man who was placed in very tough situations and he responded. He was ambitious but always wanted what was best for the Issei and Nisei and *future generations*."

Although racism remains a part of American culture, generations following the valedictorians have grown up in a society that has evolved since World War II. Anti-Japanese laws, including ones regarding property ownership, were struck down one by one. The 1952 Immigration and Nationality Act finally allowed individuals of all races to be eligible for naturalization. The Issei, the parents of the valedictorians, could finally become citizens.

After more than a decade of legal struggle and lobbying led by groups including the JACL, President Ronald Reagan signed the Civil Liberties Act of 1988. The law included a Presidential apology to Japanese Americans who were interned, as well as monetary redress, acknowledging their loss of property and civil rights during World War II.

George Inagaki (wearing bow tie, below "Welcome Mike" sign) and Mike Masaoka (right, wearing sunglasses), celebrating the JACL's successful lobby to obtain naturalized citizenship for the Issei in 1952. *Courtesy of Chris Inagaki.*

It has taken decades but the Nisei valedictorians can dream of a better America. They've seen their children and grandchildren achieve greater heights in professional fields and in American society than the students could have imagined for themselves. But while it has taken decades for the Nisei to rebuild their lives after World War II, setbacks still occur.

Since the terrorist attacks on the United States on September 11, 2001, many Japanese Americans worry about a resurgence of the fear and paranoia that led to their unwarranted imprisonment over half a century ago. Although the students support the country's fight against terrorism, some see unsettling similarities between their own experiences and those of Arab Americans in the wake of 9/11.

"Immediately following the event, people were being judged by their supposed ethnic background," said Haruko Fujita. "[There was] immediate fear of anyone looking remotely Arab."

Those kinds of fears are familiar to anyone who has been incarcerated based on their ethnicity. In the days following the September 11th tragedy, people who were presumed to be of Middle Eastern descent were attacked and even killed—despite the fact that some were neither from the Middle East, nor were they Muslim. Legislation, entitled the U.S.A. Patriot Act, that significantly erodes civil liberties guaranteed by the Bill of Rights of the U.S. Constitution, was signed into law in October 2001. A new policy requiring people from Middle Eastern countries to register with United States authorities led to the arrests and incarceration of hundreds of people without being formally charged of a crime and without being able to contact their families.

"We need to continue educating the public, reminding people to look beyond superficial appearances and reminding them to learn from the past," warned Fujita.

"The only way [to avoid another internment] is to teach ourselves to better understand our neighbors," said Pearl Kurokawa.

Joe Nakanishi added, "What happened to the Japanese Americans during World War II should not happen to people of Middle Eastern heritage." He suggested that citizens have the responsibility to write lawmakers, work with civil rights organizations such as the JACL and NAACP, and take part in peaceful protests to make sure their voices are heard.

Matilde Honda commented, "It's very critical and needs to be made clear to the American public that the 'War on Terrorism'

In Los Angeles, Frank Chuman spoke at the fiftieth year reunion of the hospital staff from the Manzanar Relocation Center in 2000. *Courtesy of Frank Chuman.*

doesn't result in discriminating against Arab Americans." She "hopes" the U.S. government has "learned its lesson."

"Our government will not again incarcerate like they did with us—one big mistake was enough!" said Kazuya Sanada.

Although some valedictorians are certain that the lessons of the past would prevent another mass incarceration, Frank Chuman cited modern technology and the connectedness of the world today as one reason Arab and Muslim Americans might face worse discrimination. "There are no guarantees or assurances that the hostile feelings towards persons of Japanese ancestry before and during World War II would not happen to persons of Middle Eastern heritage. I believe the American people will feel more hatred towards the Middle East Arab and Muslim Americans because of the rapidity of mass communication." The media, he said, would feed the "propaganda war."

Haruko Fujita was more hopeful and added that the solution is for Japanese Americans to get involved in their communities. "We need to become more politically active to help ensure that such discrimination does not happen again," she said. "And the best way is within the system."

In the 1940s the "system" was flawed and failed to protect the constitutional rights of Japanese Americans. Matilde Honda observed, as time passes, the younger generations "get distant" from the history of discrimination and the violation of civil liberties seen in the United States. To young people now, the problem "doesn't seem realistic."

"They must be kept aware," she warned, suggesting they get involved in civic groups and especially understand the Japanese American experience during World War II, in light of all that has happened since the September 11th attacks. "It is important to keep vigilant."

# PART TWO

# Orations and Essays

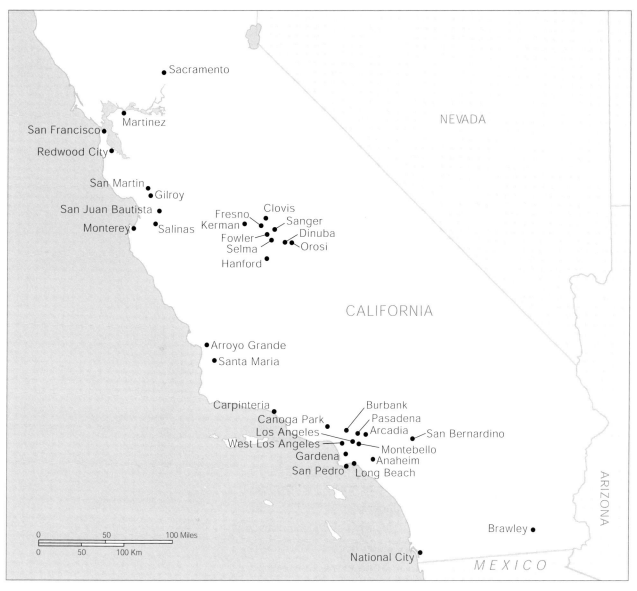

The fifty Nisei valedictorians and salutatorians in this book attended public high schools, junior high schools and grammar schools in thirty-five cities and towns all over California in the 1920s and 1930s.

# Introduction to Part 2

ORIGINALLY PUBLISHED as *Orations and Essays by the Japanese Second Generation of America* in the 1930s, part 2 features a collection of fifty speeches written by California's first Japanese American valedictorians, salutatorians and commencement speakers. The children of Japanese immigrants, these students are Nisei which means second generation.

The valedictorians were between twelve and twenty years old when they gave their speeches. By 1940, about two-thirds of all Nisei in California had been born after 1920, making these valedictorians elder members of their generation.[1] Born between 1907 and 1920, these Nisei were adults in their early twenties and thirties by the time World War II began.

While more than half are female, the students in this volume are an elite group, representing some of the best and the brightest from forty-two public schools across California in the 1920s and 1930s. Their alma maters are located as far north as Sacramento and as far south as National City near the Mexico border. Many of their schools were in the Central Valley and in Southern California near farming communities with large Japanese American populations. In 1930, the Nisei comprised only three percent of California's total school population, but about thirty-five percent of them lived in Los Angeles County.[2]

The students' orations were delivered between 1923 and 1939 with the majority given in 1932, 1933 and 1934. Nearly seventy percent of the valedictorians are high school seniors, but fifteen grammar and junior high students are also included. There is also one two-year college graduate, Helen Hirata, from San Bernardino Junior College.

Almost all the speeches were composed for graduation ceremonies and those orations given in January or February were delivered at winter commencements. John Aiso, one of the most distinguished students in this volume, became the 1926 valedictorian of Hollywood High School; however, his graduation speech is not published. Instead, the text of his prizewinning oration, "Lincoln's Devotion to the Constitution," from 1923 is featured.

Although the manuscripts are graduation speeches, the topics of the orations vary widely and were not limited to traditional commencement addresses. There are essays about education, government, international relations and social issues of the day. With guidance from their teachers, some students were allowed to choose their topics. Dorothy Yoshida, the valedictorian of Sweetwater High School, said the East Indian leader, Mahatma Gandhi, was "very much in the news" at that time so she chose to write about him. Salutatorian Chizuko Doi chose to explore feminism in her 1934 speech, "The American Woman Comes of Age."

The Olympics, held in Los Angeles in 1932, made an impression because there are a couple of essays about the games. Interestingly, there is only one speech on the topic of the Great Depression—Thomas Hirashima's oration, "Proposed Measures to Meet the Crisis." But several students spoke about the economic difficulty of the times. James Hashimoto mentioned "the stress of the present depression" and Akiko Sawada alluded to financial difficulties at her school when she said it experienced "trials and tribulations."

Growing up in California, the Nisei had to negotiate between American and Japanese cultures. Some orations compared and contrasted the two. Valedictorian Florence Akiyama shared her thoughts in "What High School Means to a Japanese Girl." In James Hashimoto's essay, he briefly compared Japan's educational system with that of the U.S. Ida Shimanouchi tried to downplay differences between races and emphasized the "oneness of humanity" in her speech, "International Peace."

Other orations covered U.S. relations with Japan. In "Prospects of Pacific Foreign Trade," Jimmie Tabata attempted to dispel myths about "cheap Japanese goods flooding the American market," explaining that Japan was one of America's "best customers" in purchasing exports. In "Education Insures Peace," Kiyoshi Nobusada argued for abolishing war and blamed "jingoistic newspapers" in Japan and the U.S. for trying to "hamper oriental-occidental relations."

Some of the students' schools set themes for graduation ceremonies and assigned speech topics. The 1932 theme for Sequoia High School's graduation program was "Adjustment of Modern Life Problems." Charles Inouye, one of the commencement speakers, wrote about the physical and social adjustments people need to make in the "machine age." Fowler High School's 1933 graduation explored the theme of leisure time in society. Ayami Onaka discussed the "Relation of Leisure to Avocations" and Toshio Yamagata spoke on the "Relation Between Leisure and Citizenship."

Reporting on what was happening in big business in the U.S., Yoshimi Nagayama and Kiyoshi Murakami of Gardena High School spoke about the problems of monopolies and unfair business practices by corporations and trusts. Mary Miyamoto and George Takaoka, salutatorian and valedictorian of Clovis Union High School, gave speeches about local areas in California. Miyamoto expounded on the beauty and majesty of the Sierra Mountains and Takaoka talked about Clovis and its neighboring communities.

The public school system had done its job well in Americanizing these Nisei and shaping their values and ideology. The students' patriotism and pride in being Americans and their appreciation for their parents and teachers are evident in many of the essays. In his book, *Growing up Nisei*, David Yoo wrote, "Rather than viewing the schools as sacred sites of democracy or instruments of the capitalist state bent on social control, the case of Japanese Americans suggests that they contained a more complex reality in which both elements were evident." He added, "In the 1920s and 1930s, perhaps no state embraced progressive education, contradictions and all, more than California."[3]

Some Issei within the intellectual community hoped the Nisei would be ambassadors of Japanese culture in America. Paul Tsunegoro Hirohata, the original editor and publisher of the students' speeches, wrote, "The Nisei can fulfill their duties as Americans and it is certain that they can contribute greatly to the cultural harmony of Japan and the United States in the Pacific era."[4] Shiro Fujioka,

Secretary of the Los Angeles Japanese Association, said in 1932, "The responsibility of fulfilling the mission of promoting goodwill between Japan and the United States has to be carried by [the Nisei]." Kay Sugahara, president of the Los Angeles chapter of the Japanese American Citizens League (JACL), felt similarly. He remarked, "In the center of this turbulent scene, the Nisei, a blend of two great cultural forces, play a prominent role in the molding of a more pacific relationship between two great powers."

In 1924 the U.S. banned all further immigration from Japan and because of this, Shiro Fujioka commented, "The future development of our race in North America fell solely upon the activity of the Nisei." After the Immigration Act, also called the Japanese Exclusion Act, was passed, the Issei viewed the second generation as increasingly significant since they were American-born citizens. Fujioka observed, "Under the circumstances, great hope has been gradually placed upon the Nisei and everyone has had much expectation of them. In light of the important mission possessed by these Nisei, I question whether our fellow countrymen and other Americans really understand them."

Some understanding of the students can be gleaned by reading their graduation speeches. Vierling Kersey, Superintendent of Public Instruction for the State of California in 1932, commented in the foreword, "This volume has for its purpose the promotion of a better understanding of the problems of the students in our California schools who would bring the traditions and the culture of other countries." Paul Tsunegoro Hirohata wrote in 1935, "Moreover, the idealism and emotion contained in the essays clearly reveal the Nisei's thoughts of the time and, as such, they constitute valuable documentation." By preserving the manuscripts, Hirohata hoped they would serve as "reference material" inspiring the younger Nisei and future generations.

## NOTES

1  David Yoo, *Growing Up Nisei: Race, Generation, and Culture among Japanese Americans of California, 1924-49* (Urbana, IL: University of Illinois Press, 2000), 5, table 2. Citing Dorothy S. Thomas, Charles Kikuchi, and James Sakoda, *The Salvage* (Berkeley: University of California Press, 1952), 575–79.

2  Yoo, *Growing Up Nisei*, 19. Citing Reginald Bell, *Public School Education of Second-Generation Japanese in California* (Stanford, CA: Stanford University Press, 1935), 7.

3  Yoo, *Growing Up Nisei*, 18, 21.

4  See appendix B for the prefaces and forewords of the 1932 and 1935 editions of *Orations and Essays*.

*Graduation Speeches of 1923–1939 by Topic*

# The Future of California

**GEORGE J. INAGAKI**
*Sacramento High School, February 1932*
*Sacramento, California*

George J. Inagaki (1914–1978). *Courtesy of Chris Inagaki.*

THE TREND of European civilization has ever been to the westward since its creation in Greece and Rome. It swept across Europe, from Italy through France, Spain and England, and not even the mighty Atlantic could stop its progress. Today it has swept across the whole of the two Americas and slowly but surely it is penetrating Asia. In every phase of the progress of this civilization some country or portion of a country at the height of this civilization has profited materially as well as culturally. Spain in her time became a world power but was succeeded by England. London was until a few years ago, the center of world culture and business, but today New York claims that title. If you will notice, each of these cities has access to the sea through good harbors or rivers and each is connected with the interior by railways, river ways, and highways.

The thought I wish to convey to you through these statements is the possibility of California profiting and advancing by this trend of civilization and culture. And why not? In its wake always comes a great demand for mechanical and agricultural products, a necessity for advancement. England profited much while America was in the process of attaining her standard of living. Spain, Italy and Greece in turn prospered before England, and now with the frontier of this civilization in Asia, the whole Pacific Coast, but especially California, is coming into its own.

George Inagaki was born and raised in Sacramento, California and was one of the first Japanese American valedictorians in Northern California. After high school he attended Sacramento Junior College but had to abandon that pursuit and help his family farm during the Depression. In 1939 he married Yukie Yagi and the couple later became one of the first Japanese Americans to adopt children, a son and a daughter.

Inagaki was a very outgoing, friendly person who was gifted with leadership abilities. Deeply concerned with the difficult Japanese American situation before and during World War II, he worked tirelessly as a spokesperson and leader for the Japanese American Citizens League (JACL). During World War II he volunteered for the U.S. Army, serving

In the near future there will come a time when America will be called upon to comply with the great Asiatic demand for products and materials, agricultural as well as mechanical. This Pacific demand will far surpass those of the past. Her demand will be the demand of nine hundred million people. And California will receive the bulk of that trade, for her position commands from the best sea ports in the 5,000 miles of the Pacific Coast of North America, the shortest route to Asia and the Pacific Islands and is reinforced by her enormous coastline. California has two-thirds of the total United States frontage upon the Pacific and nearly one-fifth of the total coastline of the United States. All this added to its relation as outlet for an enormous inland territory including not only California, but New Mexico, Arizona, Nevada and Utah gives great advantage to her Pacific commerce.

The Bay of San Francisco, with a shoreline of 300 miles, opens to the ocean only by the mile-wide Golden Gate, and receiving through the two great Central rivers the drainage of the vast interior Valley, is reckoned among the world's best harbors. Los Angeles with her artificial harbor ranks a close second to that of San Francisco. In the extreme south is the well-sheltered natural harbor of San Diego. Through these various ports annually there passes out an export of about $800,000,000. The steady increase in California's export, while that of the United States as a whole is decreasing, indicates that the Pacific Era of commerce has begun. And Theodore Roosevelt's prediction, "The Mediterranean era is past, the Atlantic rule of the sea is failing, and the Pacific will be the next arena of the world's activities," is finally becoming a reality.

Then let us pause here a moment and consider California's two leading industries, great now and destined to be greater, Agriculture and Manufacturing. California, in order to meet the great Pacific trade, must develop still further her agricultural productivity, and those products must be of the variety most needed along the far Pacific. And she should have no difficulty in accomplishing this, for fertile land she has in abundance in the Sacramento and San Joaquin valleys, extending from Tehachapi to Shasta, from the Sierras to the Coast Ranges—40,000 square miles of productive land capable of producing practically every product suited to a temperate climate. Water supply she has no fear of, for the Sacramento and the San Joaquin rivers bring down an abundant supply from the mountains. The quantity of water which annually flows down these two rivers is estimated at about 40,000,000 acre feet or a body of water 50

in the Military Intelligence Service in the Pacific Theatre. He fought in battles in Saipan, Tinian in the Mariana Islands, Iwo Jima and Okinawa. During his missions he translated documents, interrogated captured Japanese soldiers and was an interpreter on Admiral Nimitz's staff.

After the war ended he settled in Los Angeles where he owned a nursery, revitalizing the flower industry among Japanese Americans, helping many get back on their feet financially. He later worked in real estate, mutual funds and was on the board of directors of the Bank of Tokyo of California.

He aided in the welfare of the sick, the needy and the orphaned and encouraged Japanese Americans to join non-Japanese fraternal organizations. Inagaki was the first Japanese American to be accepted in the Masons and was a Rotary club member for thirty years. He was a key leader in the JACL for more than thirty years, probably contributing more than any single individual to developing the organization's financial structure. According to the JACL, Inagaki was the "personification of citizenship at its best." He always worked to prove, "It is better to light a candle than to curse the darkness."

miles square and 50 feet deep. South of the Tehachapi is more fertile land. There also is the Imperial Valley that was recently reclaimed from the desert and is now considered one of the most productive valleys in California. Along the coast and in the Sierras are countless numbers of smaller valleys whose fertility ranks close to that of the great interior.

In manufacturing also, California must always be aware of the Pacific demand if she is to make any marked progress. Her future from the standpoint of power is assured. California was greatly handicapped in her early development as a manufacturing state because of the high cost of fuel, a greater part of which had to be brought in from outside the state. But with the discovery of an abundant supply of oil, she has developed rapidly and today she ranks eighth among the manufacturing states of the Union. Although oil was the main factor in her industrial development, water power also played a large part. California has been a pioneer in hydro-electric power development. Since 1920 she has ranked first in the United States in the production of electricity by water power and is estimated to develop through her 100 hydro-electric plants more than 9,000,000 horsepower, or 14 percent of the total estimated for the United States. Yet the power of California's rushing mountain streams is far from being fully utilized. There are millions of undeveloped horsepower flowing down to the sea. Though oil may in time become scarce, California's water power will never cease, for as long as snow falls in the Sierras, she will have her rushing mountain streams.

Now then, let us consider what will be the result of this great progress in California. Eventually it is certain to bring an increase in wealth. With wealth, of course, will come better living conditions, better educational advantages and more leisure. Gathering together these three principal benefits derived from wealth, culture is created. And what state cannot benefit by culture? Moreover California has a unique setting for the development of the finer things of life. From the standpoint of art and literature the extensive coastline on the West affords inspirations in manifold forms, while on the East the lofty Sierras offer their entire selves, full of innumerable beauty and wonder spots, as a haven to all seekers of solitude and beauty to develop masterpieces. In time perhaps California may succeed the eastern states as the center of civilization and culture of America.

Does not all this seem a worthy goal for California to strive toward? To every true Californian the reply must be in the affirmative. We have speculated on the future. The full tide of this Pacific

Top: George Inagaki (right) with his best friend and life long colleague in the Japanese American Citizens League, Mike Masaoka. *Courtesy of Chris Inagaki.*

Bottom: An outgoing and friendly leader, George Inagaki enjoyed being the master of ceremonies. *Courtesy of Chris Inagaki.*

era may come in this decade, yet it may not come in the next 20
years; but it is certain to come within our lifetime. Consequently it
is in the hands of the youth of today to prepare California for the
responsibilities which will be hers when she becomes the cultural
and industrial leader of the nation.

George Inagaki in a 1968 portrait for a
testimonial luncheon held in his honor
by the JACL for more than thirty years of
"active and inspired" service. The JACL
also announced the George J. Inagaki
Citizenship Award established in his name.
*Courtesy of Chris Inagaki.*

# The Beauties of
the High Sierras

**MARY TOSHIKO MIYAMOTO**
*Clovis Union High School, June 6, 1933*
*Clovis, California*

Mary Toshiko Miyamoto (1915–1995).
*Courtesy of Ann Gorai.*

I SHALL TRY to describe for you some of the beauties of the High Sierras. We have all heard of the wonders of the Yosemite Valley and Lake Tahoe, but we seem blind to the beauties of our own mountains.

The High Sierras begin on the south at Tehachapi Pass. A day's journey to the north appears the most outstanding characteristic of the High Sierra range—the Sierra Fault. Earthquakes were numerous during the past ages. These earthquakes caused the earth to have cracks called the fault line. The whole Sierra along the fault line has a contour of a wave about to break. It swings up in long water-shaped lines from the valley of the San Joaquin. Later when the glaciers came from the north they gorged narrow canyons, such as the King's River Canyon; cut the course of rivers, range, scooped out deep caverns. Helped by the work of ice, man has constructed such lakes as Shaver, Huntington, Bass, and Florence.

After the ice went away, trees came. The stately pines swath the Sierra slopes. They march—along the watercourses they climb—up sheer walls in staggering files, like soldiers. Each tree has its own voice. The creaking of the firs, the sigh of the long-leaved pines, the whispering whistle of the lodgepole pine, the delicate tune of the redwoods—these come out for the traveler in the darkness with the night scent of the moth-haunted flowers. But there is one tree that is voiceless; it speaks, no doubt, but it speaks only to the austere

Mary Miyamoto was born in Whittier, California and grew up in Clovis, California. When she was ten years old, her mother passed away, leaving her father to raise five children between the ages of two and twelve years old. After high school Miyamoto went to Fresno State College for two years and transferred to the University of California, San Francisco School of Nursing. After she graduated, she worked at the University of California San Francisco Hospital where she was head nurse.

Because she was a professional health worker, during the war she was sent to Jerome, Arkansas while her family was sent to Poston, Arizona. She worked very hard to serve the Japanese American community in camp. In 1943 she received permission to leave Jerome and went to St. Louis.

mountaintops, to the mindful winds, and to the watching stars. This is the "big tree," the Sequoia.

When you come up through the forests you observe the flat soddy spaces of old lake basins, green as jewels, and hanging meadows gay with cascades of flowers. Here and there a stream leaps forth at the falls like a sword from the green scabbard, or higher up it may be traced as the silver wire on which are strung unrippled lakes as blue as cobalt. Great chains of such lakes lead down from the snow line to the foothill borders, banked by the silent ranks of tree.

In the spring the pines bloom. A pine forest in bloom is one of the most worthwhile things to be seen, but it is seldom seen by anyone because when the pine bloom is at its best the high passes are still choked by snow, the lakes ice-locked and the trails dangerous. When the trails are open a stain of pollen is seen on the snow, and great clouds of it fly whenever a bough is brushed by a light wind.

All our literature and mythology are filled with attempts to translate this singular impression of personality in the wind, in trees and river and rocks, and especially in mountains. High on our eastern horizon brood the Sierras. To some people they may mean land or water supply. To others they mean friendliness and comfort. There is no line of poetry more full of meaning to the people of the West than the beginning of the one hundred twenty-first Psalm:

I will lift up mine eyes unto the hills
From whence cometh my help.

In 1944 she married Takeshi "Jim" Fujisaka who served in the Military Intelligence Service and was a paratrooper. The couple had two sons.

Several years after the war ended she returned to California and became a full-time mother. The ultimate homemaker, she made every meal "from scratch" and fed the many students her husband and sons brought home from California State University, Fresno. She kept a lifelong correspondence with old classmates and hospital coworkers she had met in St. Louis and Minneapolis. An avid gardener, Miyamoto also took care of a myriad of family pets including rabbits, chickens, turtles, dogs and cats.

Her son, Steve, remarked, "[Mom's] essay indicates, perhaps, the reason why we took many camping trips to the Sierras and along the coast." He added, "Her description of clouds of pollen [in her speech] is ironic given her severe hay fever every spring!"

Left: Mary Miyamoto and Jim Fujisaka were married in St. Louis, Missouri in May 1944. *Courtesy of Ann Gorai.*

Right: Mary Miyamoto in St. Louis in 1943 after leaving the internment camp in Jerome, Arkansas. *Courtesy of Ann Gorai.*

# Clovis and Her Trade Territory

**GEORGE S. TAKAOKA**
*Clovis Union High School, June 6, 1933*
*Clovis, California*

George S. Takaoka (b. 1917) in a photo from a Japanese American newspaper in Fresno, California in 1933.

CLOVIS' TRADE territory extends south to the Fresno city limits and west to the Golden State Highway. In this area are the largest fig gardens in the world and many of the finest and oldest vineyards in the San Joaquin Valley. All the South and West territories are in a high state of cultivation. Vineyards, orchards, cotton, grain, and alfalfa are successfully grown.

Clovis is served by one of the best gravity irrigation systems in the state. She receives her water supply from the Kings River and enjoys one of the oldest water rights on that stream.

To the east of Clovis lie the lower foothills of the Sierra region which have long been the grazing ground for thousands of heads of cattle and sheep. This industry has in no small measure contributed to the prosperity of Clovis.

Beyond the foothills lies the famous Sierra Lake region. Beautiful Huntington, Shaver, and Florence are among the scores of alpine lakes hidden away among the forests of these high Sierras. Within a 40-mile radius of Florence Lake are situated twelve of the highest mountain peaks in the United States. Any one of these is higher than any mountain in Switzerland. The lakes and the mountain resorts are visited by thousands of tourists every year. These travelers from every state in the union and from many foreign lands, in enjoying our natural wonders, spend money with the businessmen of Clovis.

After high school George Takaoka went to Fresno State College and then worked in farming and sold life insurance. He was incarcerated in Poston, Arizona. He and his wife, Miyeko, live in the Central Valley in California.

These businessmen maintain homes here and contribute to the welfare of the town.

Of the nearby communities which have their influence on Clovis, Auberry has been for many years the headquarters of the San Joaquin and Eastern Railroad and was the scene of great activity during the construction of the Edison Company power project.

Toll House, so named because of the old Toll Road that lifted travelers over the mountains in the early days of the lumber industry, also has its share of interest in Clovis.

Academy, midway between Toll House and Clovis and at the edge of the foothills, is one of the oldest settlements of Fresno County. Immigrants of the "Covered Wagon" days chose this place among the oak trees for their California homes.

Today Academy is a site of the granite quarries whence comes the famous Academy blue granite found nowhere else in California. This granite is trucked to Clovis and there manufactured into fine monumented stone.

Academy also has the distinction of having been a regular stop on the old stage road leading from Stockton to Visalia. Let your imagination picture the thrilling tales the old Academy Road could tell—tales of glamour, love, and romance.

To the north and east lies Friant, situated on the banks of the rushing San Joaquin where that swift mountain stream flows its current to the valley plains. Here, cattle-raising is the chief industry.

Within ten years Friant will be the site of one of the major dams in history. This dam will provide employment for scores of men and when completed, it will benefit all the people of Fresno County. I can already see graduates of Clovis participating in the construction of this colossal dam and the need of a larger school plant here because attendance will have so increased.

Upstream a mile or so is old Fort Millerton, built as a protection against Indian raids and the site of the first courthouse and jail in Fresno County. Here too, your imagination can work wonders. You can visualize a man shut in a dark, gloomy dungeon and shudder, but you can smile when you know that the man who built the jail was the first person to be imprisoned in it. Such is *Fate*.

Just recently an organization called the Sierra Highways Improvement Association was formed. Its purpose is to bring to the attention of all Fresno County people the wonders of our Sierra regions; to bind in closer ties all the communities of Eastern Fresno County; to work for the improvement of all highways and roads leading into the mountains east of Clovis; to cooperate with clubs and the Fresno County Chamber of Commerce to establish a public camp ground at Shaver Lake; to work with government agents surveying all roads leading into the resort district; and to advertise the recreational opportunities of our Sierra regions, so that by cooperative effort, we can enjoy and utilize the incomparable values of our back country.

"Thar's gold in them thar hills"—gold that is not dug from the ground. Prosperity for One, is prosperity for All. Let us citizens of Clovis recognize the splendid efforts of the Sierra Highways Improvement Association and contribute our best to the welfare and progressive development of Clovis and her neighboring communities.

# San Pedro, the Gateway to the Pacific

**KATSUMI YOSHIZUMI**
*San Pedro High School, June 16, 1932*
*San Pedro, California*

Katsumi Yoshizumi (1913–1954). *Courtesy of Betty Kobata.*

FRIENDS, you have no doubt heard the story of the conversion of the hopeless mud flat of San Pedro to a teaming, modern seaport. To our progressive minds there now appears questions and problems concerning the future probabilities of our fair harbor and city. Let us then, for a few moments, see what the future holds for San Pedro and view the possibilities of the next several decades.

The Mediterranean, in the glamorous days of Greece and Rome, was the main thoroughfare of the world's trade and commerce. Then as the world's population gradually shifted westward for the last four centuries, the Atlantic became the international commercial highway. But the trade in the world's population still increased and moved westward and so the ocean highway has again changed, and today the Pacific has come into prominence and the Era of the Pacific has begun.

The shipping firms and the many industrialized concerns of both America and Europe realize that the Atlantic highway will soon become eclipsed in the extent of commercial traffic—they realize that within several decades the Pacific will be the super highway for international trade. Mr. Harry Fletcher, former American ambassador to Chile, refers to the Pacific as "the finest highway of the world and the richest in the possibilities of production and commercial power." During the past decade statistics show that

Katsumi Yoshizumi was born in Long Beach, California and grew up in nearby San Pedro and Terminal Island. He came from a fishing family—his father was a fisherman and his mother worked in a fish cannery. In high school he was vice president of the student body, sports editor for the school paper, and member of the football team. He was also a member of the debate team and was admired for his speaking ability. After high school he attended Compton Junior College, majoring in accounting, and after graduation he worked in the fish market in San Pedro.

When the United States entered World War II, he married his high school sweetheart and classmate, Yoneko Marumoto. To avoid internment, he relocated to Utah where he had relatives and farmed

American interest in European markets has not increased in proportion to American interest in the Pan-Pacific countries.

We have noted the increased and constantly growing merchant marine on the Pacific Seaboard, especially the increased shipping activities in our port. Our newspapers frequently herald the maiden trip of a certain ship, establishment of an Eastern or foreign branch office, or the inauguration of another shipping service. These factors show that our port is fast becoming the focal point of world commerce. The reasons for the rapid growth of commerce on the Pacific seaboard are easily ascertained. Beyond the western horizon, friends, lies the greatest potential markets for the consumption of commodities produced by any nation. The awakening Orient offers countless numbers of opportunities.

The Philippine Islands also offer many opportunities for profitable trade. To the southwest lies the great island continent of Australia, the rising queen of the Pacific, with whom a profitable intercourse is rapidly growing. Directly to the south of us are the Latin-American countries. These countries have shown their need of world trade; they have in common many necessities that the rest of the world lack and their need of foreign products is great. Thus the countries bordering on the Pacific that make up two-thirds of the entire population of the world have become the world market, and the industrial leaders of America have quickly sensed that fact.

How true the prophecy of Seward rings. That sage of American statesmen predicted that "the Pacific Ocean, its shores, its islands, and the vast region beyond will become the chief theater of the world in the world's great hereafter." Those prophetic words have become true. With the founding of the Pacific world market, the merchants of America are shipping and furnishing to the Pan-Pacific nations many commodities that are essential to all progressive countries.

Situated at an ideal and commercially strategic position on the Pacific Coast, San Pedro Harbor commands the markets of the entire world and offers to many commercial concerns shipping facilities that only a modern up-to-date port can offer.

Our port is the nearest on the Pacific seaboard for the development of commercial intercourse between this coast and Europe, and the eastern coast of South America through the Panama Canal. The Latin American and Australasian countries are nearer by 500 miles to this port than any other Pacific port and the distance to the Orient is near parity with other harbors. San Pedro is also the nearest

during the war. When Japanese Americans were allowed to return to California, he came back to San Pedro and resumed his work at the fish market. He was very creative and made furniture, built a patio and other projects. His daughter, Betty, recalled he was "stern but very fair" and was devoted to his family and friends.

In 1953 after giving birth to their third child, Yoshizumi's wife was diagnosed with stomach cancer and passed away the following year. Shortly after her death, Yoshizumi was diagnosed with lung cancer and died in October 1954, leaving behind his ten-year-old daughter, six-year-old son and baby boy. Yoshizumi's sister-in-law adopted and raised all three children, enabling the siblings to stay together as a family.

Katsumi Yoshizumi (first row, center) and his coworkers at the Mutual Fish Company in San Pedro, California in 1938. *Courtesy of Betty Kobata.*

American port on the Pacific of commercial importance to the
"Great Circle" trading lane. This route is traversed by ships that pass
through the canal coming here or are destined to the Far East. The
nearness to the route and the highly efficient fueling facilities offered
make San Pedro the principal bunkering port on the Pacific coast.
San Pedro Harbor is nearer by rail than any port on the Pacific Coast
to a majority of the great centers of population of the United States.
Thus with these important factors in mind, the merchants, exporting and importing on a competitive basis find that San Pedro Harbor
is nearest to the Pacific market which insures a quick delivery of
goods to the countries.

The back country of Southern California possesses vast quantities of undeveloped resources, though with the completion of the
Hoover Dam, development of the resources will inevitably take
place. The distribution point for these products will be none other
than this harbor. Since San Pedro Harbor and its vicinity has become
a major point of distribution for both rail and water, numerous eastern industrial concerns have established branches to accommodate
the demands of the Pacific market. The commercial and industrial
fields are, however, far from being overcrowded. Our resources are
just on the verge of being developed and the Harbor districts offer
ample room for further development of various industries. Aside
from the economic standpoint, you no doubt know of the adequate
housing and educational facilities offered here. So with these poten-
tialities at her disposal, San Pedro has a broad and endless field to
offer for new enterprises and advancements.

Thus, friends, it is inevitable that San Pedro Harbor is to be
the center of economic activities for the future development of the
Pacific highway and the Pacific southwest. Let us, friends, realize
that this city is yet in the making, and by developing to the fullest
extent our many resources, meet the call and challenge of the Pacific
era and make our harbor the Front Door of America. There's no
need for seeking opportunities elsewhere. Before our very doors lie
bountiful opportunities, "Acres of Diamonds." It is but for us to
gather the diamonds, and may we, the graduating class of Summer
1932, inspired by the vision of tomorrow, animated by our youthful
enterprising spirits, see and utilize the opportunities in making San
Pedro the Gateway to the Pacific.

Katsumi Yoshizumi and his wife Yoneko.
*Courtesy of Betty Kobata.*

# EDUCATION

# What High School Means to a Japanese Girl

**FLORENCE AKIYAMA**
*Sanger High School, June 8, 1932*
*Sanger, California*

Florence Akiyama (1914–1945) in the 1932 Sanger High School yearbook, the *Echo. Courtesy of the Sanger Depot Museum in Sanger, California.*

THE KNOWLEDGE that we have received during the four years of our high school course does not mean the same to everyone. To the preceding speaker it meant opportunity. To a student of foreign nationality it means the same, but is that all? No! To him, high school education means the absorption of the American spirit. I mean not only the attitude toward America but also the customs and the innate ability to speak and think in the English language. The American student learns these customs at home from his parents who were also raised under the stars and stripes. He also learns to speak and think in the English language there. Although a student of foreign nationality is taught to be a loyal citizen, he misses the opportunity of true American surroundings in the home, and so must acquire his American speech and attitude in school.

In another way high school has a different meaning to some. It serves as a means of comparison between our school system and the school systems of other countries. Those students, myself included, who have had the opportunity to go to schools other than our public schools know the difference in character between them and our superior school system. The school which I attended was a simple Japanese language school where I learned to read and write in a language which seems queer to Western people. Books with lines running vertically from the right side of the page to the left have often been looked upon by Westerners with curious eyes. By reading

In the 1932 Sanger High yearbook, she wrote, "I, Florence Akiyama, leave my A's to Veda Vuksan." Akiyama gave her class's valedictory address, "What High School Means to a Japanese Girl," while another student gave the salutatory speech entitled, "What High School Means to an American Boy." Akiyama went to a local four-year university and became a "talented, smart lady," as a friend described her. She spoke Japanese fluently, taught the language, and also gave piano lessons from her family's home.

When Akiyama was twenty-two, her younger sister died of tuberculosis, an illness that would eventually claim the lives of her entire family. Akiyama and her parents were incarcerated in Gila River, Arizona where in 1945 her life was cut short at the age of thirty. Her father also died that same

from these books, I have obtained a knowledge of Oriental civilization. In short, I have had to learn two languages and two customs. Although these language institutes are not very well developed, they strongly resemble the schools in the old country. By attending such a school and by reading about foreign school systems I can appreciate more the learning I have received from this high school.

Therefore, the high school must be given much credit since it endeavors to influence students of foreign nationality to become real, helpful citizens. In some cases this task may be difficult because these students who need to study more at high school are the ones who have more to do than the ordinary American student. Besides that, some students are not given an American environment at all at home, and this makes it that much harder for the public school.

Every student does not have the same difficulties at high school. Judging from my own experience and from experiences of others that I know, it seems that English is the hardest subject for students of foreign nationality. The fine points of grammar make this language difficult even for the student with an American background to master. Most students of foreign nationality do not think in their mother tongue, but there must be something wrong somewhere that makes English hard for them.

I believe that one reason why a Japanese student does not do well in oral English is because his ancestors for hundreds of years were people who talked as little as possible. There were no orators and public speakers, and those who spoke for entertainment were considered low-class people. Only poets expressed their true feelings—not by speaking but by writing. We who have inherited this characteristic from our ancestors are not, on the whole, very good conversationalists.

Many of the other subjects are not so difficult. For instance, in art the Japanese students usually do quite well. They should do especially well in printing if they have had some practice in writing Japanese characters. They should do well in other phases of art, also, since for ages their forefathers were considered artistic and skillful.

Leaving the finer arts, let us consider athletics. In this field there is no difference in race. As athletes assemble from different countries in the world Olympics, so players of different nationalities make up our football, basketball, and baseball teams.

Thus one sees that the real difficulty of the Japanese student is his handicap in learning the American language and customs. Therefore, high school opens the door of opportunity for acquiring these

year. After World War II, her mother returned to California and entered the Fresno General Hospital where she passed away in 1947. The family of four is buried together in Sanger, California.

things. It is easily seen why high school means more to us who are not able to learn these necessary things otherwise.

Aside from these facts, high school education means the same to us as it does to any American student. It should be so, for in spite of our nationality we are destined to become American citizens. High school education is like an unpolished gem which each graduate receives. The gem which I have received and the one which the preceding speaker has received are identical. Because of the social circumstances in which we are placed, they will be polished in different ways and send their rays in different directions. But each must perform its duty in beautifying the environments by which it finds itself surrounded.

# Equality of Opportunities in American Education

**JAMES HAJIME HASHIMOTO**

*Long Beach Polytechnic High School, Summer Class 1934*
*Long Beach, California*

James Hajime Hashimoto (1916–1974).
*Courtesy of Bernice Hashimoto.*

THE MOST IMPORTANT social and democratic question now appearing in American life is equality of opportunities in education.

Fortunately for the preservation of equality as a principal of democratic government, a new agency of equality was introduced. A system of free public education open to all was provided which has appealed to increasing numbers.

In the stress of the present depression, public education has been made an avenue of retrenchment. Proposals have been made to place part of the cost upon the parent, to limit the scope of public education, or to assign pupils to certain types of education on the basis of supposedly scientific tests of ability.

All such proposals must be considered not only from the point of view of the taxpayer, and especially of the wealthy taxpayer who will in any case give his own children all possible advantages; but also and even more seriously from the point of view of the believer in democratic institutions.

If public education were put on a tuitional basis, most of the poor could not afford to have their children trained. This would at once make the main body of citizens far less competent to deal with public issues and would condemn large numbers of promising children to ignorance because of the financial handicaps of their parents. The American ideal aims to give all people, in so far as is possible, a fair start in life and a chance for development.

James Hashimoto was born in Lomita, California and grew up in nearby Long Beach. His mother played the koto, a traditional Japanese instrument, and he inherited her musical gifts. He studied the violin when he was young and played music throughout his life. After high school he majored in accounting at the University of California, Los Angeles and worked in his parents' produce business.

He was incarcerated in Jerome, Arkansas where he worked in the offices and entertained those in camp by playing guitar and ukulele. He married his wife, Bernice, in 1943 and the couple had a daughter and a son. In 1944 he was drafted into the army. By the time he completed his training, the war had ended and he was sent to work in the Presidio of Monterey in 1946. After he was

Again, if society were to leave education optional instead of compulsory there would be many parents who, though financially able to provide a minimum training for their children, would be too indifferent to see that their children acquired an education. Here again the democratic ideal, with its belief in the equality of opportunity, refuses to permit the sins of the father to be wholly visited upon the children.

Charles E. Merriam, chairman of the department of political science in the University of Chicago, once stated, "Expenditure for education is self-liquidating; an investment upon which there will be rich returns. The outcome of education is not a dead loss, but a living asset."

In Japan, in order to enter high school you have to pass a most severe examination. Every year hundreds of students are deprived of an education because of the lack of sufficient schools.

We, whose parents have been educated in the Orient, have been told many times the hardships and difficulties they had to endure in order to receive an education. Therefore, through contrast, we learn to appreciate the wonderful opportunities that we are receiving from our public schools.

The Japanese members of the graduating class of 1934 appreciate the genuine education that we have received from Polytechnic High School. We have been face-to-face with problems, have examined freely and carefully controversial questions, have participated in government through organizations in school and out, causing us to know, and letting us exercise ourselves in the process by which men seek to divide the true from the false.

In recent years democracy has been severely criticized. But where in all the world can the lowly, the poor, the foreign be welcomed into the rich opportunities afforded by the public schools more cordially than in America?

honorably discharged, he settled in Cincinnati, Ohio and worked as an accountant. Hashimoto was very active in his church and twice served as president of the Cincinnati Japanese American Citizens League. For fifteen years he played bass guitar for the Paradise Islanders, a musical group that specialized in Hawaiian music. He played music every weekend until his sudden death in 1974 at the age of fifty-seven.

# Shall I Go to College?

**MATILDE SUMIKO HONDA**
*Brawley Union High School, June 1933*
*Brawley, California*

Matilde Sumiko Honda (b. 1917).
*Courtesy of Matilde Honda.*

"The time has come," the Walrus said,
"To talk of many things
    Of shoes—and ships—and sealing wax—
    Of cabbages—and kings—."

SUCH A TIME has now come to us. In the midst of the turmoil of events and the bewildering maze of unanswered social and economic questions, there comes to us today, as high school graduates, the old yet eternally new question: Shall I go to college? In comparison with our national and international contemporary problems, it may seem as trifling as "cabbages" to "kings;" but it must be answered. The future lies before us, more or less vague, but full of possibilities and promise for us if we can but direct our lives wisely.

Shall I go to college? The high school graduate should ask himself this very vital question, for which an answer is not easily found, as there are many perplexing problems that should be seriously considered before taking this significant step.

The sincere aspirant for higher education should analyze his own physical, mental, and moral conditions, as well as his circumstances, before deciding this important matter. Some of those who think they are capable of assuming college work are not qualified as candidates for higher education. But those who can answer the following searching inquiries in the affirmative would find it a very wise step to enter college: Do I love learning? How well can I read? Have I adequate knowledge and mastery of the English language? Is my family backing me? Can I pay the price? After and only after answering such self-inquiries with unfailing verity is one sufficiently prepared to answer the paramount question—Shall I go to college?

Born in Los Angeles, Matilde Honda went to junior college in Brawley, California after high school and then to the University of California, San Francisco School of Nursing. She lived with another student featured in *Orations and Essays*, Pearl Kurokawa, while they completed their post-graduate work in public health nursing. When Pearl Harbor was attacked, Honda said, "Suddenly the world turned upside down." Her father was taken by the local sheriff to the county jail and then sent to a detention center in Bismarck, North Dakota.

Honda and her younger sister left California by train in the middle of the night and went to Colorado. In Denver, Honda worked as a nurse for the Seventh Day Adventist Hospital. She married Dr. James Taguchi in 1946, and the couple lived in Dayton,

First of all, in determining whether we should go to college or not, we should ask ourselves this momentous question—Do I love learning? It is certainly essential toward a college student's success to have a love of knowledge—a strong, inherent, instinctive, intangible desire to master facts of history and literature, to know things, to study lessons, and to achieve complete comprehension of them.

Of course, there are those who go to college to have a good time, to raise their social status or to meet people, but who have no love of learning whatsoever. Possibly these have their reward, but they will never receive the full benefits of a college education, and often their fate will be similar to that of the one who after attending Granta College cried, "O Granta, sweet Granta! Where studious of ease, I slumbered seven years and then lost my degrees."

Love of learning breaks down such seemingly impregnable barriers as lack of funds, of family background, or of good health. Near the State University of Los Angeles, a young girl—a student of that institution—was recently found living under a bridge adjacent to the campus. Her father was dead; her mother, ill. No home, no job, no money—yet she was determined to elevate her status. Her love of learning was so intense that lack of financial support and family background did not hinder her from going to college.

Love of learning is revealed in the grades attained in high school, in the time spent on studies in comparison with time spent in other ways such as athletics, recreation, and social gatherings, in the voluntary use of the library and reference books, and in the number of literary and forensic activities of the school in which we have been participants.

Let us now ask this question—Do I have the ability? Those lacking in ability cannot of course, expect much from a college education. They might as well stay at home, for as Cowper says, it will only be a matter of, "How much a dunce that has been sent to roam—Excels the dunce that has been kept at home."

But, on the other hand, we should not underestimate our ability. With the aid of the present system of self-analysis—the objective tests—our native ability can be determined rather definitely.

In arriving at a conclusion, such questions as the following inevitably arise—Do I have a good memory? Do I have good reasoning ability? Am I a successful reviewer of current events? Have I made commendable marks in high school? This last query is especially consequential, for "history repeats itself," as the saying goes, and if the student has been idle and slothful during his high school

Ohio where she worked as a supervisory nurse at the Dayton Veterans Affairs Center. After almost forty years in the nursing profession, she retired in 1980.

Honda and her husband loved to ski. She only recently gave up the sport at the age of eighty-five. The couple travel extensively, play tennis and are actively involved in their church, Japanese American Citizens League, Japanese Association, Optimist Club, American Civil Liberties Union, Colorado Mycological Society, Denver Art Museum and Denver Museum of Nature and Science.

career, there will certainly be small chance for him in college. It may seem as though I am discouraging those who have failed in high school. Well, they should be discouraged. In the first place, it should be mentioned that at present over half of all students that enter college never graduate; it has been further discovered that lack of preparation for the stiff college work has been the reason for the surprising number of failures. Moreover, at present the colleges are overcrowded, and there is no place for the loafer there. The incapable, ill-prepared student would only be wasting his time, energy, and money by entering college.

A college student should not only have a love of learning and the native ability but also acquired reading ability—the ability to grasp meaning from the printed page and to apply it to life and to read with adequate speed. Bacon knew what he was saying when he wisely stated, "Reading maketh a full man." In college most of the information for the courses is derived from reading; thus to read well becomes requisite.

For the best and most efficient work, one should read about 250 words per minute on the average; less than 200 is too slow; however, not only speed but speed plus thorough comprehension is desirable. A good memory and reasoning ability encourage better and more effective reading.

Bacon again says: "Some books are to be tasted, others to be swallowed, and some few to be chewed and digested." This judgment should be applied to college reading, for the student must, for the best results, use discretion in selecting his books and in studying them.

Another inquiry should be—Is my family backing me? That is, can my parents afford to send me to college, to make this costly investment? If our parents are in comfortable financial circumstances and approve furthering our education, it is well for us to go to college, provided that we can truthfully answer in affirmative all the questions concerning our ability, dependability, and preparedness.

Can I lay out a plan and stick to it? is another inquiry which we should impose upon ourselves before deciding to enter college. We must have a definite purpose and a fixed aim in going to college. The student who has no purpose in college beyond having a good time, spending his father's money, and loafing for four years, has failed at the beginning. On the other hand, a student having a definite purpose in mind has gone far toward ensuring success.

Thus we come upon the problem of scheduling our free and study time in the best, most convenient ways, and sticking to our

Matilde Honda Taguchi in New Orleans in 2000. *Courtesy of Matilde Honda.*

program. What is the value of a good plan if it is not carried out? Lindbergh would never have crossed the Atlantic and never been received so joyously by more than one hundred thousand people who excitedly awaited his arrival near Paris, had he not stuck to his purpose and carried out his carefully prepared plans. It was Columbus' determination of purpose—"Sail on, sail out!"—that resulted in his discovery of America. Such also was the resolution of Fulton, who was laughed at and taunted when he started his experiment of creating a steamboat, but his determination persisted, and he surprised the people when he made it go. He succeeded because he stuck to his purpose.

The college student must stick to his plans. Efficiency in every activity depends not merely on plans but on dispatching activities according to the plans.

Can I pay the price? In seeking the answer, we must not forget that the cost depends largely upon ourselves. If we put little work into the investment, we reap little in return. The price of going to college may be high, but a good buyer will find his purchase invaluable. College graduates constitute the greatest percent of those listed in "Who's Who?" College education has proved a priceless investment for them and for others who have become prominent in leadership, wealth, social standing, and politics. It is impossible to enumerate all those who have gone to college and later achieved fame and prominence, for the list is a very lengthy one.

Lastly, a college student should have an adequate knowledge and command of the English language. As most of the marks in college subjects are based on written work, the mastery of many things is necessitated—grammar, sentence structure, spelling, punctuation, diction, and others. Illegible themes, examination papers and reports full of grammatical errors, misspelled words and incoherent sentences seriously handicap the aspiring college student. Thus a mastery of the English language is not only desirable but requisite.

Now, if we dubious, hesitating, pondering graduates tonight would ask ourselves these questions and analyze our standing regarding our ability to read and to reason, our financial backing, our love of learning, our dependability, and our knowledge of English, we will be ready to answer the primary question—Shall I go to college?

The school year 1933 has come to a close, and with it departs the Class of 1933 from these familiar halls. Our four years in high school will always remain a happy memory; we shall joyously recall the days we attended this dear school, and it is with an inexpressible feeling of sadness and regret that we leave. Even including the times when we were reprimanded by the teachers or when we were faced with difficult assignments, we believe that our high school days will always remain the most memorable, the happiest days of our lives.

To the teachers who have patiently taught, scolded, advised, and encouraged us during the past four years, we wish to express our sincerest appreciation. Their chidings and inspirations, we hope, have made us more industrious workers and better citizens. As we depart, there comes to us this query: Will the teachers who have labored patiently with us for the past four years bestow some passing thoughts on us when others have taken our places?

To Mr. Palmer, our principal, and to the Board of Education, we are exceedingly grateful for the kind, directing interest especially during this last year for the many valuable lessons in economy they have given us. These will doubtless be of service to us when we, in the near future, assume new ties, whatever they may be.

As we, the Class of 1933, leave Brawley Union High School to take our different ways, we feel that in temper and in spirit, we are still united as we go forth—

Strong in will
To strive, to seek, to find, and not to yield.

# The Purpose of Education

**JIMMY NAKAMURA**
*Jefferson High School, January 26, 1927*
*Los Angeles, California*

Jimmy Nakamura (1909–1996) in the 1927 Jefferson High School yearbook, *The Monticellan. Courtesy of Jefferson High School.*

FROM THE BEGINNING of mankind, since the earliest stages of civilization, education has existed. Its importance cannot be over-emphasized, for, as education goes, so goes the universe. The world of today is far more advanced than that of yesterday in many lines, such as art, music, literature, science, and transportation, only to mention a few. On the other hand, civilization has also been retarded to some extent. Why are these things so? The world must either progress or retrogress according to the amount of service that is rendered by the people. And how are we to know the manner of serving? Only through education, the purpose of which in the days of our grandfathers and their fathers was quite different than that of the present. In the days gone by, the aim was chiefly for the sake of knowledge. This is not the paramount objective today, however, for it is possible, as someone has said, to drive mere scholarship to such an extent that the scholar is crammed by knowledge instead of being freed by learning.

Today there are many who still believe that education goes just that far and stops. Others have the idea that one of the biggest reasons for going to school is to learn how to make a living, thinking that in financial power, we measure success. Friends, these are false conceptions for without the desire to do a thing the knowledge of how to do it can accomplish but little; and though we may have great financial power, we may not be happy. For, from what does

Born in Los Angeles, Jimmy Nakamura's parents grew flowers and owned a florist shop. He attended Occidental College for a year, was a produce manager of a supermarket, and helped run his parents' nursery. He was incarcerated in Rohwer, Arkansas and after the war he returned to Los Angeles and resumed working in the retail produce industry. In 1964 he married Reiko Nakagawa and they had one son.

true happiness come? The realization of genuine happiness is brought upon us by the knowledge of happiness around us. Better still, we find it by spreading cheer and goodwill ourselves.

The purpose of education must coincide with the needs of the people. That is, it must be commensurate with the aim of life. It matters not how long we live but how we live, and as we know, the purpose of living is to help make this world a finer place. Civilization is upon a much higher plane now than ever before simply because our fathers have struggled to put it there. If we are to leave this place better than we found it, we must always strive for a greater cooperative spirit among different races and religious groups. And when we are confronted by the problems of world-wide interest we must look at them from the viewpoint of a citizen of the whole world, and not from the viewpoint of a citizen of any one race or religious group. In other words, if we are striving to make the world better, we must be citizens of the world and spread love throughout, so that eventually we can realize the brotherhood of man. We must have the feeling of world endeavor. Not only must we have such beautiful sentiments, but we must strive to make them a reality. Mr. H. G. Wells says, "The task of bringing about a consolidated world-state, which is necessary to prevent the decline and decay of mankind, is not primarily the task for the diplomats, lawyers, and politicians, but it is an educational task."

Though education is principally to make us world endeavourers, we must keep in mind the other aspects which are presented to us by the now generally accepted seven cardinal principles of education. These include health, worthy home membership, command of fundamental tools, character, worthy use of leisure time, civic efficiency, and vocational efficiency. During the course of our life on earth, I believe we should specialize in a particular line of work. We must have doctors, lawyers, ministers, engineers, farmers, and teachers. Likewise we need businessmen of energy and integrity, for it matters not particularly to what field we devote our activities if we are animated by high-salaried purposes. At the same time we must realize that health is important, for without it our lives may be exceedingly miserable, and we may not be able to do justice to humanity and ourselves.

Now you may wonder why the worthy use of leisure time is so stressed. It has been said that leisure tests life, and that what one does in one's free time largely determines his character. At this point I wish to emphasize the importance of culture, which we can attain

Jimmy Nakamura in 1968. *Courtesy of Reiko Nakamura.*

in our unoccupied time. Refinement is reached when we can truly appreciate beauty, for as the great English poet Keats said, "A thing of beauty is a joy forever." Another objective of education is to produce good citizens. We are living under a democratic government, of the people, by the people and for the people, and unless we are instructed in citizenship, the privilege of voting will not help us. In fact, it would be dangerous for us to have the right of unintelligent franchise. Thus we see that a great field is included in education. However, it is not completely covered by these aspects.

Mr. Ralph Waldo Emerson said, "Education should discover man to himself, and reveal his union to God and the universe." He also said, "Self-reliance, the height and perfection of man, is reliance on God." So we see that the purpose of education is to teach us to make the most of ourselves, to bring out the latent power which we have within us, to inspire the desire to use this power toward the best, and that together with the help of the Almighty we can contribute toward making this world a more ideal place.

Now let us see how we are going to attain the goal that we have set for ourselves. There are three media through which we can do so: the teacher, the curriculum, and the student himself. The teacher, whether he be minister, school master, mother, or father, is a real maker of history. Teaching is the most important factor in determining the future of mankind. Yes, we must have teachers, but of what sort? We must have teachers who desire to see that exalted goal reached, and who know the art of living through experience and observation, as well as having a substantial knowledge of their particular subject. We need teachers who do not follow the ideas of mechanical or military discipline, but who believe in having the driving force within the student, and who are lovers of virtue and haters of vice.

The curriculum has many new features now that were unheard of in the past. The development of vocational training and the opportunity to pursue artistic abilities have opened new avenues for the high school student of today. At the same time there have been added many extracurricular activities, such as self-government, the student body store, clubs, and other organizations. This is as it should be, for the experience gained through these activities greatly supplements what is acquired from books. The fellowship that we have in the different clubs is priceless, while the cooperation displayed in athletic teams is wonderful. The course of study should be such that it not only teaches us the three R's, which are essential, but also prepare us for the game of life, by pointing out its rules and by bringing to us the desire to abide by them. The textbooks should always be the best. At the present time we find in many books that war is glorified to the extreme, while intellectual development and progress in art, music, literature, science, and in many other lines is not even considered important. Can this continue? Absolutely not. We must have textbooks which stress the importance of doing right for right's sake, which glorify that sublime end toward which we are striving, and which will guide us toward it in a manner which everyone can comprehend.

Yet, however wonderful the teacher and curriculum may be, the making or the breaking of the student depends upon himself. Each individual casts a reflection upon another so that both are influential to each other. Therefore, we conclude that if we are to help ourselves we must be considerate, cooperative, and intelligent, and as Huxley once said, "We must train the mind and the will to do the work we have to do, when it ought to be done, and learn to like it." In other words, we must grow in knowledge and character. This, indeed, is the fundamental purpose of education. Let us each and every one, graduates and older men and women too, bend our efforts toward the attainment of the day when this ideal purpose shall be fully achieved.

# American Ideals of Education

**KAZUYA SANADA**
*University High School, January 30, 1935*
*West Los Angeles, California*

Kazuya Sanada (b. 1916). *Courtesy of Kazuya Sanada.*

EDUCATION is in the process of evolution because of rapidly changing social, political and economic conditions throughout the world at the present time.

In America, the educational system has become the object of adverse criticism because it has been too impractical, too visionary, and too bound by the old academic standards of yesterday. The typical American school is built on an eight-year elementary set-up: four years of high school and four years of college—with entrance into the professional field during or at the end of college. That the period devoted to secondary education should begin earlier and should embrace much of the present college content is urged. But the curriculum which should be flexible enough to respond to new demands of the social order has, in fact, lagged, and like other social institutions has resisted innovations.

Certainly too much emphasis has been put on terminology such as grades, promotions, certificates, diplomas, passing, graduations and so forth; and youth has been crowded into a standardized mold instead of being taught "how to live" and how to be a "constructive happy producer, and an intelligent satisfied consumer, and an effective group member."

New American educational trends, although still in the experimental stage, give students and teachers a greater participation in supervision and administration. They free the high school from

Kazuya Sanada was born in San Francisco and while he was in high school, his family relocated to Los Angeles. After graduation he went to the University of California, Los Angeles and majored in political science. In 1942, after the attacks on Pearl Harbor, he married Yoshiye Sato just before entering detention. The couple had two children.

During the war he was interned in Rohwer, Arkansas where he worked for the social welfare department. He left the camp temporarily on seasonal leave and worked as a farm hand in Illinois. In early 1944 he received permission to leave Rohwer permanently. He went to Chicago and then sent for his family to join him.

In Chicago, he worked as a production engineer for Sara Lee Bakery for many years, returning

domination of colleges and universities. Since the World War, intelligence tests have come into general use in schools of all grades and these are being used with discretion and with greater regard for achievement. Subject matter is being reorganized in terms of the five life phases, namely: health, work, play, socialization and learning tools—and in accordance with the three life functions, producing, consuming and group living. Extracurricular activities are meeting with the recognition they should, and such organizations as the Hi-Y's, the Knights, the Mawandas, various school organizations, the athletic groups, R.O.T.C. and scholarship societies are fostered and encouraged.

At the crux of the whole matter lies the taxation situation. To educate fairly "all the children of all the people" the national government should undertake the control of education, with a cabinet officer at the top and equal opportunities guaranteed to every child, whether he be rich or poor, a resident of a small country district or of a large fashionable one.

At present, many modern schools are breaking away from the old methods of teaching and are introducing vital changes. Our own University High School has been a leader along these lines and it was from a brochure on a new setup for secondary education, by two members of the faculty of the school, that many of the points made in this talk were gleaned. Oakland's University High School bases its English Junior Curriculum on life situations—the 7th grade activities being built around the post office, the 8th grade the stage, and the 9th, the newspaper. Walla Walla High School of Washington has successfully placed students in charge of study halls, corridors and social groups, demonstrating that true student government is not only possible but highly desirable when well organized.

It is evident that changes are imminent and that education, in order to meet the highest American ideals, must be reorganized under a dynamic group leadership of youth and teacher and interpreted in terms of our own modern world and in the "language of experiences." It must move in an atmosphere of freedom, unhampered by worn-out academic standards. This will lead us not only toward democracy for youth and teacher but also for the nation. Crucial changes in education must come—are in fact, already here—whether we like it or not, in our altering social, political, economic universe. In the words of E.C. Lindeman, noted social worker and outstanding American educator, "Education is life—or should be."

to California in 1959. In Los Angeles he worked for several major manufacturing companies in the aircraft and consumer products industries. Since retiring in 1985, he enjoys fishing, golfing and traveling. His secret to a long life is "moderation" and "no stress."

Kazuya Sanada in 2001. *Courtesy of Kazuya Sanada.*

# An Average Day at School

Yukiko Sanwo (b. 1913). *Courtesy of Yukiko Sanwo.*

**YUKIKO SANWO**
*Kerman High School, June 6, 1933*
*Kerman, California*

OFTEN I HAVE HEARD people say, "What do those high school students do anyway? Seems to me, they play in the band most of the day, or play ball all of the time or do nothing but work in shop or sewing room."

Tonight, I would like to explain what an average day at school really means, and what value it has to all of the students. A day at school isn't easy and restful. We accomplish much that takes a great deal of thinking, worrying, courage, patience and strength. And that must be continued day after day, up to 170 days in one school term.

I would like to explain to you every step from the time we get on the bus to the close of school. The buses run on a regular schedule every day, so we always arrive at 8:15.

The first bell rings. The students hurry and bustle, going in all directions. The first period is an hour long and many classes such as Geometry, Physics, Spanish, American History, Bookkeeping and English are taught at that time.

The second period is the activity period with the exception of a few classes. Journalism is one of the subjects taught this period. This class publishes the school paper, the "Kardinal." The paper has greatly influenced school loyalty and school citizenship in our school. At the same time, the students in this class have gained literary and business experiences from editing and managing this paper.

Yukiko Sanwo, whose English name is "Doris," was born in Sanger, California and grew up in nearby Kerman. In 1933 she was chosen to be the salutatorian of Kerman High School. Several topics were suggested for her speech and she chose to write about a typical day in high school.

In 1934 she married Masaru Sakata and they had one daughter and two sons. During World War II the family was incarcerated in Jerome, Arkansas where her husband worked as a cook while she took care of the children. After the Jerome camp was closed, the family moved to the camp in Rohwer, Arkansas before returning to California.

When the family returned to Kerman, they no longer had the grocery store they owned before

The student council often meets this period to discuss school affairs while the senior band meets every Monday, Wednesday and Friday.

The third period is again a period when many classes are taught such as: American Problems, Farm Mechanics, Chemistry, English and Debate. At the beginning of the year, two teams went out for debate to compete with other schools, and they have made progress for the first time.

We, the seniors, have been taking up American problems and economics, and learned about world politics, finance, social troubles, and many problems of the world. We, as seniors graduating tonight feel much more prepared to go out in the wide open world to meet the difficulties of our life on account of this contribution.

Next is the fourth period—a period before the lunch hour. Physical education for seventh and eighth grades is taught three days a week, enabling them to build a foundation for their solid physical health which is very essential in our lives. The other two days a week, students have the opportunity to appreciate music. Students can also take Auto Mechanics, Chemistry, Art, English and Home-making this period.

At noon we have thirty-five minutes. Many rush to the cafeteria for their lunches while the others gather on the lawn to have their feast. Some study and other students rest from the previous hard studies. Just about the time when everybody seems to get settled, the bell rings for the next step of the day's program. Everybody separates and goes in all directions to their classes: Science, History, Commercial Law, Biology and English. Many students go to the library and study hall. The purpose of having a study period is to teach the students habits to study while the use of the library for reading and reference purposes also stresses greatly in the campaign for improved study habits.

The subjects taught in sixth period, which are very interesting, are Boy's Cooking and Girl's Shop. The boys are able to make all varieties of pastries and fix many common foods. On the other hand, girls are able to be of practical help by fixing tires, soldering, painting, etc.

High Algebra, Advanced Bookkeeping, Trigonometry and English are all rather difficult curriculums taught in the seventh period. This period is forty minutes long.

There are two large groups of physical education classes out playing during the eighth period. The boys have baseball, basketball,

the war. The couple performed farm labor until they were able to buy another small store and later, a farm. In addition to raising her children, Sanwo worked as a cashier for twenty years and then was employed by a department store for another twenty years. She enjoys sewing, cake decorating, embroidery, knitting and cooking.

football and tennis while the girls have paddle tennis, tennis, baseball, speedball and soccer.

This year, an extra period has been added to the schedule to give a chance for different organizations to have meetings and gatherings. This period has helped out a great deal in avoiding the use of class time which is so valuable.

Thus as the day's program ends, we find that each teacher on the average has taught 198 pupils and that 104 classes have met and have been taught.

A certain number of requirements must be met in order to graduate. They are: English, three years; History, two years; and all four years of Physical Education. The students are required to take these whether they wish to or not, but as for the rest, they are privileged to take any classes according to the ambition and vocation of each student. The success of each student depends largely upon the wise selection of their curriculum.

As you see, there are many diverse types of classes taught. This is essential to give balance and variation to an average day. Students are taught music, sewing and physical education along with academic subjects partly to relieve the monotony of the day from so-called bookish studies and partly to improve their health.

I will conclude by saying that an average day at school aims first and most importantly, to widen the scope of knowledge, second, to stimulate mental activity, and third, to preserve good health.

Yukiko Sanwo Sakata celebrated her 88th birthday in 2001. *Courtesy of Yukiko Sanwo.*

# What Junior High School Has Done for Us—Aladdin's Lamp

**NORIO YASAKI**
*Foshay Junior High School, February 1928*
*Los Angeles, California*

Norio Yasaki (1912–1988). *Courtesy of Frederick S. Yasaki.*

IN EVERY MAN'S LIFE, we find a few great moments. To me, the greatest moment comes when I stand at the height of glory and look forward to a still greater achievement. In a student's life, the greatest moment is the time of graduation. With heartfelt pleasure and contentment on one hand, I can look back upon the sweet memories of the three years of my junior high school life; and with thrilling joy and hopefulness on the other, I can look into the three years of senior high school life that is to come.

For the past three years, I have crossed day after day the threshold of Foshay. Hour after hour, I have entered various rooms of this building. In those three years, there have been joys and sorrows, excitement and weariness, hopefulness and disappointment. There is not a single corner in and around the school that does not bring me memories of some kind or other. Really, the school is so familiar to me that I feel as though the past three years have been a single stream of experiences.

Yet have you ever realized that you and I have spent three thousand and six hundred hours together at our dear old Foshay? If education means the broadening of our outlook on life, have you ever thought how much richer we have become through those three thousand and six hundred hours of school life? You and I know perfectly well how much wider an outlook we can get by climbing Mount Wilson in only a few hours. Upon the mountain trail every

Norio Yasaki, whose English name was "Frederick," was born in Korea. The eldest of six children, he had little time for extracurricular school activities because he held numerous odd jobs to help support the family. However, he did attend and graduate from Chapman College. In 1941 he earned his Masters of Theology degree from the Pacific School of Religion in Berkeley, California and became a student pastor at the Loomis Methodist Church.

His career as a minister was interrupted during World War II. He married Mary Takagishi in 1942 and they were incarcerated in Tule Lake, California and later moved to the Amache camp in Colorado. The couple had a daughter and a son. After the war Yasaki enjoyed a thirty-five year career as minister of seven churches in California, Illinois, Oregon and Washington.

upward step brings acres and acres into our naked sight; so with education. Every hour that we have spent for study has brought us into the ever-widening fields of rich experience.

Take, for instance, mathematics. When I first came upon the puzzles of algebraic equation, all the x, y, z's were horrible monsters to me. Yet when I captured and tamed those monsters, the whole system began to look like a curious circus of which I was the master trainer. The pride of mastery, the joy of triumph, and the thrills of discoveries were all mine, when I realized that the monstrous x, y, z's were merely the tools of mathematics.

In science, I was led into the mysterious regions of the universe. Astronomy taught me the unseen relationships among the silent stars in the sky. Atoms, molecules, and electrons with their strange movements and functions were fairy tales to me. Are not these microcosms fairies? Yes, they are the fairies who tickle all the universe into its gorgeous colors, sounds, and motions.

History took me through the ages to the days that are no more. Geography showed me the places that neither my parents nor I have ever seen. Foreign language is the gate through which I entered into the rich field of Spanish culture. Studies in English introduced me to such worthy men as Lincoln and Enoch Arden of Tennyson. The encouragement and inspiration that I received from those studies will never be forgotten in my life.

Education, then, is like Aladdin's Lamp. Once I got it, a slight rub with the cloth of my imagination takes me immediately to any place in the universe, to the internal structure of all things, to any part of the history of humanity, or to any person whose life I respect and admire.

In a country like this where the children enjoy good education, each child is given this magic lamp. He is taught how to use it and what to get with it. He is taught not only what is good and what is bad, but also how to get good things and how to avoid the bad things of life.

The two great missions of junior high school, as I see it, are: first, to give its students the ability to choose good things from bad things; and second, to give its students the opportunity to experiment with what he has learned. Training for various trades in the shops, independent thinking, citizenship, and leadership are merely the manifestation of those two missions.

In the old system, students had to follow blindly and were often whipped to make them memorize the things that they never

According to his son, Yasaki loved life and was an avid reader of politics, religion, statistics, history and current events. He always thought of his long life as a "gift," having faced kidney problems while young and pronounced terminally ill at the age of thirty-two. Although he was prepared to die, he outlived his wife and daughter.

understood. But today in our junior high school, we understand what we learn, and put that learning into practice as we go along. We use our stock of knowledge in our everyday lives. We are given the opportunity to experiment and the ability to choose right. We are trained to become not only good scholars but also good citizens.

All through the past three years, you and I have carried the Aladdin's Lamp of education and have been taught how to use it in the right manner. As we go along the roads of life, we shall learn more and more uses of this magic lamp; and accordingly we shall appreciate more and more the kind guidance that our teachers have given us. As we leave the halls of Foshay Junior High School, each of us with his lamp of education in his hand, let us pledge ourselves that we will ever use it rightly; and whenever we appreciate the value of education, let us recall the days that we have spent together at the dear old Foshay Junior High School.

# Why Study the English Language and Literature

**KAMEKO YOSHIOKA**
*Edison Technical High School, June 8, 1932*
*Fresno, California*

Kameko Yoshioka (1913–1978). *Courtesy of Lisa Sato.*

WE AMERICANS claim the English language as our national tongue. People of the British Empire do the same. The leading nations of the world teach the English language in colleges and high schools. The business of the world is being carried on more and more through the medium of the English language. How fortunate we who were born in America are, for we have heard this great language spoken more or less from our babyhood. It has become a part of us and helps to identify us as Americans.

However, this valuable speech, made up as it is of elements from many languages, cannot be mastered in the eight years before high school. Great linguists tell us that it is the most difficult of all languages to learn. To express our ideas intelligently in English and to enjoy fully the ideas of other English-speaking people require more than eight years of study.

The first years the American boy goes to school he is taught correct usage and given no reason for it except that *it is correct.* The poor English he has acquired before entering school is drilled out of him. He is taught to say "isn't" instead of "ain't," "have gone" instead of "have went" and "had written" instead of "had wrote." He is busy at the same time learning to spell the words he uses and gathering new words for his limited vocabulary. Day by day, he needs these words to express his new thoughts or to understand his history, his geography, his storybook, or his "funny paper." He is too busy and

Kameko Yoshioka's English name was "Alice." After high school, she became a nurse until she married David Tadao Sato and they started a family in the late 1930s. Following the attacks on Pearl Harbor, Yoshioka, her husband and five-year-old son were sent to the Santa Anita Racetrack in Southern California. The couple's second son was delivered in a horse stall barrack in June 1942. Later that year the family was sent by train to an inland camp in Rohwer, Arkansas.

After the war ended, the family settled for a short time in Chicago and then made their way to Boulder, Colorado. After leaving the camp, Yoshioka cleaned homes while her husband tried many fields of work and attempted to start a new business. Almost three years after their release, they finally returned to Los Angeles where

too young to be burdened with the difficult study of English grammar. When he enters junior high school he begins to learn English grammar, which teaches him how to know when an expression is right and when it is incorrect. This new knowledge is his only on the condition that he uses it. To use it correctly he needs more drill than the time spent in junior high school will allow.

If the eighth-grade pupil quits school to go to work, he is not mature enough to resist the influence of slang users and uneducated persons whom he meets in the street or shops where he runs errands or performs some other small jobs suited to his ability. He forgets to apply his rules of grammar. His employer feels no responsibility for the boy's speech; hence he drifts into the language of the street which is, as a rule, third- or fourth-rate English described as *vulgar* because it is incorrect and careless.

If the boy stays in high school he is under the constant supervision of teachers who correct his mistakes, and he is in the company of other pupils who are making a habit of correct speech to such an extent that they will occasionally correct his errors.

A businessman needs the vocabulary gained in high school. He needs the habit of speaking correctly. It gains him the respect of his customers. It saves him time and often, as in the use of the exact word in his business correspondence, saves him money. If a boy or girl wishes to succeed socially, he must use good English since cultured people do not enjoy associating with persons who speak in a vulgar or slangy manner. The mark of an educated man or woman is proper speech, clearly and carefully spoken. Oral English in high school, whether in a class, an oratorical contest, a high school play, or in a student body activity such as acting as president of a society or club or campaigning in an election, tends to fix proper usage as well as proper pronunciation of the words used.

Often we hear educated foreigners speaking our language correctly and even beautifully. They have learned English as it is correctly spoken in our high schools and colleges and have not been influenced by the colloquialism or slang found in English-speaking countries, America chief among them. Can we, who wish to be known as loyal and representative, master the English language? The state of California does mean that we should, for by law we are required to give three years to the study of English because we as children of foreign-born parents need to understand better the language and ideals of the American people. It is for this reason that the fourth year at Edison is spent in the study of literature.

they became cigarette wholesalers and distributors. When they tried to purchase property in Montebello, the neighborhood petitioned unsuccessfully to keep them out.

While their company became successful, their main pleasures later in life were their family and grandchildren. The couple were avid golfers and they eventually lived on a golf course in a private community in Whittier, California. They also loved fishing and clam digging. Every spring Yoshioka took her granddaughters to the local department store and bought them new patent leather Mary Janes™ for Easter. She died from pancreatic cancer in 1978 at the age of sixty-four.

Literature written in the English language boasts some of the world's greatest thinkers and writers—writers who have expressed in a simple and beautiful way the simplest as well as the most profound thoughts of men. We read in Shakespeare and in Sir Walter Scott, in Longfellow and in Whittier, in Mark Twain and in Bret Harte, in Eugene Field and in Edna St. Vincent Millay, the thoughts and emotions we have often felt but which we have found no words to express.

We also learned to understand American ideals, for every masterpiece of literature, whatever its theme, is rooted in an ideal, reflects an ideal, and thus illustrates an ideal. We, whose parents have already taught us the ideals of their homelands, should, as loyal Americans, lose no chance of learning and understanding the ideals of America, *our* country. By the interested study of literature we also gain a means of spending the leisure time of which we have so much today. With time on our hands we may, by reading a good book, find enjoyment or profit when otherwise we would spend the time in discontented complaining or in company that would be of no benefit to us. In reading good literature we have a form of entertainment that is priceless and yet which costs us nothing since books of all descriptions may be borrowed for the asking from public libraries. We are indeed wise to adopt reading as a hobby for use in spending leisure time.

We of this graduating class know the value of correct speech; we are familiar with some of the best in literature; and we believe that we as loyal Americans who wish to stand before the world as educated persons should safeguard ourselves against the use of slang or any other unlovely desecration of our national language. We believe that you will agree with us that we can ill afford to discontinue the reading of good literature which not only helps us pass many a pleasant hour but which also helps in the development of character through the presentation of American ideals.

Kameko Yoshioka Sato and her two sons, David (foreground) and Don (being held) in Boulder, Colorado in 1944. *Courtesy of Lisa Sato.*

*And now, classmates, we are at the bend of the stream—*
*the end of our course. We have paddled together up to now,*
*but each must row alone into the deeper channels to come,*
*wherever and whatever they made lead to.*

—Sakaye Saiki
Katella School, 1932

# GRADUATION

# Persistent Idealism

**FUJIO FRANK CHUMAN**
*Los Angeles High School, June 22, 1934*
*Los Angeles, California*

Fujio Frank Chuman (b. 1917). *Courtesy of Frank Chuman.*

TO US, the graduating students not only of this great institution, but of thousands of other schools throughout the nation, America hurls her challenge: that we become future citizens that the United States will be proud of, citizens who will do our part in making her the foremost among all nations of the world, not in armaments, navies or man-power, but in the advancement of education, of science, of all the fine arts.

What the nation lacks today is not a stable government or great leaders. It lacks a more vital necessity—an abundance of good citizens, citizens who are, as one of our greatest Presidents said, "lofty in purpose, resolute in endeavor, ready for a hero's deeds, but never looking down on their task because it is cast in the clay of small things, scornful of baseness, awake to their duties as well as to their rights, and in this world doing all that in them lie, so that when death comes, they may feel that mankind is in some degree, better because they have lived."

Now, the greater majority of us will take our places in the business, industrial, agricultural, and social worlds.

We, who will join the ranks of worthy service, shall in time realize that our ideals which we cherished during our high school career must be broadened and adapted to our particular station in life. We shall soon see that life is not the thing we now imagine it to be. Life is real, life is hard. Too often shall we be perilously swept

Frank Chuman was born in Montecito, California and grew up in Los Angeles. After high school he went to the University of California, Los Angeles and received his B.A. in political science. In 1940 Chuman studied at the University of Southern California Law School until World War II began. Appointed by the U.S. Public Health Service, he worked as the administrator of the 250-bed hospital in Manzanar, California where he and his family were detained.

In 1943 Chuman received permission to leave Manzanar to continue his law studies at the University of Toledo. After one year he transferred to the University of Maryland Law School and graduated in 1945.

After returning to California, he entered the law firm of Wirin,

away into the sea of adversities, hardships and misfortunes. Discouragement and failures may weigh heavily on our weary hearts.

But I believe that as we go into this turbulent world, no matter how low or how high a place we may hold in society, we must cling to two great ideals—loftiness in purpose and resoluteness in endeavor.

I interpret loftiness in purpose as being magnanimous in our thoughts and deeds. That means we should never stoop so low in our speech or action as to besmirch and defile the noble name of America. Rather, we should exert our energy, our time, our money, and if necessary our very lives, to do all that is a credit and honor to our nation.

We must also be resolute in endeavor. We must have that quality of character which makes us dig in and fight against overwhelming odds. We must have that unquenchable will, the will to come up with a smile, no matter how badly we may be beaten. We must have that same tough fiber which sustained the sturdy rugged pioneer, as he broke away from old traditions and old influences, to match his courage, brawn and wit against the unknown wilderness.

In future years, through these two ideals—loftiness in purpose, resoluteness in endeavor—we must do our utmost to make others see our true nation. Not the nation veiled and hidden behind a smoke-screen of glorified gangsters, embezzlers, and murderers, but the real, pulsating nation: kindly, fair, friendly and generous to all lofty-thinking, forward-looking men, not only of America but of the whole world.

Therefore, on our course toward honest and upright citizenship, we must be trustworthy, loyal, just, clean of motive, firm in courage, pure in purpose. We must strive to keep alive the high purposes that we have vowed to follow—"Obedience to Law, Respect for Others, Mastery of Self, Joy in Service." It is our bounded duty as well as our privilege to maintain and perpetuate these ideals of those who have gone before us.

Then, and only then, through the maintenance and perpetuation of these ideals, will we have answered America's Challenge to Youth!

Rissman & Okrand that was special counsel to the Japanese American Citizens League. He was assigned Japanese American cases including ones concerning the Alien Land Law, Commercial Fishing, and Restoration of U.S. Citizenship.

In 1948 he married Ruby Dewa and had two sons. He started a law firm in 1950 with another Nisei profiled in this book, John Aiso. In 1976 he authored *The Bamboo People: The Law and Japanese-Americans.* He has been active in the Japanese American Citizens League and was national president in 1960. He continues to be active in his law practice, business enterprises, civil activities and as an instructor in civil litigation and professional ethics at a local university. He and his present wife, Donna Karschamroon, have a daughter.

# Citizenship

**JIMMIE CHIKAO HAMASAKI**
*Santa Maria Union High School, January 18, 1934*
*Santa Maria, California*

Jimmie Chikao Hamasaki (1916–1992).
*Courtesy of Clara Hamasaki.*

WE WHO STAND tonight between a meeting of a happy past and an unknown future feel that this is only the commencement of our lives. What those lives are to be depends largely upon the foundations we have been building in our high school. We have entered, we have learned, and now are ready to go forth to serve. It seems well for us who are about to step into the arena of the world's progress to consider what our parts in the struggle of life are to be.

All through our lives we have heard of citizenship, and every citizen seems to have his own definition for it. For instance, during a political campaign one speaker will tell you that to be a true lover of your country, you must be a Democrat; another will be equally emphatic in urging the positive need of being a Republican.

This seems a very narrow view of good citizenship. Because to the person who loves his country as Washington and Lincoln loved it—to the one whose thoughts are deeper and broader—good citizenship has a much finer meaning. To this person the only true citizenship is the love of country with a lofty conception of what the nation should be, and he uses all his energy and influence and power to bring her as close to that ideal as possible.

Dear friends, we who are passing into more active citizenship feel that we have a place in this national life. We feel that each one of us has work to do in demonstrating the spirit that is within us. Under the splendid leadership of our President at the White House,

Jimmie Hamasaki was born in Guadalupe, California and grew up in nearby Santa Maria. His parents owned and ran a boarding house. After high school he worked for a year and then went to Japan. He was admitted to Meiji University in Tokyo and graduated with a law degree in early 1941. In July he accepted a job with the United States Consulate in Formosa (Taiwan) and married his wife, Clara Yamagishi. The couple lived with Vice-Consul Glen Bruner in the living quarters of the consulate building. After the Pearl Harbor attacks, the Japanese authorities kept Hamasaki, his pregnant wife and the Vice-Consul in custody in order to trade them for Japanese diplomats held by the United States. In July 1942 he was part of the first diplomatic exchange in East Africa between the United States and Japan.

we can all have a part to play. Whatever helps to make the country better and nobler; whatever serves to elevate the people of the land to a higher plane of thought and life; whatever, in any way, makes America great is the work of present-day accomplishments. We must remember that whatever elevates the individual, elevates to a greater or lesser degree the community in which the individual lives.

To you, teachers, we offer our thanks at this time for your untiring effort in all you have done for us. We know how fully you have realized that the strongest asset of the American nation, and of all nations, is its citizenship. For four years you have trained us in this spirit and we sincerely hope that in years to come we may demonstrate to your satisfaction that we were molded strongly.

Finally, classmates, let us, as we separate, go forth with the determination to prove that our high school was one of the best mills in the world for grinding out individuals that are worthwhile. Let us make loyalty our controlling spirit, and in being loyal to ourselves, to our class, and to our school, we shall of necessity be loyal to every larger claim that the American nation can demand of the most efficient of her sons and daughters. Let us prove that we are the stuff of which the best citizens are made.

According to his wife, upon returning to the United States, those with Japanese faces were detained so the U.S. government could "check them out." He was imprisoned on Ellis Island for six weeks and was shocked to learn that Japanese Americans on the West Coast, including his own parents and extended family, had been put into concentration camps. After leaving Ellis Island, he was assigned as a civilian employee of the War Department for intelligence work in foreign weapons technology at the Pentagon where he worked for many years.

He received two prestigious awards during his career: one for exceptional civilian service as a military research specialist and another for meritorious civilian service as chief of the weapons systems division in the United States Army Foreign Science and Technology Center. When he retired in 1970, he went back to Santa Maria, California. He lived in his hometown for nineteen years and then moved to Nevada, where his wife still lives.

Jimmie Hamasaki in 1970 receiving the U.S. Army's award for Meritorious Civilian Service as Chief, Weapon Systems Division. *Courtesy of Clara Hamasaki.*

# Valedictory Address

Ayame Ichiyasu (1915–1947). *Courtesy of Kiyoshi Ichiyasu.*

**AYAME ICHIYASU**
*San Francisco High School of Commerce, June 1933*
*San Francisco, California*

WE ARE ASSEMBLED tonight to receive the reward of years of study and work. We are here to bid farewell to our school, our teachers, and our friends. With hope and joy we have waited for this day to come. However, now that it has arrived, we feel a sense of sadness, a queer sense of eagerness to taste the adventures of the world, and of regret to have to break the many friendships we have formed during our stay at the High School of Commerce.

We have achieved our goal with the kindly aid of all of our teachers. Without their unceasing care and encouragement, many of us would have fallen by the wayside. We may have chided at their teachings, but now each of us looks back upon it with a profound sense of gratitude.

There is another group of people whom we must thank and love most dearly. They are those who were a haven in every storm, those who toiled unceasingly so that we might have the best. How often we realize that our education has meant many sacrifices to them. To these people who have always encouraged us in trouble or in success, we express our deep appreciation. To you, dear fathers and mothers, we extend our most heartfelt thanks.

As we are assembled here tonight, many of us wonder what the future holds in store for us. Shall it be glorious success or shall it be miserable failure? Will each boy and each girl win outstanding success and lasting greatness? To this we say "NO" for everyone cannot

Ayame Ichiyasu was born and raised in San Francisco. Even though she was top in her class, objections were raised against her during the faculty valedictorian selection meeting. According to her brother, the excuse used to reject her was that "her voice would not carry" and she would not be loud enough for her speech to be heard. The real reason for the opposition to her speaking was racism. However, non-prejudiced faculty prevailed and Ichiyasu became the school's first Japanese American valedictorian in 1933.

After high school she attended the University of California, Berkeley earning her B.A. in history, then a post-graduate degree in librarianship. After graduation, she moved to New York and worked for the Japanese Embassy as a translator until the United States entered World War II. She was escorted

be great. But, we can be real men and women, true to the truth that is in us. We can accomplish our bit toward the development of the world by being good and honest citizens of our great nation. If we follow the ideals of sportsmanship, honesty, responsibility, leadership, and diligence taught us here at our beloved Alma Mater we can be sure that we are doing our best.

The memories of the lessons learned at school will help us attain our goal. Alma Mater, no matter how great or small we may become, we shall always hold your memories in our hearts.

Memories are the priceless treasure of youth, which neither gold nor jewels can buy. No one can rob us of these. In days to come when we may be flanked with despair and bitterness we can always hold our memories most dear. No matter what other things we may carry away with us, these will be most sacred.

And now, to our alma mater, our teachers and our friends, we bid a fond farewell. May the pleasure we enjoy tonight never be clouded by the sorrows of a misspent life. May we pass all temptations so that when we reach the dark valley of the shadow of death, our fidelity to principle will be a light that will pierce the veil of obscurity and work the way to the Great Unknown.

back to California by the FBI and was incarcerated briefly in Manzanar, California where she helped set up the school system and was the director of the library from July 1942 to January 1943. Soon after, she was recruited by the University of Michigan to teach Japanese to United States military officers.

In 1944 she married Taiichi Kawase, and became a Harvard law librarian. In 1946 the Library of Congress offered her a position. At about the same time she was diagnosed with cancer and chose to return to California for medical treatment. In January 1947 the illness took her young life. She was only thirty-one years old.

# Commencement Speech

Charles Inouye (b. 1914) in a photo from the May 31, 1932 issue of the *Redwood City Tribune. Courtesy of the Redwood City Public Library, California.*

**CHARLES INOUYE**
*Sequoia High School, June 3, 1932*
*Redwood City, California*

WE GRADUATES of tonight have just completed four years of high school work. To some of us this has been a preparation to further our course in college, while for others this has just completed our preliminaries to the art of living. We are here tonight not to celebrate the successful conclusion of careers but to inaugurate the successful beginning of careers. It is not by accident that the ceremonies at high school graduation are called commencements.

In going out into this world, we wish to make a success of life. But what is success? How do we achieve success? The answer is simple, but is more easily said than done. To attain success, I believe we must adjust ourselves to our environment so that we can meet life's problems and conditions.

This might seem like an impossible adjustment, but it is not. The human machine is so made that it is usually able to adjust itself to its environment.

This life of ours has been a struggle between the human machine and its environment. Wherever man has gone throughout the earth, he has been confronted with just this problem of adjusting his habits and his social organization to the exigencies imposed upon him by the specific kind of environment which characterizes it. Man has usually been able to adjust himself to his environment.

Perhaps the first and foremost adjustment I believe we should make in the world which we are about to enter is the physical one.

Born in Santa Clara, California, Charles Inouye was one of three outstanding students chosen to speak to his 1932 senior class of 204 students and received a $100 scholarship. The theme of the graduation program was "Adjustment of Modern Life Problems." After high school he attended Stanford University, majoring in sociology. After graduation, Inouye went to Japan but returned to the United States after several months. He was incarcerated in Heart Mountain, Wyoming. He later farmed in Utah and is married and has four sons and a daughter.

When we were babies and touched the hot stove, we adjusted our-selves to that particular environment by not touching the hot stove again. When we were boys we adjusted ourselves to our environ-ment by not eating green apples twice. These were simple adjust-ments which tended toward better health. But going out into the complex world of today, we may be confronted with worries and difficulties and not allow them to impair our health because "no love, nor honor, wealth nor power, can give the heart a cheerful hour, when health is lost." Be timely wise; with health all taste of pleasure flies.

The next adjustment we must make is the social one. There was a time in this world when very little knowledge was necessary. This was in the days of the cave man. However, even the cave man had his standard of learning which he had to have to live his life more efficiently. Now our standard of learning has been greatly raised. We have up to today accumulated very little knowledge compared to what we can accumulate. But our accumulation of knowledge should not stop after we are out of school. We shall, I hope, constantly keep on accumulating more knowledge in order to be able to live a more successful life.

In going out into the world, we must become associated with many older people. As the freshman in high school feels among sen-iors, we also might feel lost among the seniors of life. After all, we shall find ourselves by losing ourselves.

It may not seem an easy task to become adjusted to this new group of people. Indeed it is not easy. However, there is a way in which we can more easily become assimilated, and that is by partic-ipation.

The effect of participation in securing assimilation can clearly be illustrated by my own personal experience. When I came to Sequoia, being ignorant of many of the American customs and not being able to speak as fluently as others, I felt somewhat out of place, and I felt that I was out of place until I became adjusted by participating in some of the many school activities of Sequoia. In my case I hope that it can easily be seen that participation led to assimilation.

When we have become socially adjusted to our environment, we the students who have been educated through the aid of the inhabitants of the world must know it to be our duty to increase the efficiency of our present deficient government, for our benefit and for the benefit of our posterity. I believe that with this political adjustment, life will become more easy and happy.

If ever there were a time when life could become more happy and easy, it is the present machine age. Whether we like it or not, machinery can liberate man if man knows what to do with them. The machine age contains all the qualities necessary for a good life. According to a recent article in the *Literary Digest,* we have 165 machine slaves apiece. In the middle ages any man with as many slaves did not often find it necessary to even move his admired self. We who are about to enter the world hope to make the machinery work for us and thereby save ourselves.

One of the opportunities that will eventually arise from the machine age is our privilege to more leisure time. We know that leisure can either break or make the man. We shall use this leisure time in worthy purpose and live the life that can be lived in the Golden Age.

Because of the radical changes that took place in our spiritual life, we have a tendency to free ourselves from immortal God. We have a tendency to become modernists. As a result, few of us spend much of our time in our spiritual adjustment. I believe that life will bring us no happiness unless we have a religion.

Without spiritual religion we shall feel that there is a vacancy in our lives and that modern civilization leaves a dusty taste in our mouths. We may be busy with many things, but one day we shall find out that we are not sure that we are doing worthy things. We shall become involved in a routine of pleasure, but it will not amuse us. It will occur to us that it is a great deal of trouble to live. All the while we shall realize that the pursuit of happiness has always been an unhappy quest, and we shall become world weary at an early age.

We wish to love the world in which we live until we are very old, so we must benefit by the advantages of a religion of faith and with a sense of certainty as to why we must work, whom we must love, whom we must honor, and where we may turn in sorrow and happiness.

In an age in which custom is dissolved, and authority is broken, the religion of the spirit is not merely a possible way of life. In principle, it is the only way which transcends our difficulties. So we, the future leaders of the world, should have a spiritual religion to guide us in happiness or in sorrow.

We, the graduating seniors of 1932 are about to enter life. Like other graduates in other places at other times, we have set our goal at success. If we reach our goal we must adjust ourselves to our environment physically, socially, economically, spiritually, and politically.

And by so doing we wish to better this world. I do not know that it is for all of us to achieve success, but we all have had an extraordinary opportunity to do so. If all of us do not reach our goal, we at least shall all be happy working toward this goal, for, "Be it jewel or toy, not the prizes gives the joy, but the striving to win the prize."

# A Pause in the March of Education

**PEARL KUROKAWA**

*Arroyo Grande Union High School, June 1932*
*Arroyo Grande, California*

Pearl Kurokawa (b. 1914). *Courtesy of Pearl Kurokawa.*

DEAR PARENTS, teachers, friends, one and all:

When we entered Arroyo Grande Union High School four years ago as the class of 1932, we found knowledge with outstretched hands, inviting and welcoming us to enter. The road has been long, and at times rough and steep, but we have patiently walked and climbed up the dreary way, and have almost reached the great goal in a high school career—the diploma.

However, this does not mean that we reached the greatest goal in our lives; it is just the same as reaching a fork in the road, the one leading to a higher education, the other to education through business. It has taken us four long years of battling with books and conquering exams to reach this starting point which leads us to the great achievement—education. We are only pausing now, just taking a rest; but we must not stop our work here. Onward we must go with perseverance until we reach the final goal for which many, many people are continuously striving throughout their lives.

As I look back on my four years of high school, I can clearly recall my teacher's enthusiasm and kind interest in advancing my classroom work by making the tedious lessons more pleasurable. In a very inspiring way, they have continuously helped me to add more and more to my library of knowledge.

Education is not confined to books alone, as most people interpret it to be. Every single minute at school or outside, whether you

Pearl Kurokawa was born in 1914 in Gilroy, California and grew up in San Luis Obispo County. Since there were no public schools in the rural farming area where she lived, she attended the Children's Buddhist Home in Guadalupe, California for first through tenth grades. After high school, she went to the University of California, Berkeley to study nursing and then did one year of graduate study in public health nursing at the University of California, San Francisco School of Nursing.

She avoided internment in April 1942 when she traveled to Camp Grant in Illinois to marry her fiancé, Dr. Samuel Kimura, who had enlisted in the United States Army. While her husband was oversees in Italy serving as a medical officer, she lived in St. Louis and worked in the clinical laboratories at the University of

are studying or otherwise, has a great deal to do toward building one's character, which is after all, education. Many of the school activities, the mingling and becoming associated with our classmates, has either directly or indirectly given us very useful points on citizenship, which is the greatest factor in building one's personality to the ability to tackle any task that comes in our path.

Many of us may not have the great opportunity of furthering our education by means of schools. Some may be fortunate enough to continue while others are prone to go out into the world of business. Whatever we do hereafter, we shall constantly come into contact with different types of people, and with numerous new problems. To smooth out all these obstacles along our road of life, we must without doubt use our education attained in high school, but also will be forced to learn new laws and ideas so that our education will not cease, but continue.

Whatever path we might take to reach our goal, if we constantly keep marching onward, we shall at the end arrive. Even if the road at times seems rough and unbearable, we must keep on looking forward with high hope and endurance remembering that:

Heights by great men reached and kept,
Were not attained by speedy flight,
But they, while their fellows slept
Toiled upward in the night.

Classmates, let us resolve anew to take up our march into the world bravely, to tackle anything that comes our way, so that we may be proud of each other for the sake of dear Arroyo High.

Let us be good citizens! The future of our country depends solely on the steps we take. The country is crying to find men and women who are willing to sacrifice their selfish desires for the good and welfare of the community and the country. We have all learned the principles of loyalty and comradeship at one time or another during our high school career. Let us use them! Let us show the past generation what a strong cooperative power we have, and how it can be used! Our mind has been schooled to accomplish the things set before us. We must not allow this phase of education to become idle. Let us pay our debt to the school by years of noble living.

Members of the Board of Trustees, and teachers, we bid farewell with sincere regret. To you we express our thanks for the privileges you have given us through our four years of high school.

Washington. After the war she was reunited with her husband and they returned to California. In 1949 her husband was invited by the Atomic Bomb Casualty Commission to go to Japan and study the effects of radiation on the eyes of the survivors in Hiroshima and Nagasaki. Kurokawa worked as his assistant and served as an interpreter. She also helped establish eye clinics and trained Japanese nurses. During her year in Japan, she became interested in ikebana, the art of Japanese flower arranging.

After the couple returned to the United States, Kurokawa claimed she was just a "lady of leisure" but she became very active in the San Francisco Bay Area Chapter of Ikebana International. She was appointed to the board of directors, served several terms as president, and remains active in the organization to this day. In 1971 her husband co-founded That Man May See, a foundation at the University of California, San Francisco dedicated to vision research and clinical eye care. Kurokawa serves on the foundation board and continues to raise funds for vision research. In 1993 the Japanese government honored her for her work in visual research and ikebana by decorating her with the Order of the Sacred Treasure, Gold and Silver Rays award.

Then here's a smile for the future,
And for our parting, a sigh.
Here's a God-speed and bon voyage,
And to all a fond goodbye.

Pearl Kurokawa Kimura in front of her arrangement of copper pipe sculpture and lavender roses for the 2000 Ikebana Flower Show Exhibit in San Francisco. *Courtesy of Pearl Kurokawa.*

# Valedictory

Helen S. Kuwada (1920–1997). *Courtesy of Agnes Sasaki.*

**HELEN S. KUWADA**
*San Martin Grammar School, June 1933*
*San Martin, California*

BEFORE US lies the future,
    But 'ere its paths we tread,
There yet remains one duty
    One word is yet unsaid.
Oh! Sheltering walls around us
    Where sacred memories dwell,
We leave you now forever
    And sadly say farewell.

Here with our patient teachers
    We gathered day by day,
They gave us kindly counsel
    And helped us on our way.
Here with our merry classmates
    The hours quickly sped,
And here our happy school days
    Like passing visions fled.

Helen Kuwada was born in Watsonville, California and grew up in nearby Gilroy. She excelled in math and skipped a grade in grammar school. In high school she skipped another grade to accelerate graduation because she needed to help her family at home. She was the eldest in a family with seven children and she was sixteen when she finished high school in 1936. In 1937 she married Frank Yamakoshi, another student featured in *Orations and Essays*. The couple eventually had five daughters. During her incarceration in Poston, Arizona, her husband became ill with tuberculosis and was hospitalized. Kuwada spent her time in camp caring for her children and in-laws, frequently visiting her husband in the hospital.

After the war, the family settled in Reedley, California where she raised her daughters and took care

Ah! Soon must we forsake thee
    Our own, our sheltering home,
But we will ne'er forget thee
    Wherever we may roam.
In years to come thy memory
    Deep in our hearts shall dwell,
Home of our happy school days
    Farewell to thee, Farewell!

of her in-laws. She worked as a domestic for ten years and then as a receptionist in a medical office for thirty-one years. Active in her Buddhist church and community, she was a Sunday school teacher for forty-two years. After her retirement in 1986, she dedicated herself to volunteer work.

Although she never fulfilled her dream of going to college and studying business, she served as a board member of the Community College Foundation. She loved to sing and was famous for her pies and *umeboshi* (pickled plums). Happily married, she passed away just three months before her sixtieth wedding anniversary.

Left: Helen Kuwada Yamakoshi and Frank Yamakoshi in a portrait taken at their 1937 wedding reception in San Jose, California. *Courtesy of Agnes Sasaki.*

Below: Helen Kuwada Yamakoshi and Frank Yamakoshi celebrated their 50th wedding anniversary in 1987. *Courtesy of Agnes Sasaki.*

# Salutatory Address

Mitsue Matsumune (b. 1917). *Courtesy of Marion Hayashi.*

**MITSUE MATSUMUNE**
*Salinas Central Grammar School, June 1932*
*Salinas, California*

PARENTS, teachers, and friends, we, the graduating class of 1932, extend to you our heartiest welcome to our graduation program—or, in a more correct sense, our commencement program. For, are we not, in reality commencing—commencing to the bigger things, the more important of life? This occasion is the completion of eight years of hard work and play, and now we are ready to advance into the higher grades—the high school. We, each of us, in a larger sense must stand alone, each for himself, to overcome obstacles that loom up in the distance. Can we do it? Yes, by cheer, hard work, by gaining success through effort. This motto, success through effort, has carried us in this last year through odds—through thick and thin. But now, what is there to guide us lest we falter in our journey through life? We can, by playing the game—and winning through effort, success.

Mitsue Matsumune was born in Salinas, California and helped in her family's laundry business. During World War II she was interned in Poston, Arizona with her parents and siblings. After the war, the family went to Chicago for a brief period and then returned to their native town of Salinas.

Matsumune gradually lost her sight during her youth and shortly after the war ended, she was totally blind. Despite her disability, after attending a school for the blind in Oakland, she went to the University of California, Berkeley and graduated Phi Beta Kappa in 1955. The following year she married Robert Rottman who was her reader in college. They had one daughter and a long and happy forty-two year marriage.

Despite being blind, Matsumune did all her own housework, was an

excellent cook and ironed beautifully due to her experience in her
parents' laundry business. She loves
to read, using audiotaped books
and Braille publications. She has
always been interested in politics
and current events, staying abreast
by listening to the radio.

Mitsue Matsumune and her husband,
Robert Rottman, picking a raffle ticket in
this 1956 photo. *Courtesy of Rebecca Green.*

# Farewell

Michiko Naito (b. 1920). *Courtesy of Michiko Naito.*

**MICHIKO NAITO**
*Lovell Grammar School, June 1934*
*Orosi, California*

PARENTS, friends and classmates, our hour of triumph has now come to an end. It means that we have passed the one mile post in our life. It doesn't mean that we have reached the end. The end! We assure you we are only beginning. We have just tasted of the fruits of knowledge. The small store of learning that we have acquired as graduates of the grammar school has only whetted our desires for a bigger one. The more you learn, the more you realize how little you know.

There is still high school and college ahead of us, and some of us will be fortunate enough to follow the course of education to its climax. But for those who formally end their schooling today, it will not mean that henceforth the mind will close itself to all new ideas.

Quite the opposite is true. That is the wonderful thing about education. It is a plant that never stops growing. Once the seed is planted, it will grow indefinitely if only its owner tends it a little.

Of course, we know that though our own efforts counted, still it was the cooperation of parents and teachers that really got us through. You are sharing our joy, and well you should, for half of it belongs to you. We especially want to thank our teacher who is with us today. Her sympathy and interest, her unceasing effort to help us, is a splendid memory that we shall never forget.

Friends and parents, accept our thanks for the deep interest and tolerance you have shown today. We cannot tell you how much we

Michiko Naito was born in Fresno and grew up in Dinuba and Orosi, California. In high school she was the junior and senior prom chairman. Her principal called her "Michi" and she continues using the nickname. After high school she attended Visalia College, majoring in economics.

Just after the United States entered World War II, she married Toru Ikeda in February 1942. They were sent to Poston, Arizona where Naito gave birth to their only child, a daughter. She received permission to leave Poston before the end of the war and went to New Jersey where she worked at Seabrook Farms. In 1948 she returned to California.

She immediately found work with an auto dealer in Reedley, becoming the first Japanese American to work in town after the war. Her

appreciate the presence of every one of you. Your generous spirit has made our graduation program a success.

We thank you with all our hearts and our final word, we say to you: GOOD-BYE.

husband went back to school to become a teacher and she worked "late into the night" to help him get his masters degree. He became the first Japanese American to teach high school in California after World War II and taught at Reedley High School for 25 years. Naito supported her husband's work to help many Issei, including her own parents, become naturalized U.S. citizens. She was very active in the Business/Professional Women's Club and helped her husband in his Kiwanis work. She loves to knit and crochet, creating towels, "scrubbies" and other kitchen accessories which she donates to fundraisers and gives to family and friends.

Michiko Naito Ikeda in 1996. *Courtesy of Michiko Naito.*

# Pioneering

Joe Masao Nakanishi (b. 1919). *Courtesy of Joe M. Nakanishi.*

**JOE MASAO NAKANISHI**
*Alhambra Union High School, June 1939*
*Martinez, California*

EACH PERSON in his own life has to do some pioneering. Even a baby goes exploring and discovering his little world. If that baby can be trained to use judgment and self-control in his exploring, his curiosity can become a big asset. He must, however, gain this judgment and self-control, or he will come to grief.

We students have continued from babyhood to explore the world around us, to learn more and more and pick and choose useful information and experience that we gain. Parents help us in this process all along. Teachers continue to help us in school to hunt facts and learn skills that satisfy human inquisitiveness so that we can try to do our part in advancing human civilization. Preceding generations and all countries of the earth have contributed to man's knowledge.

Debt of the present to the past is great. Just as we can repay our parents for their care only by giving equally good care to the generation that follows us, so we can repay this debt we owe to all who have come before us only by trying to leave an added contribution to civilization for those who will live in the future.

How can we further pioneer? In what fields can we best make our contributions? Where is there any place left for us to adventure? We say, almost no new lands are left. We say, science has surpassed man's wildest dreams already. We say, business has become a tremendous power. But our field, though an old one, leaves much to be

The eldest of four children, Joe Nakanishi was born in Martinez, California and at the age of fourteen, he lost both parents. His siblings were not able to stay together because various relatives adopted them and Nakanishi remained in Martinez. After high school he worked briefly as a farm hand, but "the hard work of farm life was the incentive to pursue the machine shop trade." To study the field, he attended California Polytechnic State University, San Luis Obispo.

Nakanishi was interned in Gila River, Arizona with his guardians but left camp in 1943 and went to Cleveland, Ohio to work in a defense plant. In 1944 he was drafted into the army and sent to Camp Blanding in Florida for basic training with the all Nisei 442d Regimental Combat Unit. He was then assigned to the

explored. Only the earliest stages of pioneering have been passed in the field of human relationships.

Great characters stand out like lonely mountain peaks among other human beings. These may have names famed for achievements like great discoveries, great inventions, great contributions to national advancement. But many have names which history does not record. Their contributions, however, come in the fundamental greatness of unselfishness and thoughtfulness of others. The spread of such simple virtues is the greatest need of men. If we of our generation can give our help to advance them, we will have pioneered much.

How can we go about such a task? We can learn well facts and skills that we have opportunity to learn. We can judge carefully how to use these abilities to take care of others as well as of ourselves and to spread benefits to all. We can show our belief in hard, earnest work for every individual. We can do in each day's work what is fair and true. We can bring to each opportunity in dealing with others, honesty and unselfishness. We can work bit by bit for greater and greater strength in standards of truth, fairness, and kindness.

This follows our country's ideals, which explain its beginnings. To those men and women who risked lives and fortunes and braved the dangers of colonizing America, we gladly give credit for unselfishness of action, for staunchness of purpose; but we honor them most for high ideals of human character. Their dream of the triumph of goodness and truth among men is our most cherished heritage. We owe the debt of making such simple but great ideals come true.

As a representative of the graduating class of 1939, I express our faith in humanitarian ideals and our hope to pioneer in the great task of furthering those ideals as much as it is in our power to do so.

Military Intelligence Service and received training at Fort Snelling in Minnesota. By the time he completed his instruction and was sent to the Philippines, the war had ended. He was transferred to Tokyo and translated Japanese military documents into English for the U.S. occupation forces. Although he served during peacetime, he said the devastation he saw in the Philippines and Japan will "always remain" in his memory.

Following his honorable discharge in August 1946, he relocated to San Francisco and married Mary Kobara. They had a daughter and son. Nakanishi worked as a machinist, die maker and foreman for many years, retiring in 1981. He is a life member of the International Association of Machinists and Aerospace Workers Union. After living in San Francisco for forty-six years, he moved to San Jose in 1992 and enjoys gardening, fishing and camping.

Joe Masao Nakanishi in 2001. *Courtesy of Joe M. Nakanishi.*

# Valedictory Address

George Nishida (1920–2001). *Courtesy of Agnes Nakamura.*

**GEORGE NISHIDA**
*Dinuba Grand View School, June 1934*
*Dinuba, California*

DEAR FRIENDS, one and all:

They say there are people who always like to have the last word. I'm sure I cannot see why they should, for to me it seems the hardest of all words to say, and I would rather somebody else should be the one to say it. For that last word must be, to many if not all of us, "Goodbye!"

We have finished the course that has been given us, and are now ready for a step forward along the pathway of life. So far we have come together, hand in hand, and we have been looking forward to this time as a glad one, forgetting that it was going to mean a time of parting. Now we are suddenly forced to remember this feature, and in spite of our triumph, it makes us sad. So I am not going to linger over the parting words.

To the board of education, as well as to our parents and friends, I would extend the thanks of the class for the privileges we have enjoyed here. We naturally feel that we are better trained and more carefully looked after than many who attend school in other places, and under other conditions, for that is the spirit of school patriotism that we have inhaled with our every breath; and so, we naturally feel very grateful to those who have made it possible for us to come to this particular school.

To our dear principal and teachers, we have much we would like to say, but that curious lump comes into our throats and we are

Born and raised in Dinuba, California George Nishida was selected valedictorian of his junior high as well as Dinuba Union High School. He attended Woodbury College in Los Angeles where he majored in foreign trade and business and became a "gold pin winner" in the annual Gregg Shorthand contest. He also played the leading role in a comedy produced by the college students.

He was sent to Poston, Arizona during the war where he taught shorthand for one year. While interned, he volunteered to serve in the army and was assigned to the Military Intelligence Service. He was sent to Guam in 1944 and Japan in 1945. He was honorably discharged in March 1946. He remained in Tokyo for about fourteen years and was involved in import/export with Iran, Korea and other countries.

choked with the unspoken thoughts that keep back the words. So we can only look at each in turn, knowing we must leave them, and brush aside the tears that we may see their faces clearly for the last time. Dear teachers, you must all know how deeply we feel this, and can realize how much we mean by the only words we can find to say—God bless you!

Classmates, there's only one word more and the last one must be to you. We did not realize how hard it was going to be to say it, did we? In our work here together, we have become very dear friends, and it is always hard to say goodbye, even for a little time to the ones we have learned to care for. We have shared our pleasures, our triumphs and our few disappointments for so long that we shall miss the old companionship more than we now realize, when we are too far apart to enjoy it any longer. Some of us may work together through some of the higher grades, but for the most of us, I feel that it is indeed the parting word. But I am sure that we shall not forget each other and that we will always think of these days as very happy ones that made us as classmates a little nearer and dearer to one another than mere friends.

Let us as we part pledge ourselves to remember all the true and lofty aims that have been formed in us in our work together here, and make our lives such as shall bring pride to our school and cause our dear instructors, every one of them, to be justly proud to remember that they had the task of teaching us how at least to begin to live.

For now our boat glides out between the rocks that guard the shore bearing the Class of 1934. To be a class no more; but looking forward with a smile of courage, strong and high, to meet in that glad afterwhile no more, to say "Goodbye!"

Nishida returned to the United States in the early 1960s and worked for the U.S. Postal Service and the *Los Angeles Times*. According to his sister, he was very generous, giving large sums of money to his relatives while living modestly. He was a private person with a great sense of humor and infectious laugh.

# Valedictory Address

**SAKAYE SAIKI**
*Katella School, June 9, 1932*
*Anaheim, California*

DEAR FRIENDS, teachers, and classmates:

Our little boat stands at rest tonight at the bending of the stream and we pause a moment before we round the corner and sail on the waters ahead. The voyage of life is through many deep and unknown channels, with many windings and turnings that often make it hard for us to tell just what we have passed by and what we are yet to meet. It seems a long course to follow, as we row through the waters; but as we rest upon our oars and look back how short the distance seems to be! How close the banks appear to be! It is pleasant to pause here at the bending of the stream, and consider the calmness of the wave-ripples through which we have been so easily rowing. But we cannot linger long, for already the murmurs of life's larger waters are calling us to row ahead out of the shallow current of this young life, and enter into the stream of a fuller life.

Dear friends, we cannot pass forever out of this quiet stream into the deeper waters awaiting us without thanking you from the bottom of our hearts for the privileges you have given us as we have begun the voyage of life. We are profoundly grateful to you who have fostered our successful eight-year voyage on the educational waters. Years may pass by, but each one of us will bear deeply in our hearts the remembrance of your dear fostership which has meant a blessing to us. The teachers have carefully sheltered us from every adverse wind of thought, and have warned us, as do light-

Sakaye Saiki was born in Orange County in California. In Illinois she met Albert Mayeda and married him in 1943. She passed away in Riverside, California in 1992 at the age of seventy-five.

houses against the evil rocks, to be within broader channels on our onward course.

Your guidance has not been wasted on us, because as we sail on into the deeper channels ahead, your eyes will be able to follow us and they will ever see our green and white as signals of promise and grateful resolution. As we push out to perform our missions in the splendid sea of a bigger opportunity, we will wave our banners of green and white high and in our hearts bear everlasting memories of your valuable support.

And now, classmates, we are at the bend of the stream—the end of our course. We have paddled together up to now, but each must row alone into the deeper channels to come, wherever and whatever they may lead to. Let us face every duty of the unknown waters bravely and boldly, the principle of honor ever turning the pilot wheel as we sail to the success no graduate of this dear school can ever fail to win.

> Onward, through deep channels,
> May we ever hold,
> Waving from all panels,
> Our royal green and white;
> May we keep them floating
> On each breeze so high,
> True ideals denoting,
> As we say, "Good-bye!"

# Welcome Address

**AKIKO SAWADA**
*San Juan Grammar School, June 9, 1932*
*San Juan Bautista, California*

MEMBERS of the faculty, fellow students, ladies and gentlemen:

It gives me pleasure to welcome you; and speaking for the class, I am gratified to know that you have honored us with your presence. It shows that you have an interest in educational matters and the welfare of the school at heart.

These occasions are joyful ones and mean much to the student who has spent his time in search of knowledge. The goal is reached, that for which we have been striving has been attained and our labor has had its reward. We hope to entertain you and trust our efforts will not fail. We feel that you, our friends, will lend us every encouragement for we know that you are interested in the graduating class.

I feel it's my duty as well as a pleasure to say something on behalf of the school. You know the trials and tribulations it has experienced. It has had periods of adversity as well as times of prosperity, but through it all the school has not wavered but gone along disseminating learning to the eager seekers. We, of the class, know the work of the school and can better appreciate the kindness and zeal of the teachers than others. I'm sure every member has a warm spot in his heart for the San Juan Grammar School, his alma mater. We can never repay our teachers, for money does not express feelings. We can only say that we recommend the institution as a moral, busy school where genuine interest is taken in all who may be enrolled.

A friend from San Juan Grammar School remembers Akiko Sawada as a "bright, smart" girl and recalled Sawada spoke several times about moving to Japan with her family. Her parents probably wanted to return to their homeland and she most likely relocated to Japan with them before World War II.

# An Appreciation for Our Education

**FRANK K. YAMAKOSHI**
*Gilroy High School, June 1932*
*Gilroy, California*

Frank K. Yamakoshi (1914–1999).
*Courtesy of Agnes Sasaki.*

WE, THE SENIOR CLASS of 1932 now leave Gilroy High School with best wishes for success to the faculty and students.

Friends, imagine that we are on an airplane ready to take off. Some of us will take off from Gilroy to obtain higher education and some of us will circle around this locality. There will be some going out into the commercial world and some going out into the agricultural world. Wherever the class of "32" lands, I wish for you much success and happiness.

You all know why Colonel Charles A. Lindbergh's flight was successful. It was because of his hard work that he was able to make his trip. There were others who had just as many chances as he had at his career. But why was Charles Lindbergh more successful, one may ask? The reply is this: was he not *industrious* at his work? was he not *reliable* at his task? We all have to struggle to go through hard work before we can stand on our feet and obtain success. Let us all try hard to aim for our wants and needs.

We have now had twelve years of our precious schooling. Some of us may have more and some of us may not, but anyway, isn't it because of our *parents*, that we were able to obtain these many years in school? When we go into higher institutions of learning or out in the business or agricultural world, let us do our utmost and show our parents our appreciation for our education and what it has taught us.

Frank Yamakoshi was born in Watsonville, California and grew up in nearby Gilroy. He graduated from high school in three years because he was needed on the family farm. Due to his financial and family situation, he was unable to go to college and fulfill his dream of becoming a teacher.

In 1933 he helped collect speeches for the second edition of *Orations and Essays* and asked Helen Kuwada for a copy of her valedictory poem for San Martin Grammar School. Four years later they renewed their friendship, fell in love and were married in 1937. She was seventeen and he was twenty-two. The couple was married for almost sixty years, had five daughters and made sure all their girls went to college.

Yamakoshi was incarcerated in Poston, Arizona where he fell ill

You may wonder first what the class of "32" may do after leaving Gilroy High School. This depends on each individual, but I am sure that we, the class of "32," will do our best for the good of our parents and the people of Gilroy.

Let us citizens of the United States not *falter*. Let us look to the future years. Let us hope that education will be the outstanding institution of the United States of America.

with tuberculosis and spent most of the war years in a hospital in Phoenix. He recovered and after the war settled in Reedley, California. Because he had lost his farm and equipment during internment, he became a self-employed gardener. Seven years later, he worked as a custodian for an elementary school and manufacturing company for thirty-four years until his retirement in 1986.

A very gregarious and friendly person, according to his daughter, Agnes, he could "easily sell raffle tickets to anyone." He collected sports caps and especially enjoyed baseball. Active and dedicated to his Buddhist church, he was a Sunday school teacher for twenty-five years and in 1984 the Reedley Chamber of Commerce named him "Man of the Year."

# INTERNATIONAL RELATIONS

# Education Ensures Peace

**KIYOSHI NOBUSADA**
*Hanford Union High School, June 1, 1934*
*Hanford, California*

Kiyoshi Nobusada (1916–1998). *Courtesy of Yemi Nobusada.*

ONE OF THE chief obstacles throughout the past of civilization has been the fear of international war between civilized nations. This is a tendency which is fostered by the ignorant masses of the universe. We must not as a people permit the past to fetter the present. Retrogression lies that way, and our duty as a nation is to be determined by the present, not by past conditions. We cannot even stand still. We must move onward. From civilization we derive inestimable rights; to her we owe immeasurable duties, and to shrink from these is cowardice and moral death. Our contribution to civilization must be international peace. The economic development of the nineteenth century has produced a solidarity of humanity which no hatred must be allowed to destroy. Each nation is his brother's keeper and the greater the power, the greater the responsibility. If this be so, no nation owes a greater duty to civilization to be an active leader of the world than the United States.

Have we forgotten those priceless words of Washington in his farewell address? "Observe good faith and justice toward all nations . . . cultivate peace and harmony with all . . . . It will be worthy of a free, enlightened, and at no distant period, a great nation, to give mankind the magnanimous and too novel example of a people always guided by an exalted justice and benevolence. Who can doubt that in the course of time and things, the fruits of such a plan would richly repay any temporary advantages which might be lost by a

Kiyoshi Nobusada, known simply as "K," was born in Armona, California. His youthful achievements foreshadowed the outstanding civic and business success he attained as an adult. He went to the University of California, Berkeley and graduated in 1938 with a B.S. in chemistry. After graduation he worked for almost two years as the chief analytical chemist at L. M. Martini Grape Products Co. in Kingsburg, California. In March 1940 he became the chief chemist in charge of production at the nine million gallon capacity Central Winery, Inc. also in Kingsburg. In 1941 he married his college sweetheart, Yemi Kono, and they had a daughter and a son.

During World War II he was incarcerated in Gila River, Arizona where he designed a vegetable dehydration plant for the War Relocation Authority. He also

steady adherence to it." For the United States to skulk and shirk from the ruling set by the Father of Our Country would be one of the great derelictions of this world.

Wars now have no real causes—they have only petty excuses and go on because nations have the habit and move by the precedent. Wars cannot settle anything . . . the strong nation, not the right nation, wins. Sensationalists in foreign nations and their counterparts in America, where freedom of the press is enjoyed, are daily influencing the citizens with their racial propaganda.

The transferring of the entire Atlantic fleet to the Pacific last year for the annual naval maneuvers increased the fear of the possibility of war with Japan. Jingoistic newspapers in both nations tried to hamper oriental-occidental relations. It is obvious that the United States had no intention of severing peaceful relations, for this year did she not order the Pacific Fleet into Atlantic waters?

Indeed both nations desire the benefit of culture and commercial relations. Therefore common sense and cooperation are greater protection than provocations due to misunderstanding caused by lack of education.

However, while not only sensationalists but munitions manufacturers exercise the influence which they now wield with government, we shall make little progress in reducing all armaments. The munitions makers break down laws; they break down government; they kill human beings; they trample upon everything which gets into their way, be it human or divine; and they do it for gain—nothing but sordid monetary gain! During the Depression, while millions of men and women have walked the streets ill-clad and half-starved, while governments have been unable to pay their just debts, while educational institutions have been starved for funds, it is a fact that munitions manufacturers have been realizing profits of 12—20—and even 30 percent during the entire period through the same cause: lack of education.

Furthermore, the recrudescence of nationalism, which seems just now to be so noticeable a product of war, is chiefly political in origin. If professional politicians could be persuaded to keep their hands off, there's no question that business interests in Europe, Asia and America would more and more "play the game" together. But today, we are living at a time when professional politicians prevail. Nationalistic leaders such as Hitler in Germany, Mussolini in Italy and Stalin in Russia have gained their supreme power through the same deficiency—lack of education.

headed the farming division of the camp and supervised the personnel, the mixing of insecticides and soil analysis for the agricultural division. In his spare time Nobusada also organized cooperative enterprises and ran educational programs sharing his knowledge in food chemistry and agriculture.

In 1944 he was cleared to leave camp and went to Denver, Colorado where he and a partner started Dehydro Products, a food processing company specializing in dehydrated products for export to Hawaii. In 1945 he returned to California, settling in the Monterey Peninsula, and established Sea Products Company with a new partner. As their business grew, they formed Consolidated Factors as a sales arm of the Sea Products Company. Over the decades the business expanded and diversified, becoming a huge processor and worldwide distributor of seafood and fruit.

Throughout his lifetime, Nobusada worked constantly as a civic leader, believing participation was the best way for Japanese Americans to gain acceptance in their communities. Nobusada was president of the California Association of Employers, the Monterey Chamber of Commerce, and the Japanese American Citizens League. He was also a co-founder and former director of the Monterey Jazz Festival. He helped establish the Youth Center in Seaside, California and was active in the development of several parks and the Little League Baseball Program. His goal was to "be as good a citizen as you can be."

However, a new star is rising in the universe to establish a pacific attitude among the people. The composite of the rays from the star are: first, an authentic knowledge of the history of all nations so that the citizen can predict how the people will react; second, the ability to form his own opinion from unbiased facts; and last, the development of his mind for the achievement of an altruistic, international interest. Not as yet has the light been fully disclosed, nor is it intended to be until the education of the people can energize these rays to penetrate the foggy mists affected by the nefarious and underhanded weapons of propagandists.

The problems that now confront nations are far too numerous, too crucial, to be tried by an arbitrament of guns and bombs; how irrational to attempt to settle them away! They call for the statesmen with education, not soldiers with guns; for reason, not submarines; for roundtables, not battlefields; reconciliation, not poison gas. Let me add they call for prayer, not because God is necessarily on our side, but because He is on the right side!

We must treat war as a sin, a crime, an inequity, an unethical institution, an impractical policy—in truth, a barbarism with no rightful place in an enlightened age.

It is true that in the actual world as we know it today, the fundamental cause of war is economic trade. Side by side with politicians who talked, ever more and more, of the rights and interests of their own nationals and increasing necessity to protect them, there was developing a class of internationally-minded manufacturers, merchants, financiers, and the like—men who had come to realize that the best self-interest is one that permits give and take competition, that thinks of the other fellows as well as of himself, that recognizes the basic economic fact that there can be no such thing as a long continued "corner" on prosperity.

The world has thus learned that trade, in the long run, is preferable to plunder because it is more expedient, because it pays; that the men of large affairs in all western nations have had new proof that a give and take international policy is better than cut-throat competition because it pays. These are the best augury for our hope that international-mindedness is becoming an increasingly potent factor in world affairs in spite of all present appearances to the contrary.

The world looks to America as the most powerful leader for guidance and progress. Thus our government authorities and our private schools must inculcate into the minds of the people a peaceful attitude, teaching them that war is not only a barbarous means of

Kiyoshi Nobusada graduated eighth grade in 1930. *Courtesy of Yemi Nobusada.*

settling disputes but one which has brought upon the world the greatest affliction, suffering and disaster. Meanwhile, we, as loyal citizens of the United States, in turn must abolish war as a means of settling international disputes.

We must extend the fields of arbitration to cover all juridical questions. We must negotiate treaties, applying the principal of conciliation to all questions which do not come within the scope of arbitration. We must pledge all the nations of the world to condemn the recourse of war. We must renounce it as an instrument of international policy. We must declare ourselves in favor of settlement of all controversies by pacific means.

A huge task? Yes! But not an insuperable one. The bravest sight in all this world is a man fighting against odds. The swimmer with his head upstream, the climber facing the storm, the soldier with his back to the wall. The light which Columbus followed has not failed. The courage that carried him on still lives. They are the heritage of the people of Washington. We must lay our voyage of exploration toward complete understanding and friendship.

The pilot of this exploration for World Peace is education for an international mind, which is nothing more than the habit of thinking of foreign relations and business; that habit which regards the several nations of the civilized world as friendly cooperating equals in aiding the progress of civilization, in developing commerce and industry, and in speeding enlightenment and culture throughout the entire world.

## Armona Lad Best Student In Kings

ARMONA, Kings, Co., June 9.— The Armona grammar school has again carried off the high point honors in the county board of education test of eighth graders up for graduation. This year Kiyoshi Nobusada carried off the highest honors in the county. This is the second consecutive year that Armona has won the highest award.

With 549 points young Nobusada stands as the highest scholarship pupil in the county. He had two gold stars on his diploma, presented at the graduation exercises.

Top: Newspaper clipping from the *Fresno Morning Republican,* June 10, 1930. *Courtesy of Yemi Nobusada.*

Bottom: Kiyoshi Nobusada graduated from the University of California, Berkeley in 1938. *Courtesy of Yemi Nobusada.*

# International Peace

**IDA IKUYE SHIMANOUCHI**
*McKinley Junior High School, June 1932*
*Pasadena, California*

Ida Ikuye Shimanouchi (b. 1916). *Courtesy of Ida Shimanouchi.*

WE ARE LIVING in a world of perplexing problems. There is one problem, however, which looms above them all in the glory and splendor that may be: the problem of International Peace.

Out of the darkness and the hopeless experiments of the Great War, we have learned to see and appreciate a higher standard of international intercourse. We have learned that goodwill, understanding and friendship are far more valuable and effective than force. The question that remains to be answered, not through words, but through action is, "Have we the will which will enable us to carry on international relations on the basis of this finer and nobler standard?"

It has been declared so often that racial or national differences have been the inexorable breeders of suspicion and hate that lead to wars. In every event, racial differences have been greatly emphasized.

By race I am Japanese. In all my school days when I have mixed and intermixed with my American schoolmates and teachers, I have found no differences. Our similarities of interest were so innumerable that they overshadowed and even hid my racial inheritance. You may lay the reason to my American education.

I have met many girls, interesting girls from Japan, girls who have received a Japanese education. But I have found so many similarities.

I correspond with a Belgian girl. She writes to me in English and I write to her in French. Through the sentiments and interests which appear in our letters, I have found many similarities.

Ida Shimanouchi was born in Oakland and raised in San Francisco and Pasadena, California. After reading her oration seventy years later, she said, "I was truly an idealistic teenager when I gave that speech." After high school she attended Mills College and earned a B.A. in English. During World War II she experienced a great deal of "worry and fear" because her brothers were living and working in Japan. The divided family had no way of communicating during the war.

Shimanouchi was incarcerated with her parents and two sisters in Topaz, Utah. During her brief stay she helped set up the camp library despite experiencing dust storms that made her eyes ill. After being in camp only one and one-half months, she was granted permission to leave as a student. She went to Smith College,

The differences I have found were in appearances, in language and certain customs; but only in degrees.

These experiences have so vividly shown me that humanity is one. We have common interests and hopes. We are all urged by the same law of life. We all have appetites, the urge to live. We all want to live abundantly. We all want peace.

True, men have fought one another for a cause. But it is equally true that men have been friendly for a cause. If our intense desire for human understanding and peace is to be attained, we must emphasize the oneness of humanity and the loyalty to the one cause of cooperating for the human benefits derived from cooperative action.

We who are students in this era of enlightenment must sense the glory of real peace; study and understand how we can further its cause; and determine our will to work for it, so that the common aspirations of all men can be effectively realized.

Northampton in Massachusetts where she received a graduate fellowship in English and earned her M.A.

She moved to New York and acquired a teaching position at Fieldaten School, a private high school. For thirty-seven years she taught grades nine through twelve. During a one-year sabbatical, she made a global journey alone with stops in India, Pakistan, Iran and Cambodia. Since her retirement she continues traveling and enjoys going to musical performances, the theatre, galleries, libraries and museums.

Ida Shimanouchi enjoyed the Luxembourg Gardens in Paris, France in 2001. *Courtesy of Ida Shimanouchi.*

# Prospects of Pacific Foreign Trade

**JIMMIE TABATA**
*Monterey Union High School, June 8, 1933*
*Monterey, California*

Jimmie Tabata (b. 1916) in the 1932 Monterey Union High School yearbook, *El Susurro.*

EIGHTY YEARS have passed since Senator William H. Seward, later Lincoln's Secretary of State, uttered his famous prophecy that "the Pacific Ocean, it shores, its islands, and the vast region beyond will become the chief theater of events in the world's great hereafter."

Seward spoke in the days of the California gold rush, when America's clipper ships were famous on the seven seas. For a half century after the Civil War his prophecy was without honor, as Americans had turned their eyes inland and were occupied in the great task of carving an empire out of a continent, but in time his vision was vindicated. He had correctly foreseen the inevitable result of American expansion to the shores of the Pacific and beyond.

Many shipping firms and industrial concerns of America have realized that great opportunities for our trade expansion lie in the Pacific area. For beyond the western horizon lies the greatest potential market offered to any nation. The awakening Orient offers countless numbers of opportunities for all merchants. The Philippine Islands also offer many opportunities for profitable trade. To the southwest lies the great island continent of Australia and directly to the south of us are the Latin-American countries. These countries have shown their need of foreign trade, and they also have many necessities that the rest of the world lack.

In the 1933 Monterey Union High School yearbook, Jimmie Tabata wrote, "I, Jim Tabata, leave my brains to Howard Lo." Tabata attended the University of California, Berkeley and majored in business. After graduating in 1937, he returned to Monterey and helped his father expand the family store called Sunrise Brothers. The business was started in 1919 by Tabata's father and sold fishing supplies in Monterey.

When the United States entered World War II, the store closed down and Tabata and his family were forced to go to Jerome, Arkansas. He received permission to leave camp before the war ended and went to Chicago. When Japanese Americans were allowed to return to California, he came back to Monterey and reopened the store. He said he

Already, the volume of trade between the United States and the Far East is much greater than is generally known and is rapidly growing. Although we hear a great deal about our great Latin-American markets, it is a fact that Japan alone, to take just one example of a Far Eastern country, buys as much goods from the United States as all of Latin-America put together. Japan is the third best customer of the United States, ranking below only Canada and Great Britain. Normally we think of close economic connections between America and Europe, but Japan buys more American products every year than does either Germany or France.

The upward movement of trade in the Pacific Area may be shown by taking as examples certain countries in this area. The growth of Japan's commerce has been tremendous. In 1913, her total commerce was valued at $674,000,000. In 1926, it was $2,000,000,000, an increase of approximately 300 percent during a short period of but 13 years. Even in 1931, with countries affected by the world-wide depression, Japan's foreign trade totaled $1,000,000,000.

It is but natural to expect that this increase in trade with the countries in the Pacific area should be reflected in the commerce of the United States and especially in the commerce of the Pacific coast ports. These ports must, in ever increasing degree, share in the expansion of the Pacific trade. In 1913, their total commerce was $264,000,000 and in 1927, it had increased to over one billion dollars. The trade of the Pacific ports in the years from 1913 to 1927, a short period of but 14 years, had increased almost 400 percent.

The striking fact in the commercial relations of the Far Eastern countries and the United States is the complementary rather than competitive character of the greater part of the trade. Indeed, between well-developed trading areas, we find few instances in which the advantages of commercial intercourse are so fully reciprocal in character. Although we often hear much about cheap Japanese goods flooding the American market, if one would study the actual figures, one would find out about 90 percent of all Japanese products shipped into United States is accounted for by silk, which cannot be produced successfully in this country, and hence, offers no competition to American industry, but, quite to the contrary, supplies a raw material which is indispensable to American industry. If it were not for Japan's raw silk, American silk mills would have to shut down.

On the other hand, we find that Japan, as the third best customer of the United States, buys great quantities of American cotton. Japan

did not experience any hostility from the community. During the 1980s, Tabata's son began running the business, becoming the third generation to manage the historic family store.

buys more than three million bales of American cotton each year, constituting nearly a quarter of the total American exports, surprising as that fact may seem.

This happy relationship of interdependence holds good in regard to commodities of minor value as well—minor in comparison but by no means insignificant. For example, Japan imports from America lumber, automobiles, wheat, steel and machinery, in any of which you will find little competition from Japanese producers. On our part, we take from Japan tea, crabmeat, and porcelain, which do not seriously compete with American products.

The economic interdependence between the United States and China has not developed to such a great extent as that between the United States and Japan, but China is a great potential market. It is possible to imagine that the 400 million people of China will come to constitute a market of first magnitude. Wu Ting-Fang, the eminent Chinese statesman, once remarked that if every Chinese were to increase the length of his shirt by one inch, the cotton mills of the world would not be sufficient to meet the increased demand. Such a market staggers the imagination.

Every businessman on the Pacific Coast is vitally interested in the acquisition of new markets for expansion of his business, and the field that we must look to for a market comparable with that of the Eastern States is the market that represents a billion people with a rapidly increasing purchasing power. That market is the whole Pacific Area. Therefore, we Americans on the Pacific Coast must take the initiative to bring about a close economic tie-up with the Pacific countries.

The outlook for trade development in the Pacific Area and the prospects for the Pacific Coast ports in commercial development are indeed bright. What has been outlined indicates at once the great opportunities and the responsibilities of the Pacific Coast. We must be aware of the strength of our trade position and take all steps in our power to bring about the full realization of these possibilities for future commerce.

# An Appeal for World Friendship

**MICHIKO YOSHIHASHI**
*Thomas Starr King Junior High School, June 16, 1932*
*Los Angeles, California*

Michiko Yoshihashi (b. 1918). *Courtesy of Eiko Sakamoto.*

WAR, just a short three-letter word, but what an important part it has played in the history of the world and of our lives! Even today we hear troubles between nations which cannot be prevented in any other way but by war. That man was born to fight, that we live in a world of strife, force and battle, is still considered human fate.

In the Armistice Day parade of the year 1918, two things that stirred the emotions of the people were the disabled veterans and the heroic band of gold star mothers marching with their heads proud and erect. The latter had sent their dearest possessions, their children, to die nobly to free humanity from some of its shackles. It is time for men and women to set their minds on reaching the goal, Peace!

The Olympic Games were not organized with the purpose of competing against other countries but that through these uniting of the nations we may have world peace.

The idea of international athletics arose in the mind of a French boy seven years of age. It was at the beginning of the Franco-Prussian war. At the age of seventeen in studying his people and the causes of wars, he found that there was much discouragement and even the loss of respect of other countries. This young Frenchman, Pierre de Coubertin, felt that outdoor sport was the first step towards the development of friendship.

This idea was accepted in 1894. It was thought that these peaceful and courteous contests would develop the best internationalism.

Michiko Yoshihashi was born in Los Angeles into a family with five children. After graduating from high school she worked for a photo company in Southern California. In 1937 she went to Japan to meet and potentially marry a young man, but she had the option to return to the United States if the "match" did not work out. The relationship blossomed and she married Yoshio Kawae in 1938. The same year, they moved to Manchuria and remained there during World War II. The couple had a daughter and a son. In 1946 she returned to Japan and worked for the United States military in the translation department at the general headquarters (GHQ) in Tokyo. She currently still lives in Japan.

George Washington, the father of our country told his people in the time of the Republic:

"My first wish is to see this plague of mankind (war) banished from earth and the sons and daughters of the world employed in more innocent amusements than in the preparing of implements, and exercising them for the destruction of mankind."

Abraham Lincoln, who was a conqueror in war tells us simply: "It never gives pleasure to triumph over anyone."

Modern inventions facilitating communications and transportations in the industrial system of specialization and mass production have made men depend not merely upon their immediate neighborhood but upon men and women all over the world. Although we in America feel that we can supply our own needs, many of our articles come from abroad. If we want to escape or avoid the serious aspects of a difficult business future, we shall have to open the markets of the world and this can be done only by the stabilization of Europe.

When the historians of the future record the events of the present period they will undoubtedly write as the keynote of this age the newly awakened interest in world affairs—the interest on the part of everybody to understand the people of other countries.

But we want to know more about the foreign-born who may be proudly called Americans. It brings a feeling of kinship when we realize that Bartholdi, a Frenchman, made our statue of Liberty; St. Gaudens, an Irishman, modeled our beloved statue of Abraham Lincoln. And when we realize that Holland gave us Edward Bok, Denmark, Jacob Riis, and Scotland, John Muir, we should feel that we are all children of one father.

The one thing that constitutes world progress is the extension of the peace era. Therefore, let us add link by link to our chain of friendship so that all nations may be part of the chain.

*We, the American citizens of Japanese origin, should make it our task to bring about a better understanding, spiritually, morally, and politically, between the two civilizations. This can best be done perhaps by living loyal, honest, and dependable lives.*

—Haruko Fujita
Arcadia Grammar School, 1932

# JAPAN

# The History of Japanese Books

**KOZUE FUJIKAWA**
*John Burroughs Junior High School, June 15, 1933*
*Burbank, California*

Kozue Fujikawa (1918–1998). *Courtesy of Chizuko Sanford.*

TODAY the world's camera eye is trained upon Japan. The wonderful accomplishments and achievements made by this nation has made her one of the outstanding countries of this world.

As we study the history of the various countries, we learn that each has some sort of background from which it grew. The history of Japan is very interesting, especially that which pertains to her literature. It is my opportunity to tell you in brief, the true history of our literature.

Since the Chinese civilization began very much earlier than that of the Japanese, our language is focused largely on the Chinese.

During the earlier days the emperor of Japan called upon some of the well educated people of China to teach this so-called Chinese language. The Chinese willingly shared their language with the representatives of Japan.

Today the true Japanese alphabet numbers only 37 letters, while the other hundreds of words which we Japanese use in conversation and writing are derived from the Chinese language.

If you really plunge into the study of the Japanese language you will find that the majority of the words are square. This is true because the words developed from picture writing, or symbols.

Until recently the Japanese were printing and binding books as they did a thousand years ago. Their books were printed on paper so thin that only one side could be used. The paper was made from

Kozue Fujikawa was born in Glendale, California and grew up in nearby Burbank. According to her sister, she was outgoing, joyous and loved people. After high school Fujikawa went to the University of California, Los Angeles and then to the Loma Linda University School of Nursing, graduating in 1940. When the United States entered World War II, she moved to Honeyville, Utah and then to Salt Lake City where she met and married Paul Toshio Tsubokura. They relocated to Idaho where Fujikawa worked as a public health nurse. She later moved to Chicago where she had her first child, a daughter. After World War II ended, she returned to Southern California and had a son.

When her children were older, Fujikawa returned to nursing. She was proud of her profession but according to her daughter,

the bark of the *kodo* tree. This bark is dissolved in chemicals and brushed out in very thin sheets. The Japanese made the sheets double with a fold instead of cutting the edge. If the paper was too thin they folded it three times. The books were put between cloth-covered pasteboards, then the leaves and cover were sewed on together. The illustrations were in the form of brush drawings in black.

The modern Japanese book differs very little in appearance from the American book. Of course, the words are written vertically and the book is read from right to left, or as Americans say, from back to front. The illustrations are usually Japanese prints.

In Japan books are valued as treasured possessions, treated with respect and carefully preserved. The Japanese people are very fond of reading and whenever possible find pleasure and recreation with their books.

Christine, "was often restless and frustrated because she had the soul of an artist." She made time for drawing, painting, ceramics and other creative work in between her roles as nurse, homemaker, mother, wife and daughter. She also did volunteer work and was always helping others. According to her sister, Fujikawa would say, "Once a nurse, always a nurse."

# Why the Japanese Came to America

**HARUKO FUJITA**
*Arcadia Grammar School, June, 1932*
*Arcadia, California*

Haruko Fujita (b. 1919). *Courtesy of Haruko Fujita.*

EIGHTY YEARS AGO when Commodore Perry came to Japan demanding the Japanese open their gates to Western civilization and friendship, the little island was actually in a state of feudalism. But since then she has opened her ports to Western goods and civilization and her heart to Western friendship and customs. Little by little, she began to realize how beneficial it was to enjoy friendship with foreign countries, especially with the new, progressive United States. Little was it realized by the majority of the Japanese people that she would benefit so greatly by doing so.

At first the Japanese people marveled at the Western ideas and civilization brought in through the port. But they could not remain passive, and began seeking the true light of Western civilization by traveling, studying, and finally emigrating to the New World.

During the last eighty years Japan has made marvelous progress through the influence of Western nations—railroads, ships, telephones, modern buildings, roads, cities, and ports have been built. Schools, colleges, factories and other institutions, modern in every detail, have been established. Science, culture, and modern methods have been assimilated.

For hundreds of years Western civilization has gradually advanced westward—first to New England and then on to the Pacific Coast. For the last fifty years, however, Eastern civilization

Haruko Fujita was born in Baldwin Park, California and grew up in nearby Arcadia. She was valedictorian of her grammar school as well as her senior class at Adolf Leuzinger High School in 1936. She was the editor-in-chief of the high school newspaper and played baseball and volleyball. Her "greatest disappointment" was being unable to attend college because she could not afford it and was needed at home. In 1939 she married Harry Tademaru. Fujita and her family were incarcerated in the Amache camp in Colorado where she gave birth to her third child.

In 1944 before the war was over, Fujita's husband left camp and worked on a beet farm for one year. He was released and drove to Chicago to find work and prepare a place for his family to live. On his drive to Chicago, some people

has been looking eastward, so that now we find California the melting pot of the two currents of civilization.

We, the American citizens of Japanese origin, should make it our task to bring about a better understanding, spiritually, morally, and politically, between the two civilizations. This can best be done perhaps by living loyal, honest, and dependable lives. I believe the work is well nigh under way. Real harmony must be brought about so that the world can eventually work together in peace and tranquility, just as in a performance of a great symphony—the soft melody of strings, with pastoral and charming woodwinds, the agitating blast of trumpet and horns and punctuating percussions. So the real harmony of the world must be that of perfect blending of different types of civilizations.

This is my utmost hope so that in the future we may accomplish this great task.

would not sell him gas and he had great difficulty finding housing in a good neighborhood. In 1945 Fujita and her children were released and reunited with her husband in Chicago. There she raised four children while working part-time in her mother's restaurant, and helping her auto mechanic husband.

Throughout her married life Fujita was a dog owner and at the age of eighty-three, she still walks the family dog. She is active in the Midwest Buddhist Temple, doing volunteer work. She enjoys reading and helping take care of her great-grandchildren.

Haruko Fujita Tademaru in 2002.
*Courtesy of Haruko Fujita.*

# Festivals of Japan

**SHIZU KOMAE**
*Lafayette Junior High School, June 1931*
*Los Angeles, California*

Shizu Komae (b. 1916). *Courtesy of Shizu Komae.*

THERE ARE MANY FESTIVALS in Japan, as there are in other countries. Japan is an old country. It is 2,500 hundred years old and has many ancient customs carried down from that time to now. There are five most important festivals, which come on January 1, March 3, May 5, July 7, and September 9. Of these five are two which we celebrate in America brought down from our ancestors.

The girls have their own festival on the third day of the third month. In many houses ceremonial shelves are covered with dolls that girls enjoy. On the top shelf are the emperor and empress dolls. They are dressed in their silk and brocaded clothes; and all the other dolls, before they are seated, must first make their bows to the rulers.

Below these august personages sit other dolls in appropriate costumes: court-ladies, musicians, babies, grandmothers, dancers and others; and lower still are doll furniture of all kinds: cabinets, cookstoves, utensils and even food. All these things are brought out only for this occasion, and they pass down from mother to daughter. On this day the girls give parties and do all sorts of entertaining things, and are taught lessons of obedience, patriotism, and honor for the emperor.

Like the girls, the boys also have a day of their own, "The Boys' Festival." The Japanese have a symbol of courage. It is a fish called the carp. The carp is a very hardy fish, not content with swimming lazily in comfortable pools. It fights its own way upward against the

Shizu Komae was born in Los Angeles and grew up there. After high school, she enrolled in the University of California, Los Angeles but did not attend because her mother became ill and Komae was needed at home. In 1935 she took a job with a Japanese bank in Los Angeles and worked there for five years.

She married Henry Yamada in 1940 and they eventually had four sons and a daughter. She was incarcerated with her family in the Arkansas camps at Jerome and Rohwer. After the war ended, she went to the East Coast to be "as far away from California as possible" since the United States government was paying the family's way. After two and one-half years in New Jersey, they returned to California. Her husband passed away in 1962.

swiftest current, and even leaps waterfalls. Japanese boys are thus taught that they must go through the stream of life and overcome all difficulties.

This festival is sometimes called the "Boys' Birthday," but it is not exactly a birthday as we understand it, for of course, all boys are not born on the same day. Their birthday celebration however, takes place on this Day of the Boys instead of on their individual birth date.

All sorts of fascinating toys and treasures are spread on the shelves which are set against the walls of the main room of the house. These treasures are put away all the rest of the year, so it is a real event to have them brought out. Some are too elaborate to play with but the children play with the simpler ones. These toys are kept so carefully that they pass down from father to son for generations. Nearly all of them are military toys.

Self-control, cheerfulness, courage, and a great and unselfish love for their country—these are the cornerstones of Japanese life, and each of these virtues is taught in its own special way on the day of the "Boys' Festival," to be made a part of their lives throughout the year.

When her daughter enrolled in junior college, Komae decided to attend college with her. Komae later transferred to the University of California, Los Angeles and graduated in 1966, majoring in Japanese. She then worked for the Los Angeles County Department of Social Services for sixteen years. In 1978 she married Roy Matsumura. Today she is active in the Japanese American community, volunteers at the Japanese American National Museum, and is a board member of the Coastal Asian/Pacific Mental Health Services in Gardena.

Shizu Komae Matsumura in her home in Southern California in 2002. *Courtesy of Joyce Hirohata.*

## LEISURE

# Relation of Leisure to Avocations

**AYAMI ONAKA**
*Fowler High School, 1933*
*Fowler, California*

Ayami Onaka (b. 1915). *Courtesy of Ayami Onaka.*

WE ARE NOT entirely certain of the ultimate hours and days of labor that will prove desirable for man. We are faced with something which only a short time ago we vainly sought and prayed that we might enjoy, that is greater leisure. It would appear that the tendency through recent years has been toward general reduction of the hours of labor. These changes follow not upon the effort to bring them about, but rather upon necessities like the one in which we now find ourselves. But however it has come about; we now face a condition in which generally the community has more leisure.

The question before us next will be, how shall the leisure be employed? We are confronted in this nation and others with a testing period. The moral fiber of the community must either stand the strain of temptation accompanying greater leisure or use it in such cultural ways as to reinvigorate the individual, to expand his life in many directions.

The focus of attention upon a specialty to the exclusion of all other things is to be found in the presence of some hobby. The joy that comes of such a leisure-time activity has long been known; its value is now more than ever recognized.

Delinquency cases show the need of an avocation to prevent the misuse of leisure. Delinquency as a rule does not occur during the hours when people are engaged in their daily tasks, but rather in

Ayami Onaka, whose English name is "Ida," was born in Fresno, California and grew up in the Central Valley. Her family owned a plantation of grapevines on land acquired before anti-Japanese laws made it illegal for her Issei parents to own land. During World War II her family managed to hold onto the property, and the vineyard is still run by relatives.

After graduating from high school, Onaka went on to Fresno State College. She met Noboru Morishige and moved to Hawaii in 1939 to marry him. During World War II, Japanese Americans in Hawaii were free and unrestricted but her parents, siblings and their children in California were incarcerated in Gila River, Arizona.

Onaka had two daughters and a son. While raising her children, she

their leisure time. That is where wholesome interests and avocations can be most effective in crime prevention.

Play is the pursuit of ideals. When released from our daily tasks, the mill we tread in order to live, we strive to become what we would if we could. When we are free we pursue those ideals that indicate and create character. If they lead us toward wholesome things such as art, drama, music, literature and all of the other things that are wholesome and good, then our lives are rounded out, balanced and significant.

The man who says there's nothing much to do is singularly unobservant. There are many amusing avocations—useful, ornamental or both. First comes working with the hands, with tools in the ancient arts and crafts and now economically displaced by machines, but cherished for their indubitable solace to the spirit.

Art makes for efficiency through the development of skills, individuality, creativity and taste. Because the ideals of art are truth, unity, balance and beauty, art makes for home and civic improvement, right attitudes towards community and international welfare. Art, therefore, leads to better citizenship.

Perhaps no recreation involves more art than the drama. Trained tastes will lead to the choice of the beautiful and not the tawdry whether in relation to the public drama, cinema or pageant. Training for taste should involve the appreciative and creative elements.

Music too, offers escape to tired businessmen and women. People who have laid aside their instruments because of lack of time to practice can begin again. Most of these activities can be pursued at little or no expense. All of them will satisfy the desire for self-expression.

Literature is an escape from actual life and a supplement to it. Books are valuable because they increase the amount of our life, refine its quality, and increase its intensity and significance. No study is surely more cultural, for it opens to the mind the view of the best that has been thought and said: the history of the human spirit. People who have had dreams of authorship may now have an opportunity to try themselves out in the field of poetry, the novel, or drama.

The creative element is especially important. Every human being demands instinctively and persistently an opportunity for self-expression. Lack of this opportunity is the cause of much unhappiness among the working classes. They are simple cogwheels in a vast system of machinery. If recognizable creative work is not supplied in

worked for the State of Hawaii in the Department of Education as an administrative secretary for twenty-six years. She also served as a volunteer for Meals on Wheels for fifteen years. After thirty-nine years in Hawaii, she returned to the mainland and currently lives in California.

the factory systems, and if leisure does not furnish an opportunity for self-expression of creative work, may we not expect all kinds of evils to develop?

Athletics probably supply the greatest part of one's leisure time, at least in one's youth. But all play and playtime occupations for men need not be for mere physical exertion. They may be applied to an undertaking that occupies the time not devoted to business or profession.

Hobbies are neither drugs nor time killers. The man with a hobby should be neither a sponge nor a jellyfish. The play that is worthwhile develops, creates, educates, gives life a new dimension. The happiest people are those who think the most interesting thoughts. Interesting thoughts can live only in cultivated minds. Those who decide to live as a means of mental development, who love good music, good books, good company and good conversation —what are they? They are the ideal persons who are desirable in the world. They are the happiest people in the world, and they are not only happy in themselves, they are the cause of happiness in others.

Top: Ayami Onaka Morishige was active in club activities in 1950. *Courtesy of Ayami Onaka.*

Bottom: Ayami Onaka Morishige volunteered for a newspaper publication in 1954. *Courtesy of Ayami Onaka.*

# Relation Between Leisure and Citizenship

**TOSHIO YAMAGATA**
*Fowler High School, 1933*
*Fowler, California*

Toshio Yamagata (1912–1998). *Courtesy of Jeannette Sanderson.*

THE PURSUIT OF HAPPINESS has been the chief goal of man from the beginning of recorded time. For the relatively few, this happiness has been achieved through the accumulation of wealth, the rise of power, and acknowledged authority that is preeminent in any field of human endeavor. These fields have been developed, through the activity of man's brain and hand creations in poetry, music, painting, sculpture and architecture. These are the great sources of pleasure and satisfaction to mankind in his leisure hours.

Leisure as a potential gateway to happiness, and its sense of achievement, has always been enjoyed by the rich and powerful. Not until the present age, however, do we find leisure enjoyed in such a great degree by all people. This leisure has much of menace; however, it may be full of blessings. Leisure is apt to relate in some ways to crime. It is a fact that the way a nation or community uses its leisure eventually determines its fate. The Roman Empire was destroyed, first by too much leisure, second by the wrong use of it. The right use of leisure is as vital to good citizenship as is the right use of toil. A good citizen is not only anxious to produce the maximum of good for society but he is also equally obligated to produce a maximum efficiency for society.

Then, who is a good citizen? To this question, Mr. M. G. Brumbaugh, former governor of Pennsylvania, answered: "A good citizen is one who loves his country well enough to obey its laws,

Toshio Yamagata was born in Fowler, California where his father was a farmer and his mother ran a boarding house. When he was six years old, both his parents died in a flu epidemic. He and his three brothers were taken to Hiroshima to stay with relatives. Nine years later, at age fifteen, Yamagata returned to the United States where he had to relearn English.

After graduating from high school, he worked for a year to pay off his debts. He then attended Fresno State College, transferring to the University of California, Berkeley and graduating in 1939 with a B.S. in commerce. In 1933 he became a member of the Japanese American Citizens League. Because he could not get work in his field, he went to Japan in 1940 in search of better opportunities. He took a job in Harbin, Manchuria and worked as a civilian employee of

promote its ideals, and keep himself fit to serve at a maximum of efficiency. His fitness is dependent upon his intellectual training, his moral sanity, and his physical condition." Then he called attention especially to the value of outdoor recreation as a means of developing a worthy citizenry for the nation. As an old proverb stated, "A healthy mind stays in a healthy man." We cannot expect a vigorous mind and a loyal spirit in a body that is unsound. Therefore, our country pays very careful attention to the recreational industry.

Idleness and loafing are alike the enemies of society. They are seedbeds of much lawlessness, unrest, disorder, and class hatred—the great sources of unstable government. Industry and wholesome constructive recreation are the effective antidote for these national threats.

Hence, all children are directed and stimulated by the moral that is attached to well-organized play. When children play, they soon learn that they must, in order to participate in any game with their fellows, surrender their individual whims, temper and will to the law of the game. They must abide by this law, or they cannot play. This is the essence of true citizenry of a nation. Unless we have earned the right to our place in the community and are willing to assume our share of the responsibility in the great game of life, we are not good citizens under the laws of society.

Again, leisure time can be devoted to study and intellectual development. Too few of our citizens are able to understand the government problems upon which they have to decide as voters. Many are apt to be led by what the "other fellow" says and does without thinking things out for themselves. Reading and study may give them intellectual training and information so that they will actually become more intelligent and therefore better citizens.

Considering these points we must all individually provide ourselves with a reasonable amount of leisure. Then we want to see ourselves educated to use such leisure for our own enjoyment and betterment, and for the strengthening of the quality of our citizenship. We can go a long way in that direction by getting out of doors and really becoming interested in nature. We can make still further progress in engaging in games and the sportsmanship that is emphasized by them. By availing ourselves of many educational opportunities offered by our libraries and schools, we can grow mentally and become better citizens.

Our country is a land of cultivated men and women. It is a land of industries, of agriculture, of schools and places of worship. It is a

the Japanese Army, translating books and other printed matter. In 1942 he married Mary Muroya, an American-born Nisei from Fort Lupton, Colorado and they eventually had three daughters.

During the war, the couple remained in Manchuria. After the war ended, Yamagata lost his U.S. citizenship because he had worked for the Japanese Army. He was captured by the Russians and survived for four years as a prisoner of war in Siberia where he worked in the coal mines. He was repatriated to Japan in 1949 and reunited with his wife. Yamagata worked for almost one year for the Kyodo News Agency and then was employed by the Showa Oil Company as an office clerk until he emigrated back to America in 1958.

When Yamagata returned to the United States he was an immigrant and spouse of a U.S. citizen. He returned to America because the mandatory retirement age in Japan was fifty-five. Although he was forty-six at the time, he needed to continue working past the age of fifty-five. He also thought Japan was overcrowded and the American higher education system would be better for his daughters.

With the help of his brothers, Yamagata began a landscape gardening business and became a member of the Southwest Los Angeles Gardeners Association. His daughter, Jeannette, said, "With relatives close by and a strong network of friends through

land of mountain and plain, of lake and river. It is our American heritage. We must make it a land of vision, a land of work, of sincere striving for the good. Let us learn to create a wholesome spirit and to train ourselves to become better citizens with the right use of leisure.

the Japanese American community, adjustment to American life went well for my parents." Yamagata eventually bought his own home near the University of Southern California where his daughters grew up.

In the 1960s Yamagata regained his citizenship through the naturalization process. "When my sister and I knew our father, he was USA all the way," Jeannette remarked. "He was very patriotic, and was very critical of those who did not appreciate the rights, privileges and opportunities enjoyed by Americans." In the 1980s Yamagata became ill with kidney disease and retired. He was an avid photographer, making numerous photo albums and filming many 8mm home movies. He also loved growing chrysanthemums and bonsai, the Japanese art of miniature trees.

Top: Toshio Yamagata (fourth from right) with his parents, Kichizo and Tsune Yamagata, and three brothers in front of the family's boarding house in Fowler, California circa 1915. *Courtesy of Jeannette Sanderson.*

Bottom: After returning to the U.S. in 1958, Toshio Yamagata began a gardening and landscaping business in Southern California and worked six days a week until the 1980s. *Courtesy of Jeannette Sanderson.*

# The Influence of the Olympic Games on Greek Art

**DORIS FUJISAWA**
*Audubon Junior High School, June, 1932*
*Los Angeles, California*

Doris Fujisawa (1918–1999). *Courtesy of Alice Shinoda.*

NO DEVELOPMENT of the Greeks has been more characteristic and of more permanent value than their art.

What were the causes of this wonderful blossoming? Some of them might be due to the moderate climate of Greece and the promotion of a robust and harmonious physical development. Some of them might be due to the mere beauty of the country, its favorable position for commerce and colonization. Yet, other races had lived under similar favorable conditions and had not attained the same results.

No clearer and more definite cause for the excellence of Greek sculpture is to be found than in the athletic habits of the people. The Greeks loved beauty. Every free-born one was an athlete from his cradle, trained in a variety of bodily exercises which developed his muscles in harmony and proportion.

It was because of the love of the people for athletics and their wish to have the winners and champions immortalized in bronze that Myron and his fellow sculptors gave to the world so many beautiful statues of athletes. In Greece, this desire greatly stimulated the production of good sculpture. The games spread a knowledge of anatomy, of the play of the muscles and of the symmetrically developed human figure. It was by the study of the human form in the race, in the dance, in the throwing of the quoit and in wrestling and boxing that the Greeks' sculptures approached so near perfection.

Doris Fujisawa grew up in Los Angeles and Redondo Beach, California, graduating from Manual Arts High School. She married Peter Fujioka right before reporting for detention in 1942. Although her sister lived less than twenty miles away, she could not attend Fujisawa's wedding ceremony because of curfew and travel restrictions placed on Japanese Americans. Making the best of the situation, Fujisawa and her husband always joked that they honeymooned at the Santa Anita Racetrack where they were incarcerated. Later they were sent to Heart Mountain, Wyoming. They left camp in 1943 and settled in Detroit, Michigan and had three daughters.

At the Olympic Games held at Olympia, the judges allowed athletes who gained first place three times to set up statues in the Altis so that men who lived in future times might know of their glory. The judges measured each statue carefully and if one was found too little, even by a little, it was knocked over and smashed to bits.

The bronze horses in the temple of Jun told of Cynisca, the first woman to win a chariot race at Olympia. Milo won the wrestling match seven times. This Milo was so sure of himself that once, he had his statue made beforehand and came to the wrestling ring with the life-sized bronze figure on his back.

In Greek paintings the artists gained from the athletes the natural clear lines of the human figure and on walls and vases they picture well-proportioned bodies. The tale of these heroes were sung as ballads, thus favoring music and poetry over narration.

In Greek art one will always find a freshness, symmetry and charm which may be sought in vain elsewhere. Simplicity, regularity, clear lines and the domination of the expression of the muscles can be found which far surpass any other ancient art.

# The Ideal of
# the Olympic Games

**SHIZUE OHASHI**
*Canoga Park High School, June 16, 1932*
*Canoga Park, California*

Shizue Ohashi (b. 1914). *Courtesy of Shizue Ohashi.*

NOTHING OCCUPIES so large a space in our conversation and in our daily press as athletics. A student may toil for many years with scholarly success, yet remain in obscurity, while his companion, a successful athlete, has become a national figure. It is sometimes believed and feared that athletics is destined to submerge learning, and that the true purpose of our schools is doomed to be lost in the crowd. The best way to judge the trend of athletics is to study and observe what athletics have done for other people.

In ancient Greece, the athletic ideal was to develop physical fitness in every person to prepare him physically for the task of a soldier. But, coupled with this idea, was the urgent desire that every Greek should develop a superb body, not possessing brute strength, but approaching perfect form; a body that could be exercised to music with gracefulness. The Greeks were not actually so concerned with prowess of contests, and the skill and the finesse displayed by the contestants. One of the most far-reaching effects of the Olympic Games was the inspiration they gave to Grecian sculptors. In those strong, graceful bodies of the contestants, artists had models of perfect beauty which could nowhere else be found.

No people have been so like the American people of today as the people of ancient Greece. No people have done so much for the higher things of life, such things as art, liberty, literature, philosophy, and science. The Greeks not only gave us names, poetry, history,

Shizue Ohashi was born in El Monte, California and was a tomboy in a family of five girls. Having grown up during the Depression, she still recalls the ice cream cones her softball team received for having won a championship in 1928. After high school she studied to become a barber and in 1934 she married Hiroshi Naramura. The couple had three sons. Prior to World War II she ran a barbershop which she closed during the war when she and her family were interned in Rohwer, Arkansas.

In 1945 Ohashi returned to West Los Angeles because her father had property that he was able to keep during his incarceration. Ohashi went back to cutting hair, raised her children and attended night school to study real estate. In 1948 she obtained her broker's license which she still has to this day.

and mathematics, but they gave us the Olympic Games as well. It was the Greeks who gave the first rank and chief honor to their athletes. Homer, the first and greatest poet of Greece, said, "A man wins no greater glory, so long as he lives, than the athletic victories he gains with his hands and feet."

From the opening of the ancient Games, the poorest and noblest citizens of Greece were urged to participate in the Games, a significant fact in the furtherance of the health and happiness of the people. These Games contributed much toward the building of a strong race.

Athletics help to overcome many undesirable traits of character, such as laziness, timidity, conceit, and lack of consideration. Thus, a good athlete is, with a very rare exception, a good citizen, and amateur athletics mold and require good character. Athletics make strong, healthy youths; strong, healthy youths make good citizens, and surely, such citizens make an ideal nation. In such nations, there should exist a spirit of fairness, a spirit of brotherhood.

The Olympic Games bring democracy and develop social distinction. Today, people of all classes, of all races gather together for the Olympic Games—men of wealth, or of poverty, men of every color, men of every creed. What a great school of learning for all is this gathering of people of all classes! What a great chance for all of us to know each other, to exchange ideas! What would create a more friendly feeling among the people of various nations?

Athletics make for fairness and honesty, and the Olympic Games gives a tremendous opportunity for all nations to learn to play the game of life in a fair way, as sportsmen play fairly in their games. These games develop that sportsmanlike attitude among nations for the rights of the antagonist, and a spirit of give-and-take which is most desirable.

Athletics makes for self-control and patience. No one who does not control or master himself can ever become a great athlete. The qualifications of a great athlete are what we need as qualifications of a great nation to promote peace.

Athletics make for temperance. No one could compete at Olympia until he had convinced his officials that he had lived a life of temperance.

Athletes who have honesty, self-control, patience, and temperance! They are the ones to represent their country! They are the ones who show what their nation is like!

Outdoor sports allow a vent for pent-up energies, and build strong and healthy bodies that give a mental ballast, something that

Of the internment she said, "The [Japanese Americans] did what the government said and some people even now say we should not have acquiesced so easily—that we had rights. But if you knew those times and that Hearst paper— they were *terrible*." She knows the younger generations have difficulty understanding why Japanese American leaders cooperated with the United States government. "But [the leaders] must have felt that was the best thing," she said. "I still think it was. If we had [resisted] and fought, we wouldn't be in the position we are now."

Shizue Ohashi in her 1934 wedding portrait taken in the Toyo Miyatake Studio in Los Angeles. *Courtesy of Shizue Ohashi.*

prevents minds from becoming warped with wrong thoughts and wrong deeds. The movement today toward increased interest in outdoor sports, toward play and its resultant building of stronger bodies and the improving of the mental outlook is due, in no small part, to Baron Pierre de Coubertin who suggested the re-establishment of the ancient Olympic Games.

With the establishment of the modern Games came the reiteration of a great ideal. "All sports for all!" Sports for all the nations. Sports for all the people. What a grand idea! The fulfillment of such an ideal would contribute vastly toward the health of the world. "All sports for all!" That is the ideal that has built up worthwhile intramural sport programs in high schools and colleges. That is the ideal that is yearly causing the increasing number of municipal golf courses. That is the ideal that has built playgrounds in large cities, and that has resulted in the setting aside of great areas for recreation and play in the state and national parks. That is the idea, earnestly followed, that should take us out of the grumpy, complaining, business-crazy life and make us happy and cheerful citizens. "All sports for all!" Above all, that is the ideal in which the nations mingle with other nations and those friendly quadrennial Games!

The Olympic Games did much to bring peace and happiness, and a feeling of pride to ancient Greece. Today it hopes to bring about friendship and goodwill in the world.

Through the Olympic Games, a medium of international competition in the halls of art and in the fields of sport, much is being done for better understanding among nations and the promulgation of peace in the world.

The world has a vision of internationalism, a law of recent origin which is the result of the growing spirit; that principle of humanity ought to govern relations among nations. What better medium is there for that vision than the modern Olympic Games?

International law is an unwritten law based upon rights and justice. It contains a set of rules or customs which have no other binding form than the consent of those who obey it. The undoubted influence of the revised Olympic Games upon the modern development of athletic sports and exercises has contributed much toward this international peace.

World peace! One of the great topics of the day. Olympic Games! Another great topic! Why not bind these two together? Let one depend upon the other. Olympic Games for international peace. What an ideal! What a measure of achievement! World peace as a light, produced from the Olympic Games, a light which must be kept burning forever and ever, to brighten and shine into the hearts of every people in every nation.

Shizue Ohashi Naramura in 2001.
*Courtesy of Shizue Ohashi.*

# Lincoln's Devotion to the Constitution

JOHN FUJIO AISO
*December 15, 1923*

John Fujio Aiso (1909–1987). *Courtesy of Emi Gauville.*

THERE WAS IN THE HISTORY of our nation, a backwoodsman destined to come forth to rededicate our government, and thus open it as a strict government of the people. This savior, as you know, is Abraham Lincoln.

It was during Lincoln's era that the Constitution was about to be defaced by ridiculous interpretations. Men were clamoring that the Constitution and the Declaration of Independence were destructive to the Union. Abolitionists did not see the great danger in immediate emancipation of the Negro. If they had carried out their thoughts of "Liberty," they certainly would have wrecked the government. Slave owners were doing their utmost to extend their rights on human property.

Lincoln was a God-like man to foresee both sides of the question. He conceived the best of both sides in the conflicting situation. He could see all men loyal in support of the Constitution, and to the government derived therefrom. No one realized more than he, the great necessity of the "government of the people, by the people, and for the people." Lincoln, both as a private citizen and as President, was an ardent defender of the Constitution. To him the Constitution was a sacred instrument, tampering with which would be of no benefit.

As a member of Congress he stated, "I wish now to submit a few remarks on the general subject of amending the Constitution.

Born in Burbank, California on December 14, 1909, John Aiso's lifetime of accomplishments were groundbreaking. He first made front-page news in 1922 when elected the first Japanese American student body president of LeConte Junior High School in Hollywood. He caused another major sensation in 1926 when he became the valedictorian of Hollywood High School. At Brown University, he majored in economics and was class valedictorian. In 1934 he graduated from Harvard Law School.

Aiso was admitted to the New York State Bar Association in 1935 and worked as a law clerk in the Wall Street firm of Patterson, Eagle, Greenough & Day. He was sent to Tokyo on business and while settling legal matters he studied Japanese law at Chuo University. While preparing to return to the U.S. in the spring of 1937, he was

As a general rule, I think we must leave it alone. No slight occasion should tempt us to touch it. Better, rather, habituate ourselves to think of it as unalterable. It can scarcely be made better than it is. New provisions would introduce new difficulties, and thus create and increase the appetite for further changes. No, sir, let it stand as it is. New hands have never touched it. The men who made it have done their work and passed away. Who shall improve on what they did?"

His strong character sympathized with those in a bondage system which all men of less judgment and lack of human sympathy accepted as an unavoidable evil. The freedom of the Negro was his great moral ambition; but the phrase, "Constitutional government," meant more to him. He believed the Constitution to be right and, therefore, saw the importance of its protection by all men.

It was this that gave the inspiration to give that marvelous address on the principles of the Constitution at Gettysburg. With these principles in mind, he never lost sight of the great importance of preserving our Constitutional government.

Slavery was wrong, he saw with perfect clearness; but as it had been accepted by the framers of the Constitution, he saw that immediate emancipation meant destruction to the Union. He had eagerly opposed the extension of slavery but, on the other hand, he vitally supported the Constitution which protected the slave-owners to continue their possession until the situation might be properly met. As he said, "A law is a law, whether it is satisfactory or not. Therefore it should be respected by all."

Thus he considered the obedience of Constitutional Rights though he knew slavery was wrong. Only once did he violate this rule and that was when he had to choose between it or the destruction of the Union. He said, "There is no moral right in the enslaving of one man by another; but above all we are violating Freedom, one of the foremost principles of the Constitution." Thus, in giving every state its Constitutional Rights, he lost many supporters.

In his debates with Douglas he said, "The excuse of our forefathers is growing of less importance. They need not carry it on longer." The earliest Congress also shared the same view. In 1794 they passed a law prohibiting the taking of slave men from the United States to sell. In 1789 the bringing of slaves into Alabama and Mississippi was prohibited.

Again, Lincoln proved his loyalty to the Constitution when he heard of the Dred Scott decision. He said that he was utterly dissatisfied with the outcome, and quoting his words, "I, however, do not

hired as resident legal counsel in Mukden (Hoten), Manchuria by the British-American Tobbaco Company.

After nearly three years, upon the insistence of his mother who traveled all the way to Manchuria to fetch him, Aiso returned to the U.S. sick with hepatitis. After he regained his health, in 1941 he was drafted into the U.S. Army and reported for duty as a buck private. He was first assigned to an outfit that repaired trucks but he was soon recruited to become the head instructor at the Japanese language school at the Presidio in San Francisco. Aiso quickly gained more responsibility and eventually became the Director of Academic Training in the Military Intelligence Service Language School. Throughout his military career he taught thousands of Japanese American soldiers who went on to make invaluable contributions to the Pacific campaign during World War II.

After the war ended, in 1946 he was transferred to General MacArthur's Headquarters in Tokyo. Aiso's assignment was to investigate and enforce activities in connection with the Political Purge decreed by the Potsdam Declaration. In 1947 he returned to the U.S. and eventually retired from the reserves with the rank of colonel, making him the highest-ranking Japanese American officer at the time. In 1965 President Lyndon Johnson decorated him with the Legion of Merit.

Aiso resumed practicing law in Los Angeles in 1947. In 1953 he became the first Japanese American, as

offer any resistance as the Constitution protects the decision of the Supreme Court. Therefore we must wait until the Supreme Court passes another ruling regarding the decision." An attack on the Supreme Court at the time might have wrecked the government, but he respected the Constitution.

When President, he said, "I do not propose to save or destroy slavery with the Emancipation Proclamation but it is to save the Union." In replying to Horace Greeley, Lincoln wrote, "I would save the Union. I would save it the shortest way under the Constitution. The sooner the national authority can be restored, the nearer the Union will be, 'The Union as it Was.' If there be those who would not save the Union unless they, at the same time save slavery, I do not agree with them. If there be those who would not save the Union, unless they could destroy slavery, I do not agree with them. My paramount objective is to save the Union, and it is not either to save or destroy slavery."

In his Gettysburg address he said that the Civil War was testing whether that nation conceived in Liberty could long endure.

Thus in his loyal support of the Constitution he passed into the next world. If Lincoln has given his life to uphold the Constitution from disgrace, surely, it is the duty of everyone present this evening to respect it and defend it against all enemies.

In conclusion, as a special privilege, I ask that every solitary member of this Student's Association become famous men like Lincoln, to stand up for rights and justice and thus set an example for the generations to come.

*John Fujio Aiso of Hollywood High School gave this speech and won first prize in an oratorical contest held on December 15, 1923, under the auspices of the Federated Japanese Young Men's Association of Southern California.*

well as Asian American, judge in the continental U.S. when he was appointed to the Municipal Court in Los Angeles. In 1957 he was elevated to the Los Angeles Superior Court and then in 1968 to the California Court of Appeal. In 1972 he retired from the bench and worked as special counsel for the law firm of O'Melveny & Meyers.

In 1987, four years after his final retirement, he passed away from injuries he received from a mugging at a gas station. Throughout his lifetime he overcame racial barriers and served as a role model to Japanese and Asian Americans. More about his life and accomplishments can be found in *John Aiso and the MIS, Japanese American Soldiers in the Military Intelligence Service* by Tad Ichinokuchi.

Before his final retirement, John Aiso was honored at a banquet held by the California Asian Judges Association and Japanese American Bar Association in December 1983. This portrait appeared on the cover of the banquet's program.

# George Washington and the Constitution

**HIDEMITSU GINOZA**
*Fowler High School, June 3, 1932*
*Fowler, California*

Hidemitsu Ginoza (b. 1914). *Courtesy of Hidemitsu Ginoza.*

AS WE LOOK BACK over American history, we are held breathless for a moment. We discover a period of uncertainty and confusion, in which the greatest political sagacity and the good temper of the people were required to save the half-built ship of state from sinking. It was the period just following the American Revolution. At this thrilling critical moment lived George Washington. He gained his immortal fame by guiding this ship of state to a splendid destination.

Immediately following the securing of independence by the American colonies, Washington retired to his home in Mount Vernon. He was retiring physically, but his mind still exercised a powerful influence on the affairs of the new nation, which he, with great sacrifice and work, had helped to create. He was anxious to know whether the thirteen freed states had enough cohesive forces to form one solid nation. But the colonists' spirit of strong unity, which had been displayed during the war, threatened to cool down again because of the inefficiency of the Articles of Confederation.

These thirteen colonies had been functioning under this first federal Constitution with each state or colony retaining its sovereignty, freedom, and independence. It was looked upon as a good defensive weapon by the whole thirteen states, but it lacked the central authority and the coherent force necessary to make them carry on as a nation. Day by day it became more and more unsuited

Hidemitsu Ginoza was born and raised in Los Angeles. Because his name was so difficult to pronounce and spell, kids in school mercilessly made fun of him. In eighth grade a friend suggested he use the name "William." He liked the idea and has been using the name ever since.

After high school, Ginoza went to the University of California, Berkeley where he earned his B.A. in science and M.A. in microbiology. He was interned with his parents in Rohwer, Arkansas. In 1944 he married and had a daughter and a son.

When the war ended, he lived in Chicago where he worked as a chemist. Later, he was a post doctorate fellow at the University of California, Los Angeles. In 1962 he began teaching at Pennsylvania

to the purpose of a national government. Internal jealousies were created. Local patriotism cast darkness upon our young nation.

Observing this critical situation, George Washington came to the rescue. He invited representatives from several states to his home to learn what the underlying causes of the difficulties were. He said, "We are either a united people under one head and for federal purposes, or we are thirteen independent sovereignties eternally counteracting each other. I can foresee no evil greater than disunion; than those unreasonable jealousies which are continually poisoning our minds and filling them with imaginary evils for the prevention of real ones." This noble quotation revealed his interest upon our nation.

Serious discussions led to the idea that the weak Constitution, the Articles of the Confederation, needed many adjustments. The result of this little meeting was the Constitutional Convention at Philadelphia, in May 1787, the consequences of which mark one of the greatest advances in political history of the human civilization. It was to settle the ideal destiny of our nation, which Washington felt was "now or never."

Because of his splendid personality, leadership and efficiency, known from the struggle for American freedom, Washington was chosen to preside at this convention composed of many able delegates from all thirteen states. After some consideration he accepted, and his acceptance meant another significant duty and his highest gift to the nation. As soon as his willingness to lead was heard, there was an outburst of joy throughout the land. At once, the growth of the confidence and dignity of the convention was noticed.

But Washington was soon confronted by problems more complicated than any which had faced him during the revolution. It is hard to realize today the enormous responsibility that rested upon him at that critical point.

The original purpose of this convention was to readjust the Articles of the Confederation, but it led to the principal problem of framing a Constitution or creating a strong centralized government for the new nation whose people possessed various sentiments and ideas in government, and a constitution that could be adapted for future generations as well. As the convention began functioning behind the closed doors of Independence Hall, the people began to fear that these leaders were working to benefit themselves by forming a tyrannical government. This bad rumor as well as many others went up and down the streets. The delegates soon became the

State University and retired seventeen years later. Today he is a Professor Emeritus of Microbiology.

object of bitter criticisms by the uninformed public. Washington countered these varied sentiments by his firm determination and confidence in achieving what he believed. He felt that a Republic government was to be the destiny of this country, and consequently he exerted all his vast influence to the exclusion of everything that might lead to the form of hereditary principle, or monarchy. This theory of his has proven to be the fundamental nature of our Constitution which still exists and which we are proud to possess.

As the convention continued, it threatened to break up several times due to the selfish interests and pride of the various delegates, but Washington, as during the war, displayed his admirable leadership and saved the convention from being fruitless. There were many delegates who possessed moral cowardice and feared to carry out the plan of creating a form of government that had never been tried before in human history. But rising from the president's chair, Washington made the statement: "It is too probable that no plan we propose will be adopted. Perhaps another dreadful conflict is to be sustained. If, to please the people, we offer what we ourselves disapprove, how can we defend our work? Let us raise a standard to which the wise and honest can repair." This noble eloquence convicted every member and braced the convention very effectively. As the chairman, he was restrained from participating in the debates, but his well-known opinions influenced our Constitution far beyond our ordinary comprehension.

After the people had waited in suspense for four long months, the new Constitution was framed and submitted for their approval. The delegates waited anxiously for their verdict. If this new Constitution failed to uproot local sentiment, pride and patriotism as it was intended, Washington's face would have been covered with disgrace. But his commanding influence over the people gradually won ratification. Naturally, its adoption met some difficulties because tyranny was still feared. But generally the new Constitution was characterized as a barrier against monarchy and as a protector of human rights.

This immortal convention, which was virtually induced and headed by George Washington, had succeeded in welding the thirteen irreconcilable states into one firm union. What this meant for their immediate future we, the people of today, all know.

Thus, we have seen that all through this convention as well as through his great career, Washington showed his abiding faith in our national future and in its people upon whom his loftiest aspirations and thoughts were centered. What higher, purer, or more thorough Americanism than this can be imagined? Let us hope that we will forever be true to the ideals that George Washington has set before us.

# Proposed Measures to Meet the Crisis

**THOMAS HIRASHIMA**
*Carpinteria High School, June 15, 1933*
*Carpinteria, California*

AS WE REGRETFULLY KNOW, there are a great many national problems which the present administration has faced and still faces. However, they can all be summed up in one problem: namely, that of keeping a gigantic interdependent system of farms, mines, factories, and public utilities going without interruption in a world in which mechanical invention has made it possible to produce all of the physical goods that man can consume with a very small number of workers. This problem is essentially one of how to distribute goods to the people rather than of how to produce. The present crisis or any other crisis which this country has faced has been caused by our poor system of distribution and not of production or consumption. We can now produce more food, shelter, and clothing than we can consume. But thus far we have not discovered how to regulate incomes so as to give all of the people the purchasing power to buy goods.

As we assemble here tonight, the Roosevelt administration has been in office nearly 15 weeks. In that time it has passed many measures in the attempt to start industry going and to raise the purchasing power of the country. Let us see what actions have been taken thus far. First, it has replaced panic-like fear for the nation's financial stability with confidence by closing all the banks and reopening but three-fourths of them under governmental control.

Second, stopped the hoarding of gold.

Thomas Hirashima was born in Santa Barbara, California in 1914. After high school he attended the University of California, Los Angeles, majoring in horticulture. During World War II he was incarcerated with his parents in Gila River, Arizona. After the war ended, he relocated to Cleveland, Ohio but eventually returned to California, where he owned and operated a nursery called the Goleta Garden Center. Active in the Japanese American community, he was president of the Japanese American Citizens League in Santa Barbara. A friend calls him a "friendly, warmhearted, generous guy." Since his retirement, he enjoys golf, ballroom dancing, traveling and his miniature train set.

Third, initiated farm relief legislation, aimed at raising prices (and hereby increasing the purchasing power of the country) by restricting the production of wheat, cotton, hogs, corn and five other farm products.

Fourth, provided for the short-time employment of approximately 240,000 men in reforestation projects.

Fifth, taken a step toward the wider distribution of jobs more generally among the people by initiating legislation guaranteeing a shorter working week in some industries.

As another step to raise prices and thereby to revive confidence, on April 19th President Roosevelt ordered an embargo on all exports of gold, thus taking the United States off the international gold standard. The value of the dollar immediately dropped, inflation was expected and as a result, all market prices rose. These measures are only a few of the many passed by the administration to meet the crisis.

This program of Presidential action, launched with astonishing dispatch and courage, has already achieved one result. It has restored the lost confidence of the people. The picture of an American President carrying out a program of swift action with imperatively little interference from Congress has replaced the dark gloom of early March by increasing optimism. The rise in prices of wheat, cotton, and other farm products, and the buying on April 20th of 7,000,000 shares on the New York Stock Exchange are crude measures of the changing temper of the people. Thus the President and his administration has met the national emergency with courage, intelligence, and effectiveness.

Now let us see what the future plans of the administration are. A huge public works program plans to "mobilize industry," which includes minimum wage laws, expansion and regulation of private industry, reorganization of the railroads and a program for reform of the banks which will protect depositors and investors.

The events of recent weeks encourage the view that the administration is willing to accept leadership in world affairs. Representatives of 53 countries have visited Washington at the invitation of the President to hold informal conversations concerning the world economic situation.

Now the insistent questions—does the Roosevelt program, as thus far revealed, guarantee permanent recovery? Do these months of April, May, and June 1933, mark "the turning of the corner?" It is too soon to predict surely. So far, the steps by the President have

been steps to meet a national crisis. The prompt manner in which
he has met that crisis deserves nothing but praise. However, months
must pass before a true evaluation of his program can be made.
Therefore, it is the obligation of every American, young or old,
to be alert to passing events and to try to understand the real tasks
before our people.

Let us judge the Roosevelt or any other federal administration
from just one point of view: has it launched a program which prom-
ises to give every man, woman and child in America in the near
future not a bare subsistence, but the abundant life (food, shelter,
clothing, recreation, aesthetic enjoyment, mental as well as physical
security) which our gigantic resources, machine technology and
skilled personnel now make possible?

# Power

**KIYOSHI MURAKAMI**
*Gardena High School, January 1934*
*Gardena, California*

Kiyoshi Murakami (1916-1993). *Courtesy of Irene Yamaguchi.*

THE SPEAKERS BEFORE ME have related the history of monopolies, big business, and other unfair business practices from the period of the Civil War to the present day. They have tried to give you a clear and concise idea of the origin, growth and especially the dangers of such individualistic practices. The purpose was, first, to unfold to you the ever-increasing menace of monopolistic practices to our great heritage of natural resources, and second, to discuss the various means by which rights may further be preserved. In brief, the previous speakers have tried to make clear to you the following facts: that monopolistic practices in business are injurious to national happiness and prosperity, that monopolistic practices have taken control of most of the natural resources, that the modern movements in conservation and various government regulations and legislations in business are absolutely necessary in safeguarding the rights of the people.

I shall discuss this evening one phase of the program of water conservation which aims to control the greatest and the most unscrupulous of all monopolies, the Electric Power Trust.

Such projects as Muscle Shoals, Niagara Falls, and Hoover Dam will break the monopoly of electric power and give to the nation cheap power to which the people have a just claim. Heretofore, the Electric Power Trusts have been the most destructive of all monopolies to the welfare of the nation. In 1925, the Federal Trade

Kiyoshi Murakami was born in Alhambra, California and grew up in the area. In addition to participating in sports such as football and soccer, he was the conductor of a harmonica band. He also loved to debate and was very interested in foreign languages.

After high school Murakami went to the University of California, Los Angeles where he majored in political science and participated in Reserve Officer's Training Corps (ROTC). Upon graduation he went to Japan and changed his last name to his mother's maiden name, Yamamoto, in order to carry on her family name. He was the first Japanese American admitted to Chuo University Law School despite having no prior education in Japan. The day he graduated, he was drafted into the Japanese Army and shipped overseas to the Java area. Later he was wounded

Commission estimated that two holding companies, the Electric Bond and Share and the Insull interests, controlled over ⅓ of the generating capacity of the country; that six groups controlled over ⅓, and 12 groups ½. In 1930 it was estimated that ½ of the electrical power generated by the larger companies in the country was in the hands of three great holding groups; that ⅔ of electrical energy was controlled by six groups; and over 90% by 15 groups. Today, less than 4% of the electricity is distributed by municipal plants. These facts indicate that the people have been largely at the mercy of selfish industrial interests. But the existence of such conditions is becoming more and more precarious. Public sentiment has been aroused to such an extent that some permanent remedy must be made.

The Muscle Shoals project, which has recently been reopened after an extended period of idleness, accomplishes a definite step toward controlling the unfair practices of the private power companies in the South, long the most powerful and obdurate interest in the section. This is made evident by the fact that the private companies have been forced, either voluntarily or involuntarily, to reduce their rates from 3% to 37½% in order to compete with cheap government power. It is a shameful thing that the homes and farms as well as the factories of the world should not have electricity in abundance; the government is trying to provide it for the whole United States. The government is trying to electrify the American home through providing inexpensive power. Its purpose is to simplify domestic work and to increase convenience by means of easily operated electrical appliances.

and sent to a hospital in Singapore where he remained for seven months. After recovery, he was discharged and returned to Japan in 1946.

The same year he married Yachiyo Kitajima. They had two sons and a daughter. He lived in Hiroshima, which was occupied by the Australian Army at the time, and worked for city hall as a translator and interpreter.

Later he worked for Nippon Suisan Kaisha, a large Japanese seafood products company, as a specialist in the foreign trade department. As a company diplomat, he traveled the world and worked with companies in Switzerland, Australia, Canada and the United States. He was very reserved, but loved to teach English to the young and elderly and his home was always filled with college students. In 1993 he passed away in Tokyo at the age of seventy-six.

Kiyoshi Murakami conducted the Homare Watanuki Harmonica Band circa 1930s in Southern California. *Courtesy of Irene Yamaguchi.*

Doubtless you have heard David E. Lilienthal, director of the Tennessee Valley Authority, in his recent radio address to the nation in which he said the government has proposed a plan whereby electrical appliances as well as electric power will be substantially lowered in cost so that the monthly electrical bill shall for the average household be a little over $5. This is including the use of every possible appliance in an average American home. This proposed plan is not theoretical but practical, and can come to pass through development of such power projects as the St. Lawrence River, Niagara Falls, Muscle Shoals, and Hoover Dam. The construction of Hoover Dam is therefore looked upon with the most welcome eye. What Muscle Shoals has done for the South in the way of freeing the people from the bondage of selfish interests, the people of the West expect hopefully of Hoover Dam.

Although the Hoover Dam is regarded as being the greatest piece of engineering ever attempted by mankind, the economic aspect involved will easily out-balance the engineering feats. This project, upon completion, will break the monopoly that private power companies in the West have enjoyed for so long. Practically all the power generated by Hoover Dam will be distributed through municipal plants, only 9% being given over to private distributors, thereby eliminating to the lowest degree the possibilities of unfair business practices. The Hoover Dam, as well as the Muscle Shoals project, will serve as a yardstick by which all other rates must be adjusted. The people will, for the first time, be afforded a chance to discover the unfair rates that have been imposed upon them by private companies.

We have tried to make clear to you this evening the general program of the Conservation movement, with special reference to the Hoover Dam project, as being a part of the great movement to prevent monopoly of our great heritage and to secure to the people their dower of rich natural resources.

Kiyoshi Murakami (third from right) worked as a translator and interpreter in Hiroshima after World War II. Murakami is shown here with the Mayor of Hiroshima (right) and a visiting Australian officer (left), surrounded by journalists. *Courtesy of Irene Yamaguchi.*

# American Government and Idealism

**GORO MURATA**
*Montebello High School, June 14, 1926*
*Montebello, California*

America, America,
God shed his grace on thee,
And crown thy good with brotherhood,
From sea to shining sea.

SO WOVEN INTO THE TAPESTRY of American history, the spirit of our American forefathers who toiled that their posterity may build a nation with strength and foundation for the development of good-will in humanity. The American idealism is expressed in a simple phrase of "brotherhood from sea to shining sea."

Where will a relentless following of facts lead us in the study of the American political institution and its idealism?

For the great majority of people, and for high school students like ourselves as well, a scholarly study of the national origins of the United States will be an excursion into the miracle of idealism, of fraternity, goodwill and peace so dear to the founders of America. A true picture of the beginnings of the American people would disclose much that is inspiring, heroic, and creative — laying a basis for a social order that was uniquely American. For this Commonwealth was founded not upon men's distinctions but on their common properties and instincts; the theory of the Revolution which in its denial of sovereign struck deeply into political problems as they were and are now; and the force of the American frontier shaping a society so measurably and with such effect that the original student of the West, Frederick Jackson Turner, declared its influence upon the American people surpassed that of the Mediterranean Sea upon the Greeks. To understand through study, the profound and permanent import of each is a mighty challenge to every student. These

Goro Murata was born in Montebello, California and went to Whittier College, graduating in 1930. A friend who knew him when she was a young girl said he was "a very handsome guy." In 1934 he went to Japan and worked for the *Japan Times*, the oldest English language newspaper in Japan. He sent articles back to the United States and wrote for the *Rafu Shimpo* and *Pacific Citizen*.

He was in Japan during World War II and afterwards was one of few Nisei who continued to be employed by the *Japan Times*. Through his work at the newspaper, he helped United States occupation officials gain perspective on postwar Japan. Another friend of Murata's who worked for United States Intelligence credited Murata and other Nisei in Japan for helping the occupation forces. Murata drove around Tokyo in a big car,

are some of the features which give cause for a justifiable pride in the past of America and at the same time supply information which suggests a way to find new idealism based upon world brotherhood and understanding.

American government and her idealism is no longer a study of one nation, but carries with it certain international implications. Concerning the humanitarianism of the time, a challenging study has been made by an American scholar, James Brown Scott, under the title, "James Madison's notes of debate in the Federal convention of 1787 and their relation to a more perfect society of nations." American social idealism of brotherhood is not confined to any one period with James Wilson speaking in 1774 and Woodrow Wilson in 1917 on the eve of another and a greater struggle. These references are sufficient to indicate that the steady undercurrent of idealism in the history of American government for two hundred years has a definite contribution to make in this day, which is calling for some sort of synthesis of nationalism and internationalism. While the United States has almost belligerently withheld her membership from the League of Nations, she has always been sincerely faithful to the principal of arbitration and her fidelity to it has been one of her greatest contributions to mankind. It is a significant fact that the major portion of the present content of international law is made up of principles evolved from a century of Anglo-Saxon methods used in settling national disputes. From the time the United States submitted to the Hague its first case to the present, the American people have experienced something of the reality of the ideal that "civilization is the capacity for cooperation."

I have indicated in brief the underlying causes of American idealism in government. The Constitution, which is the basic theme of American political life, has attributes of a living thing: vitality, growth, adaptability. So we ought to call it a living thing. The United States and her idealism is growing. It is growing in that her gestures of goodwill have stretched her greeting hands across every land and people to sing in unison:

America, America,
God shed his grace on thee,
And crown thy good with brotherhood,
From sea to shining sea.

enjoyed playing mah-jongg, a traditional Chinese game, and smoked cigars. In the mid-1950s he visited his mother in California to tell her that he had sinus cancer. He returned to Japan and died from the illness in Tokyo in 1956.

# Public Domain

**YOSHIMI U. NAGAYAMA**
*Gardena High School, January 1934*
*Gardena, California*

Yoshimi Nagayama (1915–1977) earned her B.S. in Dental Hygiene from University of Southern California in 1952.
*Courtesy of Karen Tanaka*

OUR TOPIC FOR THIS EVENING is the Hoover Dam—not only the engineering feat it represents but its social and economic significance as a part of a great movement to secure the rights of the people. Perhaps you have never thought of the conservation of natural resources as being related to monopoly or big business. My share in the program is to introduce to you the problem—the growth of monopoly or big business out of the endeavors to open up our great natural resources; to present to you briefly the relation which exists between conservation and unfair business practices which have proven to be destructive to many phases of social and economic life.

From the time of the Pilgrim Fathers to the end of the 19th century, our forefathers lived in a land of plenty. The United States at the close of the War for Independence possessed an enormous and rich domain of unsettled lands beyond the Alleghenies, and from time to time new areas have been added by purchase and conquest. It is estimated that the public domain of no less than 2,825,000 square miles—an area more than ten times the size of the German empire and more than twenty times the size of Great Britain and Ireland. In 1860 we had a public domain of 1,500,000 square miles, and in spite of the enormous grants which have been made to railway companies, corporations and private persons, the United States possessed in 1909 a national estate of 1,150,000 square miles that

Yoshimi Nagayama, whose English name was "Violet," was born in Torrance, California and grew up there. She married Taichiro Shimada in 1938 and was interned in Gila River, Arizona with her husband and son. In camp, she gave birth to another son and daughter. Her husband became ill with "valley fever" and nearly died. Because her husband was sick, three times a day she walked to the cafeteria in the extreme summer heat and wintry cold to carry heavy trays of food back to the barracks for her family. She did this even while she was pregnant.

After the war, Nagayama worked as a seamstress sewing wedding gowns and also took a job as a part-time dental assistant. In 1948 she enrolled in the University of Southern California to become a dental hygienist. To pay for her

were tremendously rich in forests, oil, mineral and potential electric power.

But where is this tremendous amount of wealth being stored now? As a result of various research work, we cannot help but realize the fact that most of these tremendous resources are now concentrated in the hands of a few great industrial leaders. The program for this evening, ladies and gentlemen, will present to you the attempts that have been made to restore the wealth to the hands of the people, or to save what we have now.

With the enormous area of unsettled public domain, opportunity was once open to all. If a man failed in one place, there was always room to move West where he was able to begin anew. Under these circumstances, it was natural that the resources of the nation should be given freely to any individual or corporation that would develop them. Why not? Many men took advantage of this opportunity and in consequence have accumulated gigantic fortunes. Many of us, had we the ability and opportunity, would have done likewise. The 18th and 19th centuries, during which the unclaimed domain of the country was most enthusiastically taken possession of, were naturally times of intense individualism. Each man took freely of the resources, did with them as he pleased, and regarded interference from any source as unwarranted. Thus, the spirit bred from our early national life prompted the unfair business practices that have caused so much unhappiness among recent generations. These great monopolies made overwhelming progress from the Civil War to the present despite efforts to stop them. We realize only too well that our natural resources are not inexhaustible but that we are facing grave possibilities of shortage.

Gradually, with the shift and changes, and with the development of fundamental economic problems, recent years have seen the greatest consolidation of business in American history. The development toward large corporations has been accompanied by a definite swing toward monopoly in many of the nation's industries. First came the pools to restrict prices and outputs. Next followed the trusts in which trusteeships were created to hold the property of the formerly competing corporations. The period of the trust proper, as it has been called, extended from 1878–1896. The first years of this period gave rise to the Standard Oil Company, the linseed oil trusts, the whiskey trust, the sugar trust and other combinations. These consolidations aroused the fear of many, and led to the passage of

tuition Nagayama continued working as a dental assistant and borrowed money from a friend. In 1952 at the age of thirty-seven, she received a B.S. in dental hygiene, and earned a certificate in dental nutrition and her teaching credentials. After graduation she worked as a hygienist and taught dental nutrition at Los Angeles City College. Her marriage eventually ended and she later married J.B. Metz and lived in Perris, California until her death. Nagayama was a devout Christian and according to her daughter, she was a humble, loving and forgiving person. She spent her life overcoming obstacles, teaching by example, and seeking achievement.

anti-trust legislation and to attacks in the state and federal courts. In 1896 Congress passed the famous Sherman Antitrust Act, which declared illegal all combinations in restraint of trade. This and other remedial legislation brought the trust movement to a temporary standstill.

Beginning with the year 1900, with the election of McKinley, however, the second and more vigorous period of combinations set in. Centralization during this period was based largely on the structure of the holding company rather than a trusteeship form of organization. During the next seven years the merger movement secured such momentum that by 1904, John Moody, in his *Truth about the Trusts*, submitted a list of 300 combinations in the country with the capitalization of over $7,000,000,000. Ten of these corporations were capitalized at $100,000,000 or over.

Then came the War—the European conflict distinctly encouraged big corporations to pool their interests for war purposes, while the Webb-Pomerene law of 1918 permitted many competitors to consolidate their exporting activities. The courts meanwhile looked on combinations with a more kindly eye. Immediately after the war the third major movement developed momentum and continued with breathtaking speed until the Wall Street Crash of 1929. During this period over 7,000 mergers were reported in the manufacturing field alone. In public utilities, the number of mergers increased from 22 in 1919 to over 1,000 in 1926, while in banking and in the field of distribution, new combinations were reported almost every day. According to Dr. Gardiner C. Means, big business had developed to such an extent by 1927, that 200 non-financial corporations did 45 percent of the non-financial business of the country.

The absolutely vital consideration is that there has been an overwhelming and rapid movement toward the consolidation of all the leading business interests, of course with a large measure of privileges for each of the giant corporations or corporation groups. Leading all the nations in this development, the United States is already far along that road.

# The Struggle against Crime

Roku Sugahara (1912–1952). *Courtesy of Setsuko Asano.*

**ROKU SUGAHARA**
*Manual Arts High School, January 30, 1930*
*Los Angeles, California*

TONIGHT MARKS THE END of our high school career. We have successfully passed our years of training. Now we are ready to be knighted as graduates of Manual Arts. As I stand on the battlement of this great Castle of Learning and face the vast expanse of life into which we are now prepared to carry the torch of enlightenment, visions of past great American torchbearers come to mind. When the life of the thirteen struggling colonies was threatened by British oppression, it was George Washington who led the host of valiant torchbearers to brighten the path. It was our honest Abe who came to the fore as the chief torchbearer when the dark clouds of secession hovered over the path of national progress. Again, it was our dashing Teddy Roosevelt who held aloft the torch of the Monroe Doctrine when the gathering shadows of foreign interference darkened the hopes of our sister American republics.

Today we are enjoying the abundant blessings of life under the immortal torches of our forefathers. But this does not mean that we can now lead a happy-go-lucky type of life. As we graduating students leave the portals of Manual Arts, each diploma that we receive symbolizes a torch of education with which we are entrusted to brighten the path of human progress.

Looking back over the diversified fields of our national life, there are blotches of darkness here and there that challenge our torches of enlightenment. Among these blotches of darkness, the

Roku Sugahara was born in Los Angeles into a family of five children. While still a young boy, his parents died and the Japanese Methodist Church looked after the five orphans. From the age of nine, Sugahara earned money delivering Japanese American newspapers on his bicycle. He and his siblings inherited money to go to college, so he attended the University of California, Los Angeles and majored in economics. After graduation, he married Viola Honda whom he had met in college.

Avoiding incarceration during World War II, the couple relocated to Colorado where they worked as domestics. Sugahara struggled to find employment and eventually made his way to the South, where he thought race prejudice would not be as severe for Asians. After the war he worked in real estate and part-time at a bookstore in

problem of crime is outstanding. President Hoover in a recent address said that crime was one of the two major problems confronting the American people today. Let me show you the appalling cost of crime in dollars and cents. The budget of our country, which is the largest in the world, totals four billion dollars a year. The cost of crime per year, my friends, is more than three times as much. This staggering sum puts into oblivion all of the other expenses of our government. But this monetary cost of crime is only a trifle in comparison to the loss of lives, grief, broken homes, and disillusionments that always accompanies crime. Crime is here and it challenges us to solve it. Here is a chance for a torchbearer to blaze the way for a solution to this vital problem.

With a true American spirit let us look into the causes of crime. Some experts suggest that crime is due to some weakness in our religious beliefs. Others say it is due to the rapid influx of foreigners in the last 50 years. Still others claim that crime is chiefly due to our competitive economic system. As knights of old went forth overcoming dragons and other forces of evil, so we graduates today seek to combat this monster, crime.

As I approach this problem with my little torch of learning, I perceive at the center of this blotch of darkness a little devil— a demon scattering the black seeds of evil. In spite of the sincere efforts of many workers to stem its growth, this blotch seems to be spreading.

Who is this devil? His treacherous strength lies in his littleness. He creeps unnoticed and often finds easy access to the hearts of the young people. He has a long name—but not a hard one. He is a spirit of "get-away-with-it." I don't know where he comes from but he is here. We all have heard of him and we all know what he has to offer. It is this spirit—this demon which, I believe, is a cause of this crime problem.

We find this demon everywhere. He has victimized both young and old. We find him in the misapplied superiority of the reckless driver. We find him in the erroneous pride of the prohibition violator. We find him in all the public connivances of our social vices. We find him in politics, in school, and in business.

We may drive him out of one phase of our life, yet immediately he lurks in another. This demon has many fountains from which he draws the source of his life. He will ever be haunting us until we have drained all of these well-hidden fountains of evil.

New Orleans. He drank a lot of milk and constantly complained of stomach ulcers. His wife was working in New York and he visited her often.

After being drafted into the army and serving in Europe, he returned to the United States and his stomach ulcers were diagnosed as cancer. His sister said "he suffered a great deal" and passed away just before turning forty. Setsuko Asano, who knew Sugahara when she was a young woman, said, "He taught me so much. He was soft-spoken, lots of fun and guided me in my future. . . . He was exceptionally wise and taught me [that] nothing was impossible."

Sugahara wrote articles for the *Pacific Citizen* and a column for the *Rafu Shimpo* entitled, "A Nisei in Manhattan." Although his older brother, Kay, became a wealthy, well-known businessman after the war, according to his sister, Sugahara was not concerned with material possessions. She said, "He was a sensitive, loving being not concerned with money, power and the usual attachments. . . . He was a most sensitive and gentle soul."

We can't kill this devil by merely pointing at him and denouncing him. We must meet him on his own ground. What we need is a torchbearer in this crime problem. He must be a man of high ideals and lofty aspirations. A man who is unafraid, courageous and adventurous. We need a man who bears the torch that is bright enough to pierce through the darkness of ignorance that conceals these fountains of evil. A man who can see things in their true proportions and whose mind can penetrate through the different fields of the social sciences. A man, who by the strength of his character, can lead this nation along the most enlightened path.

This challenge of crime and this offer to be a torchbearer in this struggle against crime is flung to the youth of America. Can youth answer the call? It is the sincere hope of all of us graduating students that the torchbearers in this battle against crime may emerge from this very group.

Here lies stretched before us the diversified paths of different careers. We all have different talents and live under different circumstances. Some of us may never see each other again. Yet I hope that the spirit of adventure—of the safari and the love of achievements bind us each in our common endeavor to be torchbearers in our respective fields.

Fellow graduates, as we leave the halls of our beloved alma mater, each bearing his little torch of education to his field of achievement, let us pledge ourselves, as a humble token of gratitude to our parents, to our teachers, and to our nation, to strive each in his own sphere, to combat this problem of crime.

*Women work for political power so that they may use this power for peace; they plan educational campaigns in order to teach the youth the wrongs of war. They know what war is. They know the value of human life. Motherhood speaks for itself.*

—Yoshiko Higuchi
Monterey Union High School, 1932

## WOMEN

# The American Woman Comes of Age

**CHIZUKO DOI**

*Edison Technical High School, 1934*
*Fresno, California*

Chizuko Doi (b. 1915). *Courtesy of Chizuko Doi.*

I WISH TO DISCUSS briefly what is considered the greatest social drama of the 19th-century—the emergence of the American woman from her repressed and sheltered place in the home with no chance at earning a living except as a domestic servant, with little chance for education, and with no legal or political rights, to the present woman, free to go where she will, free to get all the education she wants, free to work in any profession she chooses, and free to vote on all political questions. The woman of today has come of age; the woman of 1800 was a child in comparison.

In 1840, a group of women from the United States, aroused over the injustice of slavery, went to London to attend the World Anti-Slavery Conference. Perhaps you think that these women mounted the platform and aroused the convention to action. This, however, was not the case, for these women were seated in the gallery and told to remain silent, while the men—including their husbands—took active part.

Incensed by such treatment, Elizabeth Cady Stanton and Lucretia Mott decided, as they walked home together from the convention that night, to start a non-stop campaign for women's rights—a campaign which aroused the American woman to fight for rights she realized she needed.

Eight years later a group of women and fair-minded men met in New York to make a "Declaration of Rights for Women." Clause

Chizuko Doi was born in Visalia, California and grew up in nearby Fresno. As the 1934 salutatorian for Edison Technical High School, she chose to quote beside her yearbook photo, "Whatever there is to know, that shall we know some day." After graduating from high school she worked in her aunt and uncle's store. In 1935 she married Andy Campos and the couple had two children.

After Pearl Harbor was attacked, Doi, her daughter and newborn son were detained in the Fresno Fairgrounds. Her daughter was six years old and her baby boy had been born only three weeks earlier. She said her husband was very "sad and upset" to have his family taken from him and locked up. Because Doi's husband was not of Japanese heritage, she and her children were released after four months.

after clause of this "Declaration of Rights" has since been translated into law and custom, but only after a bitter struggle by women leaders.

Before a quarter of a century had passed, women forced open the doors of Western colleges and soon afterwards managed to establish women's colleges on a par with those of men. Radcliffe College, once an annex of Harvard, elected a woman for its president.

Enthusiastic over the rights to education they had gained, women wished to extend these rights to even the smallest child and so they organized kindergartens in the United States and had them made a part of the free public schools. Thousands of women now prepared for teaching as they had done before for nursing.

From 1883 to 1934 women entered into virtually all the businesses and professions which had been closed to them. They formed trade unions, which demanded and obtained better working conditions for women. They formed the Consumers' League, which is accountable for the "Do Your Christmas Shopping Early" movement and for the campaign against sweatshop conditions.

Women also developed the women's club movement, which taught women organization and led them into understanding of cultural and political questions of the day. And all the while these courageous women were being cartooned as mannish and ridiculous by the newspapers, criticized by the pulpit and press, and even insulted by men on the streets as they worked tirelessly to gain their highest goal—suffrage. Delegation after delegation of women were sent by the National Suffrage Association to Congress and to the President.

At first, President Wilson was definitely opposed to suffrage; later he gave a definite promise of help.

At last, on August 26, 1920, the battle for suffrage was won— the 19th amendment was ratified.

After gaining suffrage, women began to take active part in public and national life.

To show the progress of women since 1920, I shall name women in high positions to date. We have in law Judge Florence Allen; in aviation, Amelia Earhart; in government, Ambassador to Denmark, Bryan Owen; Chief of the Children's Bureau at Washington, Grace Abbott; and Secretary of Labor, Francis Perkins.

You may be interested in knowing that of the 29 women now holding high executive positions, 13 have been appointed since President Roosevelt came into office.

Doi says she did not experience any discrimination during the war and was treated well by her neighbors and the community. She worked for many years as a grocery clerk and "lives well" because of the "wonderful benefits" she received from her job. After almost seventy years she did not remember her high school speech. When she read it again she was surprised at what she had written and was "very impressed."

A total of 135 women serve as legislators in 34 states. Women also hold the following positions: Director of the United States Mint, Assistant Land Commissioner, Chairman of the United States Employees' Compensation Commission, Civil Service Commissioner, Special Assistant to the Attorney General, Recorder of the General Land Office, Associate Director of the United States Employment Service, Supervisor of the Narcotic Bureau, State Governor, and many other high positions.

In other words, the American woman has come of age and is making intelligent use of her citizenship.

# Women and World Peace

**YOSHIKO HIGUCHI**
*Monterey Union High School, June 16, 1932*
*Monterey, California*

Yoshiko Higuchi (1914–1982). *Courtesy of Tazu Kanda.*

WHAT IS WAR? The famous American poet, Lowell, says:

> Ez fer war I call it murder,
> There you have it plain and flat;
> I don't want to go no furder
> then my Testyment for that.

And one is inclined to agree with him. War causes more damage than anything else. Money and economic resources are consumed rapidly to furnish the fighting nation with armaments; innocent women and children are killed by unavoidable accidents so common during war time. There is not enough food to feed the hungry soldiers nor the people at home. Everywhere man is bent on destruction. Then after all, what is the result? Francis Moore's words are fitting:

> When after many battles past
> Both tired with blows, make peace at last
> What is it, after all, the people get?
> Why! Taxes, widows, wooden legs, and debt.

Above all, women feel the deepest antagonism towards war for they know and bear the cost of human life. All their sufferings are in

Yoshiko Higuchi was born in San Francisco and grew up in Monterey, California. Athletic and a natural leader, she was one of a few girls allowed to study kendo, a Japanese sword-fighting martial art. She became quite proficient and went with her team to Japan to compete in tournaments. As the spokesperson for her group, she gave a speech in Japanese to their hosts. She loved to write and kept a journal of her trip.

After high school she attended Healds College and did clerical and domestic work. In 1938 she married Yoneo Bepp and the couple had three daughters. She was interned in Heart Mountain, Wyoming with her husband, three-year-old daughter, parents and in-laws. After the war, the family relocated to San Jose, California but had difficulty finding housing. Higuchi raised her

vain if their children are brought up only to be sacrificed on the battlefield.

But women never really attempted to work for peace until fifty years ago, and at that time the only women's organizations striving for peace were about twelve groups in Europe called "Olive Leaf Circles."

The first modern attempt for the women's peace movement was made by Julia W. Howe. Roused by the suffering caused by the American Civil War and by the Franco-Prussian war which followed, she determined to organize a women's "peace crusade." She drew up an appeal to the womanhood of the world which was translated into all languages and distributed throughout the world. Mrs. Howe succeeded in arranging a large public meeting in London but the women's spirits were not aroused sufficiently. There was still something lacking to make the organization forceful. Nevertheless she worked steadily to win a place for women in the political field so that they could use their power for peace.

During the World War, another American woman, Mrs. Clara Guthrie d'Arcis, attempted to unite women into one strong attack against war. She established the World Union of Women for International Concord. In a speech before the members of the organization, Marchioness of Aberdeen and Temair appealed in a vivid accost:

> If the wild deer knows how to protect its young against the eagle hovering above, if a savage mother knows how to hide her babe from the rival tribe, cannot the mothers of today devise plans for an international understanding among themselves, whereby, they will be able to protect the children of the human race from the calamities which threaten their very existence?

Before the World War and before their attainment of political power, there were no national or international women's groups organized solely for the promotion of peace. The International Council of Women, as early as 1888, devoted part of its work for peace but not all. At about the same period, other women's organizations formed for different purposes, created special committees to work for world peace. The most outstanding was the Women's Christian Temperance Union under the leadership of Frances E. Willard. During the last quarter of the 19th century women in practically every country of the world were to be found working for peace.

daughters and worked part-time doing office work and bookkeeping for her husband's business. She also took care of her in-laws who lived with her.

Throughout her life, Higuchi was active in the Japanese American community and her Buddhist temple. A classmate still remembers "Yoshi" as the vivacious leader who organized hikes in Pacific Grove and seaside lunches, and taught her how to tap dance and go on a "banana diet."

The most outstanding leader of all was Jane Addams and ranking next, Mrs. Carrie Chapman Catt. In 1915, they called a convention of women out of which grew the first national organization of women designed solely to promote peace, the Women's Peace Party.

After America entered the war in 1917, the activities of women's organizations interested in peace practically ceased. The members turned to Red Cross work and educational activities.

Following the announcement of the Armistice, a second international congress of women, agreed upon at the Hague Conference, was called to meet in Paris in connection with the Peace Conference. By this time, the world sentiment for peace was so strong that it led from nationwide peace movements into an international one, namely, the Women's International League for Peace and Freedom. Branches were organized in 24 countries. Throughout the rest of the world without including the United States, there are according to latest estimates, 232 organizations concerned with international peace. Among these, England, France, Germany, and Japan boast more than forty each.

In addition to the American section of the Women's International League for Peace and Freedom, there are in the United States, two other national women's organizations which are devoted solely to work for world peace—the Women's Peace Union and the Women's Peace Society.

These two organizations, in the spotlight of the peace movement, stand against all participation in war on the grounds that human life should be held sacred under all circumstances. The Women's Peace Union has secured the introduction in Congress of an amendment to the Constitution making it illegal to prepare for, declare, or carry on war.

Personally, I feel that Jane Addams has been and still is the most prominent peace worker of America. Her activities can be summarized briefly. In 1915 she presided over the Women's Peace Conference at the Hague. During the war, she was an active worker for the conservation of food and human resources. She traveled from place to place presenting lectures to colleges and clubs. In 1919, after the Armistice, she attended the peace conference in Paris. At that time, Miss Addams also visited various war-torn countries with "Gifts of Love"—food, clothing, and other necessities for the starving people. She was one of the leaders of the Third International Congress held in Vienna in 1921. At the present time she is at her social settlement,

Hull-House in Chicago, and she has lost none of her ideals for the part women have in the world peace movement.

Women work for political power so that they may use this power for peace. They plan educational campaigns in order to teach the youth the wrongs of war. They know what war is. They know the value of human life. Motherhood speaks for itself.

The world interest of the last century in the Atlantic has been shifting to the Pacific base. Probably in the near future, the Pacific will be the central stage of international drama. As we are at the gateway to the Pacific countries, let us contribute to the promotion of world peace which should be the basis of the new civilization.

The eyes of the world are focused on America as one of the foremost nations of the world. They note our every movement. It is our duty to shoulder this great responsibility. Inspired by Jane Addams and other women who have devoted themselves to the cause of peace with that faith so inseparable from true Americanism, let us strive for the ultimate goal—World Peace.

*We find that enthusiasm overcomes prejudice and opposition; it spurns inactivity; it overwhelms all obstacles. It is nothing more nor less than faith in action. Faith and initiative rightly combined can remove any barrier, and achieve miraculous results.*

—Mary Fukuye Asada
Selma High School, 1933

# Enthusiasm

Mary Fukuye Asada (b. 1916). *Courtesy of Mary Asada.*

**MARY FUKUYE ASADA**
*Selma High School, 1933*
*Selma, California*

KIND FRIENDS, you are here tonight to witness our commencement which culminates our four years of study. We are grateful to you for the interest and cooperation you have shown toward us. We welcome you to our graduation, and are honored by your presence.

A good deal of the joy of one's life consists in doing perfectly, or at least, to the best of one's ability, everything he attempts to do. There is a sense of satisfaction, a pride in surveying such a work. But this perfection and this satisfaction is brought about only when it is accompanied by enthusiasm.

Enthusiasm is an impelling force, or an impassioned emotion, which causes a vigor, an earnestness and a joy in one's actions and speech.

The late Dr. David Starr Jordan of Leland Stanford Junior University has said, "My message shall be an appeal to enthusiasm in things of life, a call to do things because we love them, to love things because we do them, to keep the eyes open, the heart warm, and the pulses swift, as we move across the fields of life."

His message is an appeal to our earnestness and ardent feelings, to vim, to vigor, to admiration, to interest and to life itself. He declares that if we undertake to do a thing with enthusiasm, no matter how we may originally have disliked the idea, we will grow to love a thing and we cannot help having enthusiasm. The success

Mary Asada was born in Alameda, California and was raised in Selma, California. After high school she attended McKays Business College in Los Angeles. She was interned in Gila River, Arizona with her parents and siblings. The six of them shared one room and three beds separated by curtains. In camp she worked in the mess halls and later taught shorthand.

In October 1943 she was released from Gila River and went to Chicago where she did office work and bookkeeping. She married in 1954. After she retired, she did volunteer work for a food pantry and a nursing home. She remained in Chicago until 1995 when she moved to Texas.

results from an ability to observe closely the interesting things about us and to try to understand and sympathize with those about us, and to keep the heart actions strong and swift. Only in this fashion does life become worthwhile.

Robert Louis Stevenson said if we would take the old world by the hand and frolic with it we would have a good recipe for joyousness.

Emerson said, "Every great and commanding moment in the annals of the world is the triumph of some enthusiasm." The Arabs, from a small and mean beginning, established, because of their eagerness and confidence, a larger empire than that of Rome. Joan of Arc, in her belief in her great mission, sent a thrill of enthusiasm through the French army and so won the war for France. Her zeal had inspired others and had carried everything before it. Beethoven in his enthusiasm composed the "Moonlight Sonata." How much the world owes to the enthusiasm of such people!

Enthusiasm may be derived from many sources. The school gives us knowledge, intellectual drill, breadth of mind, business and social training. Moreover, it gives us comradeship and friendship. In school we are just getting ready for life, and we have about us the finest and richest materials that can be found. In school we learn from text-books, from discussions in classrooms, from the teacher's experience, and from our friends. All of these things are inspirational and valuable.

Another source of enthusiasm is in studying people at large. The human heart is human, no matter where it may be found. Even a savage may be a perfect gentleman. Primitive people who had no such advantages or opportunities as we have, had a joy for accomplishment, and a satisfaction in that accomplishment.

Someone has declared that a wise young man ought never to shun men and women; he should mingle freely with them. He needs to get their point of view.

From nature we also derive a desire for action. How can we look at the many beautiful things about us—the flowers, the clouds, the trees, the mountains—without feeling a joy of living? How can we listen to the birds, to the wind in the trees, without a feeling of response within our own hearts?

Travel permits us to have contacts with people and thereby gives us greater breadth of vision. A traveler gets his mind full of a large and varied store of delights. Pictures constantly rise before him, magnificent, solemn, bold, or charming.

Literature provides a means of inspiration. The more one can become acquainted with good prose and poetry, the more he will feel an inspiration and an aspiration. Some students say we ought to read a bit of poetry every day for spiritual refreshment. Literature touches every feeling, every hope, every craving of the human heart.

Other arts, such as music, painting, and sculpture give one not only satisfaction but strength to live more highly. With a devotion to them comes a feeling of dedication to the highest purposes and ideals.

Man's business is to work, to surmount difficulties, to endure hardships, to solve problems, to overcome the inertia of his own nature—in fact, to live. Sometimes our labor is a mere repetition of acts; this has a tendency to result in staleness and monotony. We must go through the same motions and the same expressions again and again. What drudgery it is if there is no enthusiasm to enliven the labor. Enthusiasm is the one necessary ingredient in the recipe for doing good work.

Exercise only the highest and the best, else you may give strength to habits and inclinations that may master you, to your own great disadvantage.

We should be happy in our daily job, but we should, too, give happiness to others with whom we come in contact. We should be radiant, reflecting to others our own health, cheerfulness, courage, and goodwill. Set the germ of enthusiasm afloat in any kind of place. Carry it in your attitude and manner; it will spread like contagion and will influence all those about you; it results in greater produc-tion with less effort; it means joy and pleasure and satisfaction.

Summing up the whole subject, we find that enthusiasm over-comes prejudice and opposition; it spurns inactivity; it overwhelms all obstacles. It is nothing more nor less than faith in action. Faith and initiative, rightly combined, can remove any barrier and achieve miraculous results.

Thus, then, should one create for himself an enthusiasm. For so long as enthusiasm lasts, so long will youth endure.

Mary Asada in 2000. *Courtesy of Mary Asada.*

# The Voice of Nature

Helen Hirata (1913–1983). *Courtesy of Phyllis Mizuhara.*

**HELEN H. HIRATA**
*San Bernardino Junior College, June, 1932*
*San Bernardino, California*

MY MIND IS ILLUMINATED upon this memorable occasion by my incapability to do justice to the honor bestowed upon me. For the past few days I have been cudgeling what serves will "stick." Of course, it must be worth sticking or it will be unacceptable, and therein lies the difficulty.

One does not wish to place before you a series of bromidiums, no matter how beautifully phrased or how sincere they may be; nor to repeat to you that which can be read every day in the papers about the Depression, the problems of the college graduate, or even about the coming presidential election.

So, after casting about for something real and different, I have chosen to speak this evening concerning the voices of Nature—Nature who has played so important and vital a role in the development of the mental, moral, and physical qualities of man since the dawn of history. It is proper and fitting that we should listen to the voices of Nature, for Nature is always speaking to us, presenting principles so clear, so sound, so proven, as to be worth stating.

There is nothing fanciful in speaking of Nature's voices, for even those of us who refuse to admit that Nature has a divine purpose, or that this includes being a warning and encouragement to man, will confess that we can learn something from Nature. When we recognize not only man's place in Nature but his commerce with Nature for good and ill for many thousands of years, we cannot

Helen Hirata, the only junior college valedictorian included in *Orations and Essays*, was born and raised in San Bernardino, California. She was friendly, outgoing and loved to dance and sing. She went to the University of California, Berkeley and studied languages, particularly French. According to her sister, because Hirata was of Japanese heritage and female, finding meaningful employment after college was virtually impossible. Even though her test scores were high, she was not able to get a civil service job. Although she was a college graduate, she attended Healds College for secretarial training and worked for a lawyer. She also earned extra income as a ghostwriter before World War II.

Hirata was interned in Poston, Arizona and taught high school Latin, Spanish, typing and shorthand in

but discern some way-posts and danger signals. Man transcends Nature, but he has much to learn from her ways.

The voices of Nature have no audible sound; yet they resonate all over the world. There are many voices of Nature, but those in which we are interested are those which point the way towards a successful future.

When the Hebrew poet first listened to the voices of Nature, he heard the wind—a symbol of appeal to the practical side of man. What it says to us is, "Struggle. Endeavor. Push!" Everyone is familiar with the rather trite old saying, "He pushed his way to success." That phrase always recalls to my mind the story of a certain college professor who was to address a graduating class. To reach the stage he had to pass through a door which was labeled "Push." Using this as the text of his address he said, "In one word you will find the true secret of success," and so saying he pointed to the door on the inner side of which was emblazoned the word "Pull." Such embarrassing situations are usually attributed to be characteristic of the absent-minded professor, but his philosophy of success is that which the first voice of Nature expresses to us in innumerable ways—through the wind which pushes its way through the valleys and forests, the wind that tells the sailor when to furl and unfurl his sails, and through the little shoot that pushes its way through the solid cement out into the life-giving sunshine. All through the ages it is the men who have heeded this first voice of Nature and "pushed" ahead who have realized their hopes and ambitions. What is worth gaining is worth striving for, and the training that we have received and are going to receive in the years to come will enable us to push. In some ways this is the loudest voice of Nature—for it is the voice of the struggle of existence.

The second voice of Nature is to be found in the singing of the birds, the blossoming of the flowers, and in the passing of a fleecy cloud across the azure sky. It is the voice that is forever urging us to reach for the highest things in life. It tells us to "Enjoy, wonder, and inquire." We are led to wonder about every little thing that we enjoy. Wonder is of human value in arousing curiosity and in stimulating thought. Every cloud is a challenge to science, prompting inquiry. One of the reasons that we should listen to this second voice of Nature which says so insistently, "Wonder, enjoy, inquire," is that thereby we come to a better understanding of man's place in the world. It is the voice that tells man to enter more and more fully into the life of the world.

camp. She was also the advisor to the senior class. After the war ended, she moved to Los Angeles and worked for the War Relocation Authority, helping Japanese Americans released from the camps find housing and jobs. She later worked for the State of California in the Department of Human Resources for decades and passed away in 1983 before she was ready to retire. Hirata appreciated the creative arts, visiting museums and attending plays and musical productions. She also enjoyed traveling and fine dining.

The third voice of Nature is well known to those who have attended this institution of learning. It is the voice that tells us to serve. The voice of service is that voice through which Nature expresses her regard for man. Through the stalks of golden corn in the fields, through the brightly colored fruit that grows on the trees, through the luscious grapes that hang on the vine, comes to us the most compelling of all of Nature's voices: "Serve." Those of us who have been permitted to withdraw for several years of sequestered study must not forget those who were working to make it possible for us to become, as Emerson put it, "the favorites of heaven in earth, the excellency of our country and the happiest of men." Aye, even were there no questions of duty to our parents, to our professors and to our community, our lives should shower into service from sheerest gratitude for the opportunities given us thus far. The luscious fruits of Nature are no more a matter of ornament than the heed to Nature's call of service a matter of sentiment. Scholarship is a trust, and woe to the steward who turns a miser. The proper pursuit of place and fortune is most laudable, but it is the end in view that gives character to the man and his work. If place and fortune do not sway him, if success means wider service, then life itself becomes a holy thing.

Let us therefore heed the voices of Nature. First, let us push ahead toward the fulfillment of our ambitions. Let us perform our tasks in a way which will exceed all previous attempts, for true progress towards any end comes only as an improvement upon the things that we want to do. Let us also heed the second voice which urges us to seek the highest thing in life, to seek facts, and, to look ahead. Let the first two voices of Nature abide in our hearts, but let the voice of service become so integral a part of ourselves that every fiber of our bodies reacts to its call. For only in forgetting ourselves and dedicating ourselves to a life of service in whatever branch of life's work we may select, can we ever pay back our debt to our community, to our teachers, and to our parents.

# The Simplified Calendar

Charlotte Shimidzu (1914–1981). *Courtesy of Marie Nakamura.*

**CHARLOTTE SHIMIDZU**
*Lafayette Junior High School, June 1928*
*Los Angeles, California*

ALL CHILDREN KNOW the convenient old rhyme for telling the number of days in a month:

> Thirty days hath September,
> April, June and November
> February twenty-eight
> Thirty-one the others rate.

How did the world ever come to have such an unsympathetic arrangement for keeping the records of time?

The purpose of a calendar is to arrange in advance what days shall be Sundays, work days and holidays; to measure and to register the passage of days throughout the year. Neither the length of the year or day can be altered, as these units are astronomically fixed.

The present calendar had its origin in the calendar devised by the Egyptians. It was developed through years of study of the length and direction of the noon-day shadows cast by the pyramids. It is now thought that they were built for that purpose. The Egyptians determined that the true length of the year was 365.242 days, and they divided it into twelve months of thirty days each. The five extra days (or six days in leap years) were devoted to festivals. The month was divided into three ten day periods.

After the conquest of Egypt in 46 B.C., Julius Caesar adopted the Egyptian calendar for the Roman Empire, except that he distributed

Charlotte Shimidzu was born and raised in Los Angeles. She was the elder sister of Lincoln Shimidzu, a Nisei also in this book. After high school Shimidzu attended Chapman College, majoring in sociology. She then attended the University of Southern California where she earned a masters degree in sociology. After graduation she relocated to Hawaii to accept a job with the YWCA in Honolulu.

In 1942 after the United States entered World War II, she married Michael Ikehara. Meanwhile, her parents and siblings in California were put in concentration camps. In 1943 she gave birth to her first son and eventually had two more sons and one daughter. Later she earned a teaching degree from the University of Hawaii and became a teacher. She chose teaching so that her work schedule would coincide with her children's school hours,

the five extra days to every other month, because odd numbers were supposed to be lucky, and took one day off of February.

The Julian calendar was based upon a 356.234 days with leap year every four years. As the actual year is 365.242 days, .008 of a day was accumulated. By 1582 the accumulation had amounted to 10 days, and Pope Gregory in that year ordered the ten days from October 5 to October 15 dropped from the calendar, and adopted the present rule for leap year.

Of late the magazines have published articles upon "The Thirteen Month Year," and lecturers have been explaining it throughout the world.

Do not get excited, boys and girls. It does not mean another month of vacation.

From 185 calendar suggestions from thirty-eight nations, the League of Nations' Committees of Inquiry selected two proposals to establish a thirteen-month year. A new month would be inserted between June and July. The 365th day would be December 29, to be known as "Year Day" inserted between Saturday, December 28, and Sunday, January 1. In Leap Year the extra day, July 29, would be placed between Saturday, June 28, and Sunday, the first day of the new month.

Some of the advantages of the simplified calendar are:

Pay days would recur on the monthly date, which is an advantage, both to business and home life. Holidays and other permanent monthly dates would always occur on the same weekday. All holidays could be placed on Monday, and Easter could be fixed. The reckoning of the lapse of time for interest and other purposes would be greatly simplified.

Few reforms come as quickly as reformers would like to have them, but it is true, as Tennyson says, that many times—

"The old order changeth yielding to the new."

so she could spend more time with her family. She was employed as a teacher for twenty-three years and pursued her interests in music and art. After retirement, she enjoyed traveling and attending symphonies and plays.

# New Clues to
the Mayan Riddle

**LINCOLN SHIMIDZU**
*Lafayette Junior High School, February 1930*
*Los Angeles, California*

Lincoln Shimidzu (1916–1999) *Courtesy of Marie Nakamura.*

SOARING OVER the tropical jungles of Central America, the man who has become the living symbol of one of the latest phases in human progress looked down upon the crumbling remnants of the oldest American civilization.

In twenty-four hours of flying over Honduras, Guatemala and Yucatan, Colonel Lindbergh accompanied by Mrs. Lindbergh and scientists of the Carnegie Institute of Washington, D.C., discovered the ruined cities of the Ancient Mayan Empire of 613 B.C. which could not have been reached by land in five years.

Once more Lindbergh had played the part of the trailblazer. A few years ago the famous aviator, on his superb flight over the Atlantic, linked two continents. On his recent survey, made at the close of a journey with which he opened the West Indies–South American airmail route, he established the initial aerial link between the present and the past. This was the first major expedition ever undertaken by air. The new method proved so successful that many others are certain to follow.

From the cabin of his big amphibian, Colonel Lindbergh and his passengers saw the photographed columns of white rising from the jungle growth. They saw the decaying walls of majestic temples, remains of stately pyramids and a group of twenty-five lofty buildings. In all, they found the ruins of what centuries ago were four beautiful cities. It is believed that of these four, three have never

Lincoln Shimidzu, younger brother of Charlotte Shimidzu, was born and raised in Los Angeles. He loved to sing, was often a soloist in the church choir and was very artistic. After he graduated from high school, he went to the University of California, Berkeley and majored in agricultural economics. After graduation he went into the U.S. Army but following the Pearl Harbor attacks, he was released because of his ancestry.

He was incarcerated in Rohwer, Arkansas with his parents and sisters. While imprisoned, he married Mary Fujita in April 1943. He left the detention center in October that year and went to Chicago. After a difficult time, he finally found housing near the University of Chicago and worked at a wholesale drug chain. He was then able to bring his bride out of camp.

been seen by white men. Further investigation of the Lindbergh discoveries will, archeologists hope, shed new light upon the mystery of the Mayas who ruled Central America for centuries before enterprising Europeans, in quest of gold and power, discovered the "New World."

Much of the history and evidence of their amazing culture have come to light in recent years, principally through the efforts: of Dr. H. J. Spinden, curator of Ethnology of the Brooklyn Museum and formally connected with the Peabody Museum and Harvard University; Dr. Sylvanus G. Morley and other scientists of the Carnegie Institution; Thomas W. F. Gann, the British archeologist; and Gregory Mason, American journalist-explorer. But the investigators are well aware that their present knowledge forms but a fraction of what remains unknown.

Step by step, along trails of remains, science has been able to trace the Egyptians back to the earliest and crudest beginnings. But not the Mayas. They might have dropped down from Mars or other planets.

What disaster befell this ancient race, that was sturdy in body and keen in mind? Did it fall victim to a civil war? Did its food supply give out? Experts say that yellow fever had much to do with it, but nobody really knows. Should the finds of Lindbergh and the "tomb of the kings" at Chichén Itzá tell the answer to the riddle of their origin, another problem might be solved.

The Mayas were the Greeks of the West. They were the inventors of skyscrapers which showed that they were architects of extraordinary ability.

In the art of painting and sculpture they are considered superior to the Egyptians. Their extraordinary system of hieroglyphics was more complicated than the Roman and Greek alphabet and as serviceable as the Egyptians' system.

The Mayan population consisted of about 14,000,000 prosperous people, of whom a few thousand poor and ignorant Indians are left as descendants.

The Mayas were also good business men and artisans. Along trade routes compared with those of the ancient Phoenicians and Sumerians, Mayan merchants imported pearls from Colombia and turquoise from distant Mexico and exported their pottery and textiles in exchange.

As agriculturalists, the Mayas surpassed the Europeans. To them the world owes its corn, potatoes, sweet potatoes, lima and kidney beans, cocoa, cotton, tobacco and many other fruits and vegetables.

According to his sister, he was a "quiet, low-key person," but showed great compassion and concern for others. A few years after leaving the Rohwer camp, he began to help other Japanese Americans who came to Chicago from the detention centers.

In the 1960s he was president of the Japanese American Citizens League and from 1957 to 1967 the Japanese American Citizens League Credit Union. He also served as board chair of a social welfare and community organization for Japanese Americans and on the board of a group working to preserve Japanese culture. An avid golfer, he was president of a golf club and member for thirty years. After forty years in Chicago, he returned to Southern California and settled in Gardena where he passed away at the age of eighty-two.

Also a number of medical goods such as quinine, cocaine and cascara sagrade. They were the first planters of rubber and discoverers of chicle, the base of chewing gum. The Mayas were up-to-date in their domestic arrangements. A "clean up week" was inaugurated similar to the Japanese New Year tradition. For thirteen days every Maya was compelled to clean and repaint his house and clean his furniture and household utensils. The women of the Mayan Empire did most of the farm work, as they had no draft animals to work with.

In sports the Mayas played a game similar to tennis in which a ball was knocked back and forth across a court with a racquet.

The Mayas were undoubtedly the best astronomers of their time. They worshiped several gods. They had a system of priesthood and sisterhood in which the members were pledged. They were peace loving and their cities were not fortified.

In the 16th century the Spaniards who "discovered" the strange Mayan country and its people were also religious in the extreme. Unfortunately Spanish priests destroyed most of the ancient lore in trying to stamp out the Mayan works.

Only three books survived the bonfires of the old Spanish Padres. From these and Mayan inscriptions science has pieced together a story as fascinating and romantic as any of the histories of the human race.

Several chapters of this story are missing. Perhaps Colonel Lindbergh's discoveries and those of the Mexican archeologists will provide the world with information of the mystery of the Mayas' origin and tragic passing.

# Mahatma Gandhi

**DOROTHY CHIYE YOSHIDA**
*Sweetwater High School, February 1932*
*National City, California*

Dorothy Chiye Yoshida (b. 1914) in the 1932 Sweetwater High School yearbook, *Red & Gray. Courtesy of the National City Public Library, California.*

AT THE ROUNDTABLE CONFERENCE held in London last fall, interest was centered in a singular little man, Mahatma Gandhi. He is one of the most forceful, picturesque, and influential personalities in the world today; a leader who has achieved a greater following than that of any living man. The bare-legged Mahatma, clad in loin cloth, with his spinning wheel, who holds the fate of 350,000,000 people in his frail hands, what is he? To one group of extremists he is just a half-naked fanatic and a virulent anti-British agitator; to another, he is a saint who can do no wrong. To the third group, who try to see him with unprejudiced eyes, he seems a man of sincerity and great courage, deeply concerned for the poor and the oppressed.

Throughout the world, this man and his meaning are eagerly discussed, and nowhere with greater eagerness than here in the United States.

Mohandas Karamchand Gandhi was born in the northwestern part of India in 1869. His family belonged to the third or the merchant caste, and were followers of the Jain faith, a branch of Hinduism which requires a doctrine of non-injury to any form of life as one of its basic principles.

As a boy, he went to the village school and according to the orthodox Hindu custom, was engaged at eight years of age and at thirteen, was married to the woman who remained his devoted partner for nearly fifty years.

Dorothy Yoshida was born in Santa Ana, California and grew up in Orange County, California. She was valedictorian of her high school and chose the topic for her speech. Mahatma Gandhi was "very much in the news" at that time, so Yoshida wrote about him. When the 1932 edition of *Orations and Essays* came out, she was very disappointed with the printing of her oration because she had accidentally submitted a draft that still had errors. She was very happy to correct the mistakes for this new book.

After high school she helped on her father's farm until she married Tsuneshiko Morioka in 1936. They had two daughters. The family was incarcerated in Poston, Arizona and after the war they came back to Los Angeles. She modestly admits her only accomplishment in life was that she "raised two daughters."

At nineteen, he went to the University of London to study law. Upon his return to India in 1891 there occurred the event that was to be the turning point in his life. He was invited by a Hindu firm to conduct a case for them in South Africa where some 150,000 Indian immigrants were settled principally in Natal. The white population resented their presence and the government passed a series of oppressive measures designed to prevent the immigration of Asiatics, and to oblige those already there to leave.

Thus began an epic struggle between spiritual power on one side and governmental power and brute force on the other. He founded a settlement in the open country near Durban and placed the Indian people on the land. The Indians withdrew from the industries in the cities, gradually paralyzing the industry of the country. In this way, he tested his doctrine of nonviolent resistance which was to be carried out on a much larger scale in his own native land. Finally after twenty years of suffering and self-sacrifice, the long and bitter struggle ended in a victory for Gandhi and the repeal of the oppressive measures. When Gandhi returned to India, he had the prestige of a leader.

What the Mahatma attempted and achieved in South Africa, great as it was, shrinks into insignificance in the light of his later nonviolent, noncooperative campaigns against the British Empire in India.

Since the beginning of the twentieth century, the movement for Indian independence has been gaining ground. In 1918 when promised reforms were not granted to them, the natives revolted. Gandhi became their leader. It should be noted that when Gandhi stepped into the political field as a leader, it was only from a desire to spare the country from violence. The revolt was bound to come. He knew there was no possibility of avoiding it; and the point, therefore, was to turn it into nonviolent channels. The conviction that the British rule worked for the good of the Indian people was definitely discarded by Gandhi after the massacre at Amritsar in 1919.

Straightaway, he began to work for a boycott of the English government. Noncooperation meant the surrender of all titles and honorary offices, settling of disputes outside of British courts, boycotts of schools and all English goods. All this must be carried out without lifting a finger in violence. For the first time, all classes of India united in the same ideal. Gandhi had awakened the national consciousness in a way that no other man could.

His nonviolent resistance is based on a vast and unshakable foundation of religion. He became a political leader only through necessity to give practical political expression to his religious doctrine. He endeavored to teach his people the doctrine of returning love, not violence, for evil. Gandhi maintained that self-rule can be attained only by "soul-force." This is India's real weapon.

If cooperation with England ceased, on what would India live? With what would she clothe herself? Gandhi's solution was simple. He undertook to establish the old Indian industry of home spinning. In order to raise the economic level of the Indian people, cloth must be produced at home not with the use of modern machinery where millions are left out of work but with the ancient spinning wheel in every home. Thus Gandhi hoped to achieve a complete boycott of foreign cloth. Today spinning and weaving bid fair to take their places once again as the popular industries of India.

In 1921, Gandhi's power was great. His authority as a moral leader was widely recognized and almost unlimited political power was placed in his hands. When Gandhi proclaimed civil disobedience in 1921 by refusing to pay taxes, violence broke out in Chauri Chaura. He immediately suspended his campaign, refusing to go on and thereby disappointing many of his more radical followers. In spite of his efforts to curb violence, a number of riots occurred. Noncooperation, his weapon of peaceful defense, disappointed him because India could not attain the ascetic spiritual level of his vision and dominant will.

Soon after these events Gandhi was arrested and accused of preaching disaffection toward the British government. He pleaded guilty to all charges and was sentenced to six years in prison.

Because of illness, he was released two years later in 1924. He abandoned the political field to other and lesser men and devoted himself to the task of spiritual regeneration of his people and to the many social and economic problems of his country. At this period, Gandhi became what he had been, in essence, from the beginning: a religious teacher. He believes in the religion of his people, Hinduism. However, he does not consider it the only religion. His most characteristic remark is, "In my religion, there's room for Krishna, Christ, Buddha, and Mohammed." "Mahatma" is a title given to him by the Indian people, meaning a "great Soul." As a religious leader, he comes nearer to St. Francis of Assisi perhaps than to any other.

Gandhi wants his people to shake off the yoke of western civilization and lay down a foundation of truly Indian culture. He declares the modern civilization has set material well-being as the only goal of life, scorning spiritual values. Thus he endeavors to

create a really independent, Indian spirit. As a result of the muddle
over the Simon Commission in preparing for a revision of the Indian
Constitution, and the failure of England to grant India Dominion
Status, Gandhi returned again to the political field in 1929 and led
the people, reviving noncooperation. He renewed his civil disobedience by marching 165 miles to the sea and making free salt. Thus he
defied the British government's tax on salt. Two months later, in
May, 1930, he was arrested and imprisoned.

Finally a temporary truce was signed on March 4, 1931 and
Gandhi was released from jail. He suspended the civil disobedience
campaign and consented to represent the nationalist party at the
Round Table Conference on India in the fall of 1931.

If today, the masses of India follow him with intense devotion,
it is because they see him as a leader who not only has merged himself with their ambitions but also lives and suffers as they live and
suffer, since he allows himself no more clothing nor better food
than the poorest outcast can afford.

He is a small frail man of 62, weighing less than 100 pounds. He
literally eats only to live, his food consisting of goat's milk, fruit and
nuts. There is nothing ridiculous about him in spite of his peculiar
costume; there is too much true dignity in him to allow any specta-
tor to retain the impression that he is a ridiculous figure. A modest
and unassuming man, his chief characteristics are his utter simplicity
and unaffectedness. He begins and ends the day with one hour of
prayer and meditation. One day every week he keeps complete
silence, not broken under any circumstances. He is and looks an
ascetic, but there is nothing gloomy or funereal about him. He has
a keen sense of humor and a spontaneous laugh. This is the man who
has stirred over 300 million people to revolt, and who has shaken
the foundation of the British Empire in India.

Gandhi had come to the Indian Round Table Conference with
intentions of working for complete independence for India. The
Mahatma's dream of an independent India is not to come true for
the time being at least for the conference adjourned December 1
after having failed to reach an agreement. Upon his return from
England, he found his country in turmoil. He was arrested again for
renewing his noncooperation movement on January 4. His arrest
aroused great resentment in the Indian people and it remains to be
seen how this Indian problem will be solved.

India was floundering in the morass of her own traditions when
Gandhi came. Out of these he has organized a coherent doctrine

and a forward movement. He has brought to light the true desires of the people of India; he is their greatest leader. Whether or not he attains his ideal, he will take his place in history as the creator of the Indian nation that shall eventually emerge!

Dorothy Yoshida Morioka celebrated her 88th birthday in 2002. *Courtesy of Dorothy Yoshida.*

# APPENDICES

# Statistics and Original Materials

Toshio Yamagata's father, Kichizo Yamagata,
and mother, Tsune, in a 1918 portrait in
California with their sons (left to right)
Haruo, Shunji, Goro (standing on stool),
Jiro and Toshio. *Courtesy of Jeannette
Sanderson.*

# Appendix A

## 50 STUDENTS SORTED ALPHABETICALLY BY NAME

| Student | Speech Topic | School | City | Page |
|---|---|---|---|---|
| John Fujio Aiso | U.S. Government | Hollywood H.S. | Los Angeles | 191 |
| Florence Akiyama | Education | Sanger H.S. | Sanger | 107 |
| Mary Fukuye Asada | Other | Selma H.S. | Selma | 221 |
| Fujio Frank Chuman | Graduation | Los Angeles H.S. | Los Angeles | 133 |
| Chizuko Doi | Women | Edison Technical H.S. | Fresno | 213 |
| Kozue Fujikawa | Japan | John Burroughs Junior H.S. | Burbank | 173 |
| Doris Fujisawa | Olympics | Audubon Junior H.S. | Los Angeles | 185 |
| Haruko Fujita | Japan | Arcadia Grammar School | Arcadia | 175 |
| Hidemitsu Ginoza | U.S. Government | Fowler H.S. | Fowler | 194 |
| Jimmie Chikao Hamasaki | Graduation | Santa Maria Union H.S. | Santa Maria | 135 |
| James Hajime Hashimoto | Education | Long Beach Polytechnic H.S. | Long Beach | 110 |
| Yoshiko Higuchi | Women | Monterey Union H.S. | Monterey | 216 |
| Thomas Hirashima | U.S. Government | Carpinteria H.S. | Carpinteria | 198 |
| Helen H. Hirata | Other | San Bernardino Junior College | San Bernardino | 224 |
| Matilde Sumiko Honda | Education | Brawley Union H.S. | Brawley | 112 |
| Ayame Ichiyasu | Graduation | San Francisco H.S. of Commerce | San Francisco | 137 |
| George J. Inagaki | California | Sacramento H.S. | Sacramento | 95 |
| Charles Inouye | Graduation | Sequoia H.S. | Redwood City | 139 |
| Shizu Komae | Japan | Lafayette Junior H.S. | Los Angeles | 177 |
| Pearl Kurokawa | Graduation | Arroyo Grande Union H.S. | Arroyo Grande | 143 |
| Helen S. Kuwada | Graduation | San Martin Grammar School | San Martin | 146 |
| Mitsue Matsumune | Graduation | Salinas Central Grammar School | Salinas | 148 |
| Mary Toshiko Miyamoto | California | Clovis Union H.S. | Clovis | 99 |
| Kiyoshi Murakami | U.S. Government | Gardena H.S. | Gardena | 201 |
| Goro Murata | U.S. Government | Montebello H.S. | Montebello | 204 |
| Yoshimi U. Nagayama | U.S. Government | Gardena H.S. | Gardena | 206 |
| Michiko Naito | Graduation | Lovell Grammar School | Orosi | 150 |
| Jimmy Nakamura | Education | Jefferson H.S. | Los Angeles | 117 |
| Joe Masao Nakanishi | Graduation | Alhambra Union H.S. | Martinez | 152 |
| George Nishida | Graduation | Dinuba Grand View School | Dinuba | 154 |
| Kiyoshi Nobusada | International Relations | Hanford Union H.S. | Hanford | 161 |
| Shizue Ohashi | Olympics | Canoga Park H.S. | Canoga Park | 187 |
| Ayami Onaka | Leisure | Fowler H.S. | Fowler | 179 |
| Sakaye Saiki | Graduation | Katella School | Anaheim | 156 |
| Kazuya Sanada | Education | University H.S. | West Los Angeles | 121 |
| Yukiko Sanwo | Education | Kerman H.S. | Kerman | 123 |
| Akiko Sawada | Graduation | San Juan Grammar School | San Juan Bautista | 158 |
| Ida Ikuye Shimanouchi | International Relations | McKinley Junior H.S. | Pasadena | 165 |
| Charlotte Shimidzu | Other | Lafayette Junior H.S. | Los Angeles | 227 |
| Lincoln Shimidzu | Other | Lafayette Junior H.S. | Los Angeles | 229 |
| Roku Sugahara | U.S. Government | Manual Arts H.S. | Los Angeles | 209 |
| Jimmie Tabata | International Relations | Monterey Union H.S. | Monterey | 167 |
| George S. Takaoka | California | Clovis Union H.S. | Clovis | 101 |
| Toshio Yamagata | Leisure | Fowler H.S. | Fowler | 182 |
| Frank K. Yamakoshi | Graduation | Gilroy H.S. | Gilroy | 159 |
| Norio Yasaki | Education | Foshay Junior H.S. | Los Angeles | 126 |
| Dorothy Chiye Yoshida | Other | Sweetwater H.S. | National City | 232 |
| Michiko Yoshihashi | International Relations | Thomas Starr King Junior H.S. | Los Angeles | 170 |
| Kameko Yoshioka | Education | Edison Technical H.S. | Fresno | 129 |
| Katsumi Yoshizumi | California | San Pedro H.S. | San Pedro | 104 |

## Students Sorted by School—42 Schools

| School | Student | Speech Topic | City | Page |
|---|---|---|---|---|
| Alhambra Union H.S. | Joe Masao Nakanishi | Graduation | Martinez | 152 |
| Arcadia Grammar School | Haruko Fujita | Japan | Arcadia | 175 |
| Arroyo Grande Union H.S. | Pearl Kurokawa | Graduation | Arroyo Grande | 143 |
| Audubon Junior H.S. | Doris Fujisawa | Olympics | Los Angeles | 185 |
| Brawley Union H.S. | Matilde Sumiko Honda | Education | Brawley | 112 |
| Canoga Park H.S. | Shizue Ohashi | Olympics | Canoga Park | 187 |
| Carpinteria H.S. | Thomas Hirashima | U.S. Government | Carpinteria | 198 |
| Clovis Union H.S. | Mary Toshiko Miyamoto | California | Clovis | 99 |
| Clovis Union H.S. | George S. Takaoka | California | Clovis | 101 |
| Dinuba Grand View School | George Nishida | Graduation | Dinuba | 154 |
| Edison Technical H.S. | Chizuko Doi | Women | Fresno | 213 |
| Edison Technical H.S. | Kameko Yoshioka | Education | Fresno | 129 |
| Foshay Junior H.S. | Norio Yasaki | Education | Los Angeles | 126 |
| Fowler H.S. | Hidemitsu Ginoza | U.S. Government | Fowler | 194 |
| Fowler H.S. | Ayami Onaka | Leisure | Fowler | 179 |
| Fowler H.S. | Toshio Yamagata | Leisure | Fowler | 182 |
| Gardena H.S. | Kiyoshi Murakami | U.S. Government | Gardena | 201 |
| Gardena H.S. | Yoshimi U. Nagayama | U.S. Government | Gardena | 206 |
| Gilroy H.S. | Frank K. Yamakoshi | Graduation | Gilroy | 159 |
| Hanford Union H.S. | Kiyoshi Nobusada | International Relations | Hanford | 161 |
| Hollywood H.S. | John Fujio Aiso | U.S. Government | Los Angeles | 191 |
| Jefferson H.S. | Jimmy Nakamura | Education | Los Angeles | 117 |
| John Burroughs Junior H.S. | Kozue Fujikawa | Japan | Burbank | 173 |
| Katella School | Sakaye Saiki | Graduation | Anaheim | 156 |
| Kerman H.S. | Yukiko Sanwo | Education | Kerman | 123 |
| Lafayette Junior H.S. | Shizu Komae | Japan | Los Angeles | 177 |
| Lafayette Junior H.S. | Charlotte Shimidzu | Other | Los Angeles | 227 |
| Lafayette Junior H.S. | Lincoln Shimidzu | Other | Los Angeles | 229 |
| Long Beach Polytechnic H.S. | James Hajime Hashimoto | Education | Long Beach | 110 |
| Los Angeles H.S. | Fujio Frank Chuman | Graduation | Los Angeles | 133 |
| Lovell Grammar School | Michiko Naito | Graduation | Orosi | 150 |
| Manual Arts H.S. | Roku Sugahara | U.S. Government | Los Angeles | 209 |
| McKinley Junior H.S. | Ida Ikuye Shimanouchi | International Relations | Pasadena | 165 |
| Montebello H.S. | Goro Murata | U.S. Government | Montebello | 204 |
| Monterey Union H.S. | Yoshiko Higuchi | Women | Monterey | 216 |
| Monterey Union H.S. | Jimmie Tabata | International Relations | Monterey | 167 |
| Sacramento H.S. | George J. Inagaki | California | Sacramento | 95 |
| Salinas Central Grammar School | Mitsue Matsumune | Graduation | Salinas | 148 |
| San Bernardino Junior College | Helen H. Hirata | Other | San Bernardino | 224 |
| San Francisco H.S. of Commerce | Ayame Ichiyasu | Graduation | San Francisco | 137 |
| San Juan Grammar School | Akiko Sawada | Graduation | San Juan Bautista | 158 |
| San Martin Grammar School | Helen S. Kuwada | Graduation | San Martin | 146 |
| San Pedro H.S. | Katsumi Yoshizumi | California | San Pedro | 104 |
| Sanger H.S. | Florence Akiyama | Education | Sanger | 107 |
| Santa Maria Union H.S. | Jimmie Chikao Hamasaki | Graduation | Santa Maria | 135 |
| Selma H.S. | Mary Fukuye Asada | Other | Selma | 221 |
| Sequoia H.S. | Charles Inouye | Graduation | Redwood City | 139 |
| Sweetwater H.S. | Dorothy Chiye Yoshida | Other | National City | 232 |
| Thomas Starr King Junior H.S. | Michiko Yoshihashi | International Relations | Los Angeles | 170 |
| University H.S. | Kazuya Sanada | Education | West Los Angeles | 121 |

## STUDENTS SORTED BY CITY IN CALIFORNIA—35 CITIES

| City | Student | Speech Topic | School | Page |
|------|---------|--------------|--------|------|
| Anaheim | Sakaye Saiki | Graduation | Katella School | 156 |
| Arcadia | Haruko Fujita | Japan | Arcadia Grammar School | 175 |
| Arroyo Grande | Pearl Kurokawa | Graduation | Arroyo Grande Union H.S. | 143 |
| Brawley | Matilde Sumiko Honda | Education | Brawley Union H.S. | 112 |
| Burbank | Kozue Fujikawa | Japan | John Burroughs Junior H.S. | 173 |
| Canoga Park | Shizue Ohashi | Olympics | Canoga Park H.S. | 187 |
| Carpinteria | Thomas Hirashima | U.S. Government | Carpinteria H.S. | 198 |
| Clovis | Mary Toshiko Miyamoto | California | Clovis Union H.S. | 99 |
| Clovis | George S. Takaoka | California | Clovis Union H.S. | 101 |
| Dinuba | George Nishida | Graduation | Dinuba Grand View School | 154 |
| Fowler | Hidemitsu Ginoza | U.S. Government | Fowler H.S. | 194 |
| Fowler | Ayami Onaka | Leisure | Fowler H.S. | 179 |
| Fowler | Toshio Yamagata | Leisure | Fowler H.S. | 182 |
| Fresno | Chizuko Doi | Women | Edison Technical H.S. | 213 |
| Fresno | Kameko Yoshioka | Education | Edison Technical H.S. | 129 |
| Gardena | Kiyoshi Murakami | U.S. Government | Gardena H.S. | 201 |
| Gardena | Yoshimi U. Nagayama | U.S. Government | Gardena H.S. | 206 |
| Gilroy | Frank K. Yamakoshi | Graduation | Gilroy H.S. | 159 |
| Hanford | Kiyoshi Nobusada | International Relations | Hanford Union H.S. | 161 |
| Kerman | Yukiko Sanwo | Education | Kerman H.S. | 123 |
| Long Beach | James Hajime Hashimoto | Education | Long Beach Polytechnic H.S. | 110 |
| Los Angeles | John Fujio Aiso | U.S. Government | Hollywood H.S. | 191 |
| Los Angeles | Fujio Frank Chuman | Graduation | Los Angeles H.S. | 133 |
| Los Angeles | Doris Fujisawa | Olympics | Audubon Junior H.S. | 185 |
| Los Angeles | Shizu Komae | Japan | Lafayette Junior H.S. | 177 |
| Los Angeles | Jimmy Nakamura | Education | Jefferson H.S. | 117 |
| Los Angeles | Charlotte Shimidzu | Other | Lafayette Junior H.S. | 227 |
| Los Angeles | Lincoln Shimidzu | Other | Lafayette Junior H.S. | 229 |
| Los Angeles | Roku Sugahara | U.S. Government | Manual Arts H.S. | 209 |
| Los Angeles | Norio Yasaki | Education | Foshay Junior H.S. | 126 |
| Los Angeles | Michiko Yoshihashi | International Relations | Thomas Starr King Junior H.S. | 170 |
| Martinez | Joe Masao Nakanishi | Graduation | Alhambra Union H.S. | 152 |
| Montebello | Goro Murata | U.S. Government | Montebello H.S. | 204 |
| Monterey | Yoshiko Higuchi | Women | Monterey Union H.S. | 216 |
| Monterey | Jimmie Tabata | International Relations | Monterey Union H.S. | 167 |
| National City | Dorothy Chiye Yoshida | Other | Sweetwater H.S. | 232 |
| Orosi | Michiko Naito | Graduation | Lovell Grammar School | 150 |
| Pasadena | Ida Ikuye Shimanouchi | International Relations | McKinley Junior H.S. | 165 |
| Redwood City | Charles Inouye | Graduation | Sequoia H.S. | 139 |
| Sacramento | George J. Inagaki | California | Sacramento H.S. | 95 |
| Salinas | Mitsue Matsumune | Graduation | Salinas Central Grammar School | 148 |
| San Bernardino | Helen H. Hirata | Other | San Bernardino Junior College | 224 |
| San Francisco | Ayame Ichiyasu | Graduation | San Francisco H.S. of Commerce | 137 |
| San Juan Bautista | Akiko Sawada | Graduation | San Juan Grammar School | 158 |
| San Martin | Helen S. Kuwada | Graduation | San Martin Grammar School | 146 |
| San Pedro | Katsumi Yoshizumi | California | San Pedro H.S. | 104 |
| Sanger | Florence Akiyama | Education | Sanger H.S. | 107 |
| Santa Maria | Jimmie Chikao Hamasaki | Graduation | Santa Maria Union H.S. | 135 |
| Selma | Mary Fukuye Asada | Other | Selma H.S. | 221 |
| West Los Angeles | Kazuya Sanada | Education | University H.S. | 121 |

## STUDENTS SORTED BY YEAR (1923–1939)

| Year | Student | Speech Topic | School | Page |
|---|---|---|---|---|
| 1923 | John Fujio Aiso | U.S. Government | Hollywood H.S. | 191 |
| 1926 | Goro Murata | U.S. Government | Montebello H.S. | 204 |
| 1927 | Jimmy Nakamura | Education | Jefferson H.S. | 117 |
| 1928 | Charlotte Shimidzu | Other | Lafayette Junior H.S. | 227 |
| 1928 | Norio Yasaki | Education | Foshay Junior H.S. | 126 |
| 1930 | Lincoln Shimidzu | Other | Lafayette Junior H.S. | 229 |
| 1930 | Roku Sugahara | U.S. Government | Manual Arts H.S. | 209 |
| 1931 | Shizu Komae | Japan | Lafayette Junior H.S. | 177 |
| 1932 | Florence Akiyama | Education | Sanger H.S. | 107 |
| 1932 | Doris Fujisawa | Olympics | Audubon Junior H.S. | 185 |
| 1932 | Haruko Fujita | Japan | Arcadia Grammar School | 175 |
| 1932 | Hidemitsu Ginoza | U.S. Government | Fowler H.S. | 194 |
| 1932 | Yoshiko Higuchi | Women | Monterey Union H.S. | 216 |
| 1932 | Helen H. Hirata | Other | San Bernardino Junior College | 224 |
| 1932 | George J. Inagaki | California | Sacramento H.S. | 95 |
| 1932 | Charles Inouye | Graduation | Sequoia H.S. | 139 |
| 1932 | Pearl Kurokawa | Graduation | Arroyo Grande Union H.S. | 143 |
| 1932 | Mitsue Matsumune | Graduation | Salinas Central Grammar School | 148 |
| 1932 | Shizue Ohashi | Olympics | Canoga Park H.S. | 187 |
| 1932 | Sakaye Saiki | Graduation | Katella School | 156 |
| 1932 | Akiko Sawada | Graduation | San Juan Grammar School | 158 |
| 1932 | Ida Ikuye Shimanouchi | International Relations | McKinley Junior H.S. | 165 |
| 1932 | Frank K. Yamakoshi | Graduation | Gilroy H.S. | 159 |
| 1932 | Dorothy Chiye Yoshida | Other | Sweetwater H.S. | 232 |
| 1932 | Michiko Yoshihashi | International Relations | Thomas Starr King Junior H.S. | 170 |
| 1932 | Kameko Yoshioka | Education | Edison Technical H.S. | 129 |
| 1932 | Katsumi Yoshizumi | California | San Pedro H.S. | 104 |
| 1933 | Mary Fukuye Asada | Other | Selma H.S. | 221 |
| 1933 | Kozue Fujikawa | Japan | John Burroughs Junior H.S. | 173 |
| 1933 | Thomas Hirashima | U.S. Government | Carpinteria H.S. | 198 |
| 1933 | Matilde Sumiko Honda | Education | Brawley Union H.S. | 112 |
| 1933 | Ayame Ichiyasu | Graduation | San Francisco H.S. of Commerce | 137 |
| 1933 | Helen S. Kuwada | Graduation | San Martin Grammar School | 146 |
| 1933 | Mary Toshiko Miyamoto | California | Clovis Union H.S. | 99 |
| 1933 | Ayami Onaka | Leisure | Fowler H.S. | 179 |
| 1933 | Yukiko Sanwo | Education | Kerman H.S. | 123 |
| 1933 | Jimmie Tabata | International Relations | Monterey Union H.S. | 167 |
| 1933 | George S. Takaoka | California | Clovis Union H.S. | 101 |
| 1933 | Toshio Yamagata | Leisure | Fowler H.S. | 182 |
| 1934 | Fujio Frank Chuman | Graduation | Los Angeles H.S. | 133 |
| 1934 | Chizuko Doi | Women | Edison Technical H.S. | 213 |
| 1934 | Jimmie Chikao Hamasaki | Graduation | Santa Maria Union H.S. | 135 |
| 1934 | James Hajime Hashimoto | Education | Long Beach Polytechnic H.S. | 110 |
| 1934 | Kiyoshi Murakami | U.S. Government | Gardena H.S. | 201 |
| 1934 | Yoshimi U. Nagayama | U.S. Government | Gardena H.S. | 206 |
| 1934 | Michiko Naito | Graduation | Lovell Grammar School | 150 |
| 1934 | George Nishida | Graduation | Dinuba Grand View School | 154 |
| 1934 | Kiyoshi Nobusada | International Relations | Hanford Union H.S. | 161 |
| 1935 | Kazuya Sanada | Education | University H.S. | 121 |
| 1939 | Joe Masao Nakanishi | Graduation | Alhambra Union H.S. | 152 |

# Appendix B

### ENGLISH TRANSLATION OF THE 1932 PREFACE
### OF *ORATIONS AND ESSAYS*

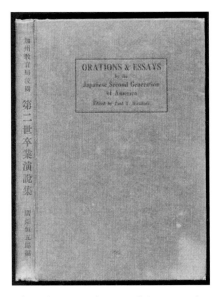

The red cover and spine of *Orations and Essays* with text printed in black ink. The English translation of the spine reads: *A Collection of Speeches by Nisei*, Compiled by Tsunegoro Hirohata, Reviewed by the California Department of Education.

## Preface

STUDENTS who deliver prestigious graduation speeches are restricted to those with exemplary conduct and excellence in scholarship. From amongst the Nisei who are studying together with the other nationalities, it is a pleasant phenomenon to note the increase in those who have been given the honor of presenting these speeches. As for myself, I did not have the opportunity to attend these auspicious graduation ceremonies this year, but in imagining these glorious moments, I could not help but feel a racial pride.

However, with the exception of a few people, many do not know what these Nisei spoke of or what thoughts were expounded at these graduation ceremonies. Therefore, I have felt it to be a worthy project to preserve these excellent orations and introduce them to the public so I have searched for these manuscripts and have come to publish this volume, *A Collection of Graduation Speeches by Nisei*.

Many of the essays contained in this book are useful as educational reference material in various ways. They are the product of individual endeavor coupled with suggestions from teachers and are rich in content. They are flawless from the standpoint of an oration. Also, since the speeches amply incorporate the feelings of the Nisei themselves, they serve as valuable research material about the second generation Japanese Americans.

I hope that this book will serve as reference material for the younger Nisei and act as a stimulant for study and mental cultivation. In publishing this book, my good friend Mr. Chikara Takeda rendered much assistance in collecting the material. I have imposed on Japanese Consul Satow, Mr. Shiro Fujioka, and Mr. Kersey with the California Department of Public Instruction in writing the prefaces. Mr. Toyosaku Komai, president of the *Rafu Shimpo*, assisted in every way in its publication. I am deeply grateful to all of these individuals for finalizing this book.

[Paul Tsunegoro Hirohata], Editor
October 1932

自 序

名譽の卒業演說をする學生は品行方正にして學力優等のものに限つてゐる、他國人種兒童と共に學ぶ第二世の中からこうした演說の榮譽を荷ふものが殖えるのは實に愉快な現象だ、自分としては今年一度々々の目出度い卒業式に列する機會はなかつたが、その名譽ある場面を想像するとき民族的の誇りを感ぜずに居られなかつた。

然し卒業式で第二世が何を語つたか如何なる思想を發表したか極く少数のものを除く外に知るものはない、私は此等の第二世の名論卓說を保存し未知の方々に紹介するのは意義のある事業と思つたのでその原稿を求め「第二世卒業演說集」とて公にするに至つた。

本書に收めてある論文は多岐に亘つて教育上の參考資料となるものが多い、自己の努力と先生達のサゼスションと相俟つて何れの論文も内容の充實を示してゐる、それらを演說の要素から見ても完全なものである、更に論文の中には第二世自身の氣分が充分に織り込まれてゐるので第二世の研究資料としても貴重なものである。

私は本書が後進の第二世への參考資料となり勉學の刺戟劑となり修養の友とならば幸ひと思つてゐる。本書を上梓するに當つて親友竹田力君は材料の蒐集に盡力して吳れた、序文に就ては佐藤領事、藤岡紫朗、加州教育局のカーシイ氏の諸氏を煩はした、出版に關しては羅府新報社長駒井豊策氏より一切の御助力を戴く、本書の完成に當つて諸氏に厚く謝する。

千九百三十二年十月

編  者  識

Paul Tsunegoro Hirohata's preface written in Japanese as it appeared in the 1932 edition of *Orations and Essays.*

## ENGLISH TRANSLATION OF THE 1935 PREFACE OF *ORATIONS AND ESSAYS*

### On the Publication of the Second Edition

WHEN this book was first published in November 1932, it received much praise from the intellectual community everywhere and it gave me much pleasure to learn that it was serving as educational material on the Nisei.

At present the Issei are sacrificing their all and are making every effort for the maximum development of the Nisei. All of the enterprises now held by the Issei must be eventually inherited by the Nisei, but if the Nisei are not possessed with self-awareness and sound will, it will be impossible to achieve a fulfillment of the foundation built by the Issei.

As a guiding principle for the development of Nisei as successors for our countrymen, there are two keys: first, the Nisei should be educated to be good American citizens and the other should be the cultivation of cultural awareness as a member of the Japanese race. Thus, the Nisei can fulfill their duties as Americans and it is certain that they can contribute greatly to the cultural harmony of Japan and the United States in the Pacific era. Fortunately, the Issei understand the position of the Nisei and are endeavoring in their development as good American citizens. This is demonstrated by the fact that the Nisei far excel the other nationalities in scholarship in the public schools and there are many distinguished students who are delivering prestigious graduation speeches.

This book has supplemented more recent speeches to the first edition with approximately twenty more manuscripts. Moreover, the idealism and emotion contained in the essays clearly reveal the Nisei's thoughts of the time and, as such, they constitute valuable documentation. When it is realized that these essays incorporate the sacrificial spirit and suggestions of parents and teachers, their value is extremely profound. In believing that by preserving these documents, they will serve as a reference and act as a stimulant for study by the younger Nisei, I have decided to supplement and republish this book.

In its republication, I wish to express my deepest appreciation for the kindness extended by the following people: Mr. Toyosaku Komai, President of the *Rafu Shimpo*; the former Los Angeles Japanese Consul Toshito Satow; Mr. Shiro Fujioka, Secretary of the Los Angeles Japanese Association; Mr. Kersey, Superintendent of the

再版に際して

千九百三十二年拾一月本書を公にするや各地の同胞識者より多大の讃辭を受け第二世敎育資料として稗益するところがあつたのは誠に欣快とするところである。

今や第一世は身心を犠牲にして第二世の完全なる發展のため揮心の努力を拂つてゐる。今日在るところの第一世の總ての事業は第二世に繼承せしめなければならぬが、若し第二世に自覺と健全なる意思がなかつたならば第一世の基礎に有終の美を收めしむるのは全く不可能であらう。

第二世をして同胞の後繼者たらしむる指導方針には二つの鍵が必要ではあるまいか、即ち一は第二世を善良なる米國市民たるべく敎育する事と他は日本民族の一員としての修養を施すことである。斯くしてこそ第二世が米國市民としての義務を完ふし、太平洋時代に於ける日米兩國の文化融合に大貢獻をなし得るは明かである。幸ひにして第一世は第二世の立場を理解して善良なる米國市民の養成に努めてゐる。此の一事は公立學校に於いて第二世が他人種兒童より遙に優る成績を示し名譽の卒業演說をなす優秀兒童の多くあるを見ても證明さるゝのである。

本書は第一版の二十有餘名の原稿に最近榮譽を荷ひし二十有餘名の演說を增補したものであるが、總ての論文に含まれてゐる理想、感情及び意識等は盡く第二世の時代思想を表はす尊き文獻と云ふべきである。尙此等の論文の中には父母及び先生達の犠牲的精神とサゼスションが織込まれてある。此等の文獻を保存し、後進の第二世達への參考に資し勉學の刺戟劑たらしむることは誠に意義あることゝ信ずるので增補の上再版するに至つた。

再版するに至つて羅府新報社長駒井豊策、前羅府領事佐藤敏人、羅府日會書記長藤岡紫朗、加州敎育局長カーシー、羅府市民協會曾々長菅原敬、羅府基督敎會附屬學園長竹田力、羅府新報布市支社主任荒木政雄の諸氏の寄せられた御厚意に對し深く茲に謝意を表す。

一九三五年七月

編者識

Paul Tsunegoro Hirohata's preface written in Japanese as it appeared in the 1935 edition of *Orations and Essays*.

California Department of Public Instruction; Mr. Kay Sugahara, President of the Los Angeles JACL; Mr. Chikara Takeda, Principal of the Los Angeles Christian Church Supplementary School; and Mr. Masao Araki, chief of the *Rafu Shimpo* Fresno Branch.

[Paul Tsunegoro Hirohata], Editor
July 1935

## ENGLISH TRANSLATION OF A MESSAGE FROM THE SECRETARY OF THE LOS ANGELES JAPANESE ASSOCIATION

WITH THE ENFORCEMENT of the new congressionally enacted immigration law on July 1, 1924, the immigration of Japanese was completely banned and the future development of our race in North America fell solely upon activity of the Nisei. Also, the responsibility of fulfilling the mission of promoting goodwill between Japan and the United States had to be carried by them.

Under the circumstances, great hope has been gradually placed upon the Nisei and everyone has had much expectation of them. Thus the Nisei issue has come to be viewed with increasing importance. In light of the important mission possessed by these Nisei, I question whether our fellow countrymen and other Americans really understand them. In reflecting upon this matter, I had certain misgivings.

Just about this time, Mr. Tsunegoro Hirohata, whom I regard with deep respect, decided to collect the manuscripts of orations of more than twenty Nisei who graduated with distinction and had the honor of delivering commencement speeches at grammar schools, high schools and junior colleges throughout California. He published the speeches in a single book. I can say without reservation that this is truly a timely and worthwhile undertaking. There is no doubt that this is valuable documentary material whereby with careful reading one will be able to gain a certain understanding of the thoughts and aspirations of the Nisei.

Based on this conviction, I would like to recommend this book to the general public.

Shiro Fujioka
[Secretary of the Los Angeles Japanese Association]
Mid-October 1932

千九百二十四年七月一日、米國議會の制定せる新移民法が實施され日本移民は絶對に禁止されて以來北米の天地に於ける我が民族の發展は一に第二世の活動に俟たざるを得なくなつた。更らに又日米親善の使命を完うするの責任をも彼等は主として双肩に荷ふことになつた。

於茲乎第二世の前途は彌々多望視せられ、何人も彼等の將來に期待すること甚だ大なりである。斯くして第二世問題は一段と價値づけられ重要視せらるゝに至つたのである。斯かる重大なる意義と使命とを有する彼等を、我が同胞及び米國民は果して能く理解してゐるであらう乎。念ひ一たび此の事に逴べば頗る心もとなく感ずるのである。

恰かも良し、今回私の敬愛する廣畑恒五郎君は、今度全加州各地の グランマー、スクール。ハイ、スクール。ジュニヤ、カーレッヂ。等を優等の成績を以て卒業し、コムメンスメント、スピーカーの名譽を荷ひし二十有餘名の第二世諸君に乞ひて其の演説の草稿を蒐集し、之れを一册の書物として出版することにした。眞に機宜に適したる有意義な企であるといふに憚らぬ。之れを熟讀頑味することに依て第二世の思想なり、抱負なりを或る程度まで諒解し得る尊き文獻であることを信じて疑はぬ。

私は此の信念から本書を汎く江湖諸賢に推薦する次第である。

昭和七年十月中澣

藤 岡 紫 朗

Shiro Fujioka's statement in Japanese as it appeared in the 1932 and 1935 editions of *Orations and Essays.*

## FOREWORD IN THE 1932 AND 1935 EDITIONS OF *ORATIONS AND ESSAYS*

NEVER in the history of America has it been so important that a knowledge of world affairs be available, especially to our youth. This volume has for its purpose the promotion of a better understanding of the problems of the students in our California schools who would bring the traditions and the culture of other countries. The graduation addresses, essays and other contributions written by Japanese students in our California schools have been collected and compiled into a book which stresses the idea of world friendship. This may be constantly strengthened by the association of young people from various countries. The friendship that was developed this summer by the Olympic Games should be a continuing process carried on by the working together of students of different nationalities. Where there is a desire for understanding and an aim to promote friendship by the use of all means available to that end, we may be assured that no mere barrier of race or language can stand in the way of unity of spirit and purpose.

Human beings must set to work making peace as earnestly as they have in the past made war. The quickest means of doing this is to put an end to fear and distrust, and this may be accomplished only as more information and more accurate information is given to everyone. This is one of the peculiar problems in our public schools. To the students working together, there is the greatest opportunity of appreciating and understanding the manners, the customs, the temperament and the problems of other countries. Patriotism is no less real or effective because students seek to understand real situations and resolve not to obscure the vision of helpfulness and friendliness. Students are neighbors to all of like spirit throughout the world.

If this book will encourage other students to understand the spirit of those who are working together, it will be effective in helping to break down barriers and create this genuine spirit of friendliness.

Vierling Kersey
Superintendent of Public Instruction, State of California
Sacramento, California
October 1932

## THE CONSUL OF JAPAN'S RECOMMENDATION
## PUBLISHED IN *ORATIONS AND ESSAYS* IN 1932 AND 1935

I AM VERY HAPPY to know that there are so many gifted writers among our second generation. The articles contained in this publication are excellent both in subject matter and in manner of presentation.

They do credit to any aspiring writer.

A gift of self-expression is particularly important to the second generation. The Americans of Japanese parentage have unique opportunities to promote understanding and friendship between America and Japan. In order to make the most of these opportunities, they must be able to express themselves. Because of this reason, I am delighted to see that they are becoming more and more interested and skilled in the art of self-expression. I hope that they will continue to develop this highly important ability and, by using it, will add another strong link in the chain of friendship between America and Japan.

Toshito Satow
Consul of Japan
Los Angeles, California
October 1932

## JAPANESE AMERICAN CITIZENS LEAGUE'S MESSAGE IN *ORATIONS AND ESSAYS* IN 1935

ECONOMIC DISTURBANCES and cultural clashes have caused misunderstanding and unrest to ruffle the even tenor of our daily lives. Thrust in the center of this turbulent scene, the Nisei, a blend of two great cultural forces, play a prominent role in the molding of a more pacific relationship between two great powers. This interweaving of our Oriental and Occidental background, manifested in the particular angle of approach to problems, represents an epic in the making of America. The sublime moments of inspiration in the academic life of contemporary Nisei are recorded for posterity through this collection of oratorical and essay efforts.

We who bring a new contribution to the building of these United States can gain renewed confidence in our chosen task by sharing the choice thoughts of other gifted Nisei trailblazers. May we never lose sight of our higher goal; may we ever be blessed with the same indomitable courage of our pioneer forefathers.

Kay Sugahara, President
Japanese American Citizens League, Los Angeles [Chapter]
1935

## STATEMENT FROM THE OFFICE OF THE PRESIDENT OF WHITTIER COLLEGE FROM *ORATIONS AND ESSAYS* IN **1932**

THE CITIZEN of modern times faces a world economically unbalanced, intellectually disturbed, and spiritually confused. In view of this fact modern education is challenged, perhaps as never before, with the task of furnishing leadership in the solution of the problem of showing the individual how he can succeed without disrupting the enterprises of the group, and the group how it can make progress without unnecessarily curtailing activities of the individuals. American education, through the acceptance of many new ideals and methods of procedure, has definitely assumed this responsibility. All progressive educators are participating in this forward movement with a spirit of loyalty that guarantees stability of the social order and of modern democratic government.

Walter F. Dexter
Whittier, California
October 17, 1932

# Appendix C

## Mary Muroya Yamagata's Letter

*In 1997, Toshio Yamagata's Nisei wife, Mary, wrote a letter to a friend about her ordeal in Harbin, Manchuria after World War II. She decided to send her daughter, Jeannette, a copy of the letter. "It was heart-wrenching for me to relive those days," she wrote Jeannette. "I'm sure you would like to learn about a sister you never knew, or an aunt your children never knew."*

## Mary Muroya Yamagata's Post War Experience in Manchuria

"AFTER JAPAN SURRENDERED, all Japanese men employed by the Japanese military were rounded up by the Red Army and taken as prisoners to Siberia. Therefore, we mothers and children had to fend for ourselves.

About four to five families moved as a group into military housing and spent one whole year struggling to make a living. At first we sold whatever we could of our meager possessions, then some found menial jobs, and some remained at home to care for the children.

I started teaching English by going to private homes until one night I was almost raped but was saved by a barking dog! Thereafter, I carried six-month old Miyoko on my back and went to work. At night we propped our doors; stayed in complete darkness lest the Red soldiers tried to get in to rob and rape us.

Finally, a year later in mid-August we were the first group to be evacuated to Japan by the Red Cross. We had to walk about four miles to reach the Sungari River as the bridge across was bombed. It was pitch dark when we were ferried across the river to the other side. We had drunk all the water we carried from Harbin, so we immediately replenished ourselves with so-called "fresh" water. Then we were all given cholera shots.

The flat freight cars arrived while we were all asleep. At last we were on our way south to Shinkyo [Changchun] and on to [Japan]. Upon arrival in Shinkyo, we feasted on *kabocha* [Japanese pumkin] which was delicious. That night many of us became very ill—vomitting and diarrhea—three days and three nights and you're dead. Fortunately, that one shot at the riverbank saved my life after only one day and one night.

Miyoko, in the meantime, was cared for by a man who had volunteered. It turned out that he stole all my valuables, brought Miyoko back to my isolation ward, and continued on home with the healthy [babies].

We were finally able to resume our trip south to Hoten and finally to Dairen. We were packed like sardines in houses until the American L&T's arrived to take us to Sasebo, Japan. From Sasebo we were parked standing into those small Japanese freight cars, arriving at last to [Toshio Yamagata's] Aunt's home in Kabe, Hiroshima. Miyoko died a week later on October 25 of starvation. When we left Harbin, the authorities told us that they could not guarantee the lives of children under the age of five!

I spent a few months at my cousin's home in Hiroshima City, another few months at another cousin's home in Fukuoka. After recovering from malnutrition, I joined my brother George in Tokyo. He was an army doctor serving in China and was evacuated right after [Japan's] surrender.

[Yamagata] was released as a POW about three or four years later. Having lost his U.S. citizenship, he returned [to the U.S.] as my spouse and became a naturalized citizen later. It's only a few years ago that I finally started to eat a "pumpkin" pie and *kabocha*! And to this day I hate to go out at night after that one year of darkness! Miyoko will always remain in my memory as a six-month old baby, not a fifty-two year old mother and maybe a grandmother!"

Mary Muroya Yamagata, 1997

# Interviews and Oral Histories

Abe, Mas. Telephone conversation with Joyce Hirohata. 11 December 2001.

Asada, Mary. Written information sent to Joyce Hirohata. 24 October 2001.

Asano, Setsuko. Letter sent to and tape recorded interview with Joyce Hirohata. 12 March 2002.

Bepp, Ellen. Written information sent to Joyce Hirohata. 15 March 2002.

Campos, Chizuko Doi. Conversation with Joyce Hirohata. Fresno, California, 28 March 2002.

Chuman, Frank. Tape recorded interview with Joyce Hirohata. Los Angeles, Caifornia, 4 January 2001.

Fujisaka, Steven. Written information sent to Joyce Hirohata. 1 April 2002.

Ginoza, Hidemitsu. Written information sent to Joyce Hirohata. 16 December 2002.

Gorai, Ann Miyamoto. Written information sent to Joyce Hirohata. 10 March 2002.

Green, Rebecca Rottman. Written information sent to Joyce Hirohata. 3 July 2000.

Hamasaki, Clara Yamagishi. Written information sent to Joyce Hirohata. 21 April 2000.

Hashimoto, Bernice. Written information sent to Joyce Hirohata. 27 June 2000.

Ichiyasu, Kiyoshi. Written information sent to Joyce Hirohata. 7 March 2002.

Ikeda, Michiko Naito. Written information sent to Joyce Hirohata. 20 November 2001.

Inagaki, Chris. Written information sent to Joyce Hirohata. 1 March 2002.

Inouye, Charles. Telephone conversation with Joyce Hirohata. 4 April 2000.

Kimura, Pearl Kurokawa. Tape recorded interview with Joyce Hirohata. San Francisco, California, 1 November 2000.

Kobata, Betty Yoshizumi Nishino. Written information sent to Joyce Hirohata. 16 January 2002.

Matsumura, Shizu Komae. Tape recorded interview with Joyce Hirohata. Gardena, Caifornia, 5 January 2001.

Mizuhara, Phyllis. Written information sent to Joyce Hirohata. 24 September 2001.

Morioka, Dorothy Yoshida. Tape recorded interview with Joyce Hirohata. Orange, California, 15 March 2002.

Morishige, Ida Onaka. Written information sent to Joyce Hirohata. 4 October 2001.

Nakamura, Agnes Nishida. Written information sent to Joyce Hirohata. 14 November 2001.

Nakamura, Marie Shimidzu. Written information sent to Joyce Hirohata. 27 November 2001.

Nakamura, Reiko Nakagawa. Written information sent to Joyce Hirohata. 26 March 2002.

Naramura, Shizue Ohashi. Tape recorded interview with Joyce Hirohata. Los Angeles, Caifornia, 5 January 2001.

Nakanishi, Joe M. Written information sent to Joyce Hirohata. 2 February 2002.

Nobusada, Yemi. Written information sent to Joyce Hirohata. 17 October 2001.

O'Connell, Masa. Written information sent to Joyce Hirohata. 29 December 2001.

Sakata, Doris Sanwo. Written information sent to Joyce Hirohata. 19 February 2002.

Sanada, Kazuya. Tape recorded interview with Joyce Hirohata. San Pedro, Caifornia, 4 January 2001.

Sanderson, Jeannette. Written information sent to Joyce Hirohata. 28 January 2002.

Sanford, Chizuko Fujikawa. Written information sent to Joyce Hirohata. 4 April 2000.

Sasaki, Agnes. Written information sent to Joyce Hirohata. 20 November 2001.

Sato, Lisa. Written information sent to Joyce Hirohata. 16 June 2000.

Shimanouchi, Ida. Written information sent to Joyce Hirohata. 18 January 2002.

Shinoda, Alice Fujisawa. Written information sent to Joyce Hirohata. 15 February 2002.

Sunada, Yutaka. Written information sent to Joyce Hirohata. 6 August 2000.

Tademaru, Haruko Fujita. Written information sent to Joyce Hirohata. 26 October 2001.

Taguchi, Matilde Honda. Written information sent to Joyce Hirohata. 24 April 2000.

Takahashi, Hiro. Letters to Joyce Hirohata. 26 December 2001, 23 January 2002.

Tanaka, Karen Nagayama. Written information sent to Joyce Hirohata. 16 January 2003.

Tsubokura, Christine. Letter sent to Joyce Hirohata. 17 May 2000.

Yamaguchi, Irene Murakami. Written information sent to Joyce Hirohata. 20 March 2002.

Yasaki, Frederick. Written information sent to Joyce Hirohata. 11 October 2001.

# Selected Bibliography

Burton, Jeffery and others. *Confinement and Ethnicity, An Overview of World War II Japanese American Relocation Sites*, vol. 74 of *Publications in Anthropology*. Tucson, Arizona: Western Archeological and Conservation Center, 2000.

Chuman, Frank F. *The Bamboo People: The Law and Japanese-Americans*. Chicago, IL: Japanese American Research Project, Japanese American Citizens League, 1981.

Harrington, Joseph. *Yankee Samurai: The Secret Role of Nisei in America's Pacific Victory*. Detroit, MI: Pettigrew Enterprises, 1979.

Hosokawa, Bill. *Nisei: The Quiet Americans*. New York, NY: William Morrow, 1969.

Ichinokuchi, Tad. *John Aiso and the MIS*. Los Angeles: MIS Club of Southern California, 1988.

Inada, Lawson Fusao, ed. *Only What We Could Carry: The Japanese American Internment Experience*. Berkeley, CA: Heyday Books, 2000.

Nakano, Mei. *Japanese American Women: Three Generations 1890–1990*. Berkeley, CA: Mina Press Publishing, 1990.

Takahashi, Jere. *Nisei/Sansei, Shifting Japanese American Identities and Politics*. Philadelphia: Temple University Press, 1997.

Tateishi, John. *And Justice for All: An Oral History of the Japanese American Detention Camps*. New York, NY: Random House, 1984.

Uchida, Yoshiko. *Desert Exile: The Uprooting of a Japanese-American Family*. Seattle, WA: University of Washington Press, 1982.

Yamada, David. *The Japanese of the Monterey Peninsula: Their History and Legacy*. Monterey Peninsula Japanese American Citizens League, 1995.

Yoo, David. *Growing Up Nisei: Race, Generation, and Culture among Japanese Americans of California, 1924-49*. Urbana, IL: University of Illinois Press, 2000.

# Index